T0207180

Communications
in Computer and Information Science   1430

More information about this series at http://www.springer.com/series/7899

Miguel Félix Mata-Rivera ·
Roberto Zagal-Flores (Eds.)

Telematics and Computing

10th International Congress, WITCOM 2021
Virtual Event, November 8–12, 2021
Proceedings

 Springer

Editors
Miguel Félix Mata-Rivera ⓘ
Instituto Politécnico Nacional
México, Mexico

Roberto Zagal-Flores ⓘ
Instituto Politécnico Nacional
México, Mexico

ISSN 1865-0929   ISSN 1865-0937 (electronic)
Communications in Computer and Information Science
ISBN 978-3-030-89585-3   ISBN 978-3-030-89586-0 (eBook)
https://doi.org/10.1007/978-3-030-89586-0

This Springer imprint is published by the registered company Springer Nature Switzerland AG
The registered company address is: Gewerbestrasse 11, 6330 Cham, Switzerland

Preface

The COVID-19 pandemic still affects the whole world, research work in remote mode continues, and this volume shows some of the advances in various fields of knowledge, such as artificial intelligence techniques, deep and machine learning methods, approaches of cybersecurity, and analysis of communications protocols, with applications to different study scenarios, including educational and health.

The International Congress of Telematics and Computing (WITCOM) series aims at fostering interdisciplinary discussions and research in all aspects surrounding telematics, computing, geospatial science, communications, and artificial intelligence. WITCOM 2021, in its tenth edition and for the second time online, attracted numerous students, researchers, and entrepreneurs to share experiences and digital experience, new interaction mechanisms that have made it possible to continue with various tasks where research in involved. These proceedings contain selected research papers, where submissions went through a peer-review process. We received 48 research papers; three members of the Program Committee reviewed each submission, and 19 papers were accepted (an acceptance rate of 40%).

The conference was held virtually during November 8–12, 2021, and the program featured a broad set of session topics that extend beyond the documents contained in these proceedings. Materials for all sessions are available on the conference website at www.witcom.upiita.ipn.mx and www.witcom.org.mx.

All the tracks and workshops at WITCOM 2021 contributed to make a consistent program. We want to thank God and all those who contributed to this effort, especially ANTACOM A.C., which supports the enrollment of all authors and mainly students. Of course, thanks also to UPIITA-IPN, including all staff, managers, administrators, and the Geospatial Intelligence and Mobile Computing Laboratory, article authors, session presenters, coordinators, members of the Program Committee, and our sponsors. Without your help and collaboration, the event could not be successful.

November 2021

Roberto Zagal-Flores
Miguel Félix Mata-Rivera

Organization

Organizing Committee

General Chair

Miguel Félix Mata-Rivera   UPIITA-IPN, México

Co-chair

Roberto Zagal-Flores   ESCOM-IPN, México

Cybersecurity Track Chair

Cristian Barria-Huidobro   Universidad Mayor, Chile

Local Manager

Jairo Zagal-Flores   UNADM, México

Staff Chair

Sergio Quiroz Almaraz   FES-ACATLAN, México

Program Committee (Research Papers)

Christophe Claramunt	Naval Academy Research Institute, France
Cristian Barria	Universidad Mayor, Chile
Lorena Galeazzi	Universidad Mayor, Chile
Claudio Casasolo	Universidad Mayor, Chile
Alejandra Acuña Villalobos	Universidad Mayor, Chile
Clara Burbano	Unicomfacauca, Colombia
Gerardo Rubino	Inria, France
Cesar Viho	IRISA, France
Jose E. Gomez	Université de Grenoble Alpes, France
Kenn Arizabal	Delft University of Technology, The Netherlands
Mario Aldape Perez	CIDETEC-IPN, México
Anzueto Rios Alvaro	UPIITA-IPN, México
Ludovic Moncla	INSA Lyon and IRIS CNRS, France
Jose Lopez	Hochschule Furtwangen University, Germany
Shoko Wakamiya	Kyoto Sangyo University, Japan
Patrick Laube	ZAUW, Switzerland
Sergio Ilarri	University of Zaragoza, Spain
Sisi Zlatanova	TU Delft, The Netherlands
Stephan Winter	University of Melbourne, Australia
Stephen Hirtle	University of Pittsburgh, USA

Sponsors

ANTACOM A.C.
UPIITA-IPN

Collaborators

FES ACATLAN
Alldatum Systems
CISCO Systems

Contents

An Artificial Neural Network for Depression Screening and Questionnaire Refinement in Undergraduate Students

Mauricio Gabriel Orozco-del-Castillo[1,2(✉)] [iD],
Esperanza Carolina Orozco-del-Castillo[3] [iD], Esteban Brito-Borges[1,2] [iD],
Carlos Bermejo-Sabbagh[1,2] [iD], and Nora Cuevas-Cuevas[1,2] [iD]

[1] Departamento de Sistemas y Computación, Tecnológico Nacional de México/IT de Mérida, Mérida, Mexico
mauricio.orozco@itmerida.edu.mx
[2] Association for the Advancement of Artificial Intelligence, AAAI Student Chapter at Yucatán, México (AAAIMX), Mérida, Mexico
[3] Departamento de Matemática Educativa, Cinvestav-IPN, Mexico City, México

Abstract. Depression is unfortunately a very common illness, affecting over 264 million people worldwide, which in extreme cases can lead to suicide. While there are treatments for mental disorders, including depression, many people do not receive adequate treatment or even psychological attention due to lack or resources, social stigmas, inaccurate assessments, and lack of trained mental health professionals. In this paper, a system for screening depression using an artificial neural network is proposed. A true/false questionnaire consisting of 117 items was designed by a medical health professional based on the Diagnostic and Statistical Manual of Mental Disorders (DSM-5). This questionnaire was applied to 157 undergraduate students, and their answers served to train the neural network to fit the related physical symptoms of depression, showing encouraging results in comparison with other machine learning techniques. Posterior principal component analysis and genetic algorithms-based approaches were used to propose methodologies to refine questionnaires, identifying some items which could prove to be more relevant than others, increasing the quality of the results in future survey-related applications.

Keywords: Depression · Machine learning · Screening · Artificial neural networks · Mental health prevention

1 Introduction

Depression, which could lead to major depressive disorder (MDD), is unfortunately a very common mental disorder, with an estimated 4.35% of the world population suffering from it [1], and 17% experiencing it at some stage in their lives [2]. The Diagnostic and Statistical Manual of Mental Disorders (DSM-5) describes nine different symptoms, some with physical (weight change, change in sleep, change in activity,

M. F. Mata-Rivera and R. Zagal-Flores (Eds.): WITCOM 2021, CCIS 1430, pp. 1–13, 2021.
https://doi.org/10.1007/978-3-030-89586-0_1

fatigue) and others with psychological manifestations (irritability, decreased interest, guilt/worthlessness, concentration problems, suicidality) [3]. In addition to being one of the leading causes of disability worldwide [4], depression has also been identified as the main precursor for suicide [5]. Therefore, screening for depression, particularly in vulnerable groups, is crucial in terms of suicide prevention. Yucatán is the state in Mexico with the highest number of suicides with respect to the total number of violent deaths in the country [6], a phenomenon which is particularly affecting a large number of adolescents in the state, the country [7], and worldwide, ranking as the second leading cause of death in 15–29-year-olds [4].

Screening is normally based on self-report measures or clinical interviews, which are particularly time-consuming for mental health professionals and that could delay priority attention to high-risk individuals. There are several ongoing challenges in screening and diagnosis of MDD. One of them is that patients' symptoms and pathophysiology are too diverse, varying considerably in genetics, neurobiology, presentation, processes, and responses to treatment [8]. Another challenge is that current diagnostic practice relies heavily on professional mental health expertise and time-consuming interviews, which evidently requires close cooperation from patients [8]. In many cases this diagnostic practice is unfeasible, for instance, during the COVID-19 pandemic. Because of this, self-report questionnaires have been widely used for assessing and screening MDD and its severity [8]; while diagnosis requires personal professional medical expertise, a first step of screening is possible with self-report questionnaires [9]. However, the information which questionnaires need to collect to efficiently serve as a screening tool, often requires a large number of items to be addressed [10], and it has been identified that the larger the number of items that need to be addressed, the lower the quality of the answers [11].

Artificial intelligence, and particularly machine learning (ML) techniques, have been successfully applied in several areas of science as analytical approaches to uncover hidden and complex patterns [12]. This has been used to help generate actionable predictions in medicine [8], including psychology [13], and particularly MDD-related applications for localization of clinical manifestations [1], correlation with other afflictions [14] and prediction of treatment outcomes [15], persistence and severity [9].

In this paper we propose a depression screening system based on an ANN which uses as input the responses of 157 undergraduate students to a self-report questionnaire. In order to develop a system which minimizes the need for interviews with professional mental health experts, the responses of the questionnaire, instead of personal interviews, serves as the target for the ANN: the reported physical symptoms commonly associated with depression. The data and the results of the ANN are then used to propose a refinement of the questionnaire using two distinct approaches: principal component analysis (PCA) and genetic algorithms (GAs).

2 Theoretical Background

2.1 Depression

Depression is a very common illness, affecting over 264 million people worldwide [16]; it is also different from temporary mood fluctuations and normal emotional responses, and may become a serious health condition [4], leading even to suicide [12]. While there are treatments for mental disorders, including depression, many people do not receive adequate treatment due to lack of resources, social stigmas, inaccurate assessments, and lack of trained mental health professionals [4]. People who are depressed are commonly misdiagnosed, or not even assessed at all.

Depression has been categorized according to the number and severity of symptoms, including recurrent depressive disorder, bipolar affective disorder, and MDD [16]. An individual may experience mild episodes, which lead to difficulties with ordinary work and social activities, or may experience a severe depressive episode, in which it is unlikely for the sufferer to continue a normal life, which worsens the depression itself [4].

Depression both 1) results from, and 2) causes a complex interaction of social, psychological, and biological factors, i.e., there are interrelationships between depression and physical health. Many people affected with depression also suffer from sleep and appetite irregularities, feelings of guilt or low self-worth, concentration issues and some even unexplainable symptoms [4].

There are effective treatments for depression, including psychological treatments, psychosocial treatments, or antidepressants which should be used with extra caution in the case of adolescents [4].

2.2   Machine Learning

AI is a science that englobes both mathematics and computer science. Its purpose is to grant digital computers the ability to perform tasks that are normally related to intelligent beings [17]. There are many methods and models used to provide these capabilities to a computer, such as genetic algorithms (GA), informed or uninformed search techniques, finite state machines, among others. Also, data-driven techniques exist to create or structure knowledge, which are generally concentrated under the subfield of AI called ML.

ML techniques are based on learning from big amounts of data, allowing a model to be constructed automatically by feeding it several examples on how to solve a problem, instead of manually or arbitrarily changing its parameters. Supervised ML techniques can be used to mainly fulfill two different tasks: regression and classification. In the first, ML models aim to predict values of a continuous variable. Classification tasks, on the other hand, consist in predicting values for a categorical variable. The knowledge needed to perform these tasks can be compacted inside diverse mathematical models, like nested conditionals present in decision trees or universal function approximators, such as ANN, a model which, given enough data and computing power, has proven to be more effective than other ML models in many applications [18].

ANN are ML models designed to behave in a similar manner as neurons in biological brains do [19]. They are composed of several artificial neurons, every single one of them resembling a weighted function; when combined, neurons give birth to complex decision functions that comprise the knowledge to solve regression or classification problems. Moreover, they are supported by an algorithm that, during training time, calculates the prediction errors and tries to slightly change the parameters of an ANN to ensure better prediction in the future [20]. ANNs have been used to support many AI achievements in the last decade, such as real-time object detection in images [21] and near human conversational agents [22].

2.3 State of the Art

Due to the priority depression implies, along with the technical challenge it poses, several approaches have been presented to use AI and ML techniques in prediction, screening, diagnosis, and treatment of depression. In terms of prediction, multivariate logistic regression was used to localize clinical manifestations of MDD in survey data [1], while other ML techniques have been used to predict the occurrence of co-morbid afflictions from correlations with depression [14]. Another approach predicted treatment outcome in depression in cross-clinical trials [15]. Other approaches include acoustic and linguistic analysis of speech using ML techniques [12, 23, 24], screening of depression using deep convolutional neural networks on electroencephalogram data [25, 26], data from internet behaviors [27–29], and ML models on self-report questionnaires [8, 9], particularly for prediction of persistence and severity of depression.

3 Development/Methodology

3.1 Questionnaire Design

A questionnaire was designed by a professional medical health expert, based on the diagnostical criteria symptoms of the DSM-5 [3], and consisted of three types of items: 1) demographic information, particularly age and sex, 2) items directly related to MDD (34 items) and other mental illnesses: Generalized Anxiety Disorder (34 items) and Antisocial Personality Disorder (34 items), and 3) physical health questions that were indirectly related to depression, such as weight changes, sleep level, and sleep regularity (5 items).

3.2 Data Collection and Analysis

The participants comprised 157 undergraduate students at Tecnológico Nacional de México (TecNM)/Instituto Tecnológico de Mérida (ITM) from May 2020 to December 2020. Relevant guidelines and regulations were followed, and all students consented to participate in the study. The students who participated were 30 females and 127 males, ranging from 17 to 23 years of age.

The students were asked to fill out the true/false questionnaire through a local website and their answers were collected into a spreadsheet. The 107 total items (102 psychological, and 5 physical) were shuffled so they would not appear clustered together in terms of the different disorders and the nature of the symptoms (psychological/physical).

The collected data was organized into the CSV file reporting the students' registration number, age, sex, and their answers to each one of the items arranged in the same order of the items in the questionnaire. Since all the items were marked as required, basically no other data cleaning technique was necessary. A "true" answer was associated with the value 1, and a "false" one to 0.

Due to the COVID-19 pandemic, it was impossible to gather information for a complete diagnosis of depression through personal interviews between the students and medical health professionals, therefore, the answers to the physical items were used as substitute for a first stage in the screening process. The answers to the physical items of each student were compared to the expected answers provided by a mental health professional showing physical symptoms of MDD (shown in Table 1), and a depression score was quantified as follows: the number of coincident items between the actual answers and the expected answers. In other words, if all the actual answers coincided with the expected answers, a score of 5 was determined; if none, a score of 0, and so on. This depression score was used as the target for the ANN, as discussed in the following section.

Table 1. The items associated with physical symptoms of MDD.

Item description	Answer associated with MDD
I have noticed that my weight in the last month has changed	True
I have more cravings than usual; they are generally unhealthy foods	True
My sleeping habits are definitely not the same as they used to be	True
I have a hard time waking up	True
I have always been interested in eating well to maintain good health	False

According to this quantification, 6 students were assigned a depression score of 1, 53 of 2, 53 of 3, 33 of 4, and 12 of 5; no students without any coincidences were reported. We considered this as a regression task, instead of a classification one; this is because there are no true 5 distinct classes, but rather different degrees of the same variable (depression score). Despite this, there was a marked imbalance between the samples lying on the different scores. We used the SMOTE technique [30] to deal with this imbalance; this technique allows to oversample the minority "classes" (particularly 1 and 5) in the training sets after partitioning the data. After balancing the minority classes samples, we ended up with the final dataset, consisting of 265 samples, 53 for each case.

3.3   The Artificial Neural Network for Regression

A shallow feed-forward back-propagation ANN to fit the data was designed, having an input layer of 102 elements (one for each item of the questionnaire), one hidden layer of 10 elements –empirically determined– and an output layer of one element, a value ranging between 0 and 5, where the depression score is calculated. To avoid overfitting, a common training-validation-test split was used [31]: of the 265 total samples, 70% (185) were used for training, 15% (40) for validation, and 15% (40) for test, uniformly and randomly distributed. The ANN performance function was set to minimize the mean squared error (MSE), the average squared difference between outputs and targets. Due to random initialization of the ANN's weights, a variation in the results every time the ANN is trained is to be expected. To account for this, 100 instances of the ANN with the same previously defined architecture and parameters were executed. The ANN with the best performance was chosen from the set of experimental designs, in which training was halted after six epochs using the Levenberg-Marquardt training algorithm [32] due to the performance gradient falling below 1×10^{-7}. The results are discussed in the following section.

4 Results

4.1 Major Depression Disorder Screening

After training was halted, the ANN showed a performance MSE of 1.3625×10^{-10} for training data, 0.0945 for validation, and 0.2530 for testing. Low MSE for training samples is evidence of the ANN accurately fitting the data, while low MSE for the validation and testing samples show that the ANN is learning and not just memorizing. Additional values of root mean squared error (RMSE) and regression R values, which measure the correlation between outputs and targets, are shown in Table 2.

Table 2. Performance of the different ML techniques. RMSE, MSE and R^2 values are shown. Additionally, for the ANN, these values are specified for the training (Train), validation (Val) and Testing (Test) data. For the other ML techniques, 5-fold cross-validation was employed.

	RMSE			MSE			R^2		
--	Train	Val	Test	Train	Val	Test	Train	Val	Test
ANN	1.85e−20	0.0089	0.0089	1.36e−10	0.0945	0.2530	0.9999	0.9623	0.9038
LR	3.6085			13.021			−5.44		
SVM	0.67341			0.45348			0.78		
RT	0.62575			0.36533			0.81		
GPR	0.38914			0.15143			0.93		

The linear regression plots between the targets and the outputs of the ANN for the training, validation, and testing data are shown in Fig. 1. Considering that the output of the ANN corresponds to a depression score, the analysis of the error distribution is particularly important. As can be observed in the error histogram with 10 normally distributed bins in Fig. 2, the errors of the ANN are mainly localized very close to zero, particularly in the −0.1137 bin, and are distributed similarly to the original distribution for training, validation, and testing.

The performance of the ANN was compared against four others ML regression techniques: linear regression (LR), support vector machines (SVM), regression trees

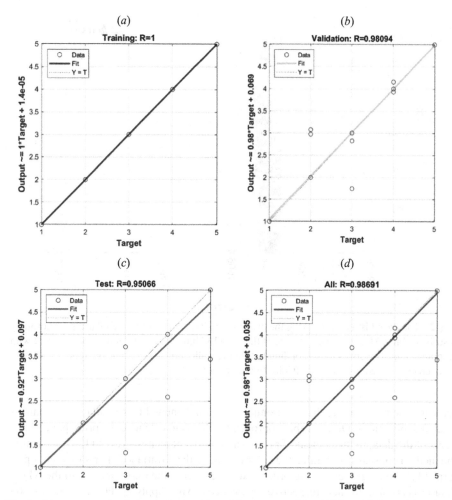

Fig. 1. Linear regression between the targets and the outputs of the ANN on (*a*) the training data, (*b*) the validation data, (*c*) the test data, and (*d*) considering all data (training, validation, and test). The coefficient of correlation (*R*) between the targets and the outputs for each case is also shown. The actual data is plotted using circles, while the fitting line is shown in blue for training, green for validation, red for testing, and black for all data. (Color figure online)

(RT) and Gaussian process regression (GPR). For all these techniques, 5-fold cross-validation was employed. Prediction performance was assessed using root mean squared error, mean squared error and R^2. The results of the comparison are shown in Table 2.

4.2 Questionnaire Refining

Principal Component Analysis Approach. It has been reported that an excessive number of items can reduce data quality [11], therefore finding the optimal items and thus

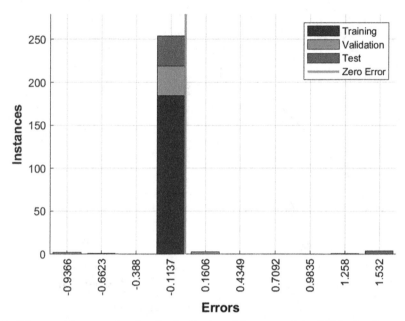

Fig. 2. The error histogram showing the distribution of the errors of the ANN using 10 normally distributed bins. Most errors are located at the −0.1137 bin, close to the zero error, depicted with an orange line. The errors corresponding to training, validation, and testing, are represented with blue, green, and red, respectively. (Color figure online)

reducing their quantity in the questionnaire is a fundamental task in all questionnaires-related applications. One possible approach for this is to calculate the principal components of the data, in the context of principal component analysis (PCA) [33]. Basically, the method consists in obtaining the eigenvectors of the covariance matrix of a set of patterns [34]. The eigenvectors are ordered with respect to their contribution to the whole dataset according to their respective eigenvalues. After applying PCA, a total of 265 eigenvectors are obtained (one for each sample), with their respecting eigenvalues. Each eigenvector has 102 elements, each one of the values representing the contribution of that item in the questionnaire to that respective vector. To determine the most relevant items in the questionnaire, we multiplied each eigenvector with its respective eigenvalue, and arranged the results in a 102×265 matrix. We then summed the absolute values of each one of the rows of the matrix to find the pondered contribution, score, of each item; higher scores correspond to a higher contribution of said item to the dataset. In other words, we find the most relevant items of the principal components. Similar approaches for identifying and removing superfluous survey items have been proposed [11]. The three items with the highest and lowest scores, along with their descriptions, are shown in Table 3.

Genetics Algorithms Approach. An ANN is capable of mapping inputs and outputs by adjusting its connection weights. When inputs are altered, the output is perturbed, and while sensitivity analysis of ANNs' output to input perturbations is expected to

Table 3. The three most and least relevant items according to the PCA, their description, and their respective score

Item	Description	Score
17	I feel guilty about the decisions that I have made	486.5932
20	It is difficult for me to make decisions even if they are simple	483.8825
41	I am bothered by insignificant things that were not important before	477.3076
98	It is normal to change jobs several times a year	90.9514
85	I have a hard time controlling myself when I get angry	89.5482
79	It is easy for me to work in a team	37.3646

provide explanations about the generalization abilities of said ANNs, it is recognized that alterations of more relevant input neurons of the ANN are related to higher perturbations of its output [35]. Therefore, detecting the highest perturbations when inputs are altered could be useful to determine the most relevant input neurons. In this manner, the item selection could be posed as an optimization problem, trying to maximize the perturbation to fixed alterations of the input of the ANN. Our methodology is described as follows.

The alteration of the inputs consisted in randomly swapping 10 of the answers to the items of a given sample; the perturbation is then calculated as the RMSE between the output of the input unaltered and the output of the altered input. This metric was defined as the cost function of a GA. GAs, originally proposed by Holland [36], represent a means to emulate the process of natural evolution through improvement of new individuals via sexual reproduction and survival of the fittest [37]. GAs are well-suited for optimization problems where no derivative information is available and the search space is particularly large. To find the most relevant items of the questionnaire through this approach, the problem consisted in finding those items which maximized the RMSE between the outputs of the original and altered inputs; the GA thus was designed to find the 10 items which maximized this metric. 1000 different instances of the GA attempting to maximize the perturbation of the ANN, given all the 265 inputs, were carried out.

The three items which appeared the most during the 1000 instances while trying to maximize the RMSE were items 33, 97, and 29, appearing in 53%, 48%, and 45% of the GAs instances, respectively. The description of these items is shown in Table 4. The distribution of how often an item appeared (histogram) while trying to maximize the RMSE during the 1000 instances of the GA is shown in Fig. 3.

The problem of finding the least relevant items is then easily approached by multiplying the output of the cost function of the GA by −1. The corresponding analysis to minimize the RMSE, and therefore identifying the least relevant items was also performed. The three items which appeared the most during the 1000 instances while trying to minimize the RMSE were items 59, 95, and 54, appearing in 51%, 34%, and 34% of the GAs instances, respectively. The description of these items is shown in Table 5. The distribution of how often an item appeared (histogram) while trying to minimize the RMSE during the 1000 instances of the GA is shown in Fig. 4.

Table 4. The three most relevant items according to the GA, and their respective percentage of appearance during the GA analysis

Item	Description	Percentage (%)
33	I have trouble remembering things easily	53
97	People who commit crimes have their reasons for doing it	48
29	I am able to carry out my activities as I have always been	45

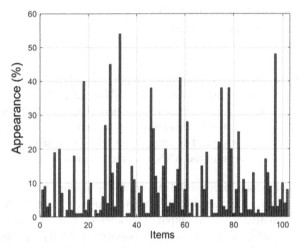

Fig. 3. The histogram showing the percentage of appearances of a given item during the 1000 instances of the maximizing GA. Higher values represent most relevant items of the questionnaire.

Table 5. The three least relevant items according to the GA, and their respective percentage of appearance during the GA analysis

Item	Description	Percentage (%)
59	I consider myself good at controlling my emotions	51
95	Neighbors must put up with each other's noises without complaining	34
54	I do not usually get upset if something does not go as expected	34

As can be observed in Fig. 3 and Fig. 4, results of both the maximization and minimization problems appear to be consistent, since the items which appeared the most when trying to maximize, appeared in very few instances when minimization was intended, and vice versa. For instance, items 33, 97 and 29 appeared in 53%, 48%, and 45% when maximization was intended, and 1%, 0%, and 0%, respectively, when minimization was intended. On the other hand, items 59, 95 and 54 appeared in 51%, 34%, and 34% (Table 5) when minimization was intended, and just 2%, 9%, and 4%, respectively, when maximization was intended.

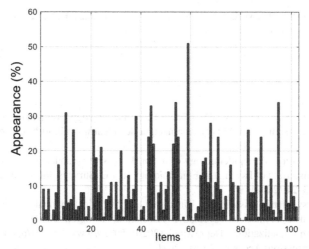

Fig. 4. The histogram showing the percentage of appearances of a given item during the 1000 instances of the minimizing GA. Higher values represent least relevant items of the questionnaire

5 Conclusions

A system for screening depression using an ANN, is proposed. A true/false questionnaire consisting of 117 items was designed by a medical health professional based on the diagnostical criteria symptoms of the DSM. This questionnaire was applied to 157 undergraduate students of the TecNM/ITM. The answers to the psychologically related items served to train an ANN to fit the items related to physical symptoms of depression. The ANN showed encouraging results which outperformed other common ML techniques. Posterior PCA and GAs approaches were used to propose methodologies to refine questionnaires, identifying some items which could prove to be more relevant than others, increasing the quality of the results in future applications of the revised questionnaire.

There appears to be a pattern in psychological items of different mental health disorders which relates it to physical symptoms commonly associated with depression. Whether or not this pattern is also related directly with depression and could be useful for a professional diagnosis, is yet to be confirmed through personal interviews with mental health professionals and was out of the scope of this work. However, our very encouraging results provide a first step in an automated screening process which does not require mental health professionals to embark in the time-consuming tasks which prelude depression diagnosis.

Follow-up studies are now ongoing at TecNM/ITM to apply and integrate different techniques (e.g., acoustical, statistical, signal processing) to the one presented in this work. The ultimate goal of this and future research is to develop a more robust, integral, reliable and explainable screening/diagnostic system that can be utilized in students enrolling at the institute.

Acknowledgements. This work was supported by project 10428.21-P from Tecnológico Nacional de México/IT de Mérida.

References

1. Oh, J., Yun, K., Maoz, U., Kim, T.S., Chae, J.H.: Identifying depression in the National Health and Nutrition Examination Survey data using a deep learning algorithm. J. Affect. Disord. **257**(April), 623–631 (2019)
2. Andrade, L., et al.: The epidemiology of major depressive episodes: results from the International Consortium of Psychiatric Epidemiology (ICPE) Surveys. Int. J. Methods Psychiatr. Res. **12**(1), 3–21 (2003)
3. American Psychiatric Association: Diagnostic and Statistical Manual of Mental Disorders (DSM-5), 5th edn. American Psychiatric Association, Arlington (2013)
4. World Health Organization: "Depression" (2020). https://www.who.int/news-room/fact-she ets/detail/depression. Accessed 29 Apr 2021
5. France, D.J., Shiavim, R.G.: Acoustical properties of speech as indicators of depression and suicidal risk. IEEE Trans. Biomed. Eng. **47**(7), 829–837 (2000)
6. INEGI: Porcentaje de muertes por suicidio con respecto al total de muertes violentas por entidad federativa (2019). https://www.inegi.org.mx/app/tabulados/interactivos/?pxq=Salud_ Mental_08_bd8fe10b-59ce-4856-8e4f-fcd46c4f25cf. Accessed 29 Apr 2021
7. Comisión de Derechos Humanos del Estado de Yucatán: Informe Especial sobre el Suicidio en Jóvenes del Estado de Yucatán (2010). https://www.codhey.org/sites/all/documentos/Doc tos/Investigaciones/Suicidio.pdf. Accessed 04 May 2021
8. Choi, B., Shim, G., Jeong, B., Jo, S.: Data-driven analysis using multiple self-report questionnaires to identify college students at high risk of depressive disorder. Sci. Rep. **10**(1), 1–13 (2020)
9. Kessler, R.C., et al.: Testing a machine-learning algorithm to predict the persistence and severity of major depressive disorder from baseline self-reports. Mol. Psychiatry **21**(10), 1366–1371 (2016)
10. Greene, R.L.: The MMPI-2: An Interpretive Manual, 2nd edn. Allyn & Bacon, Needham Heights (2000)
11. Brosnan, K., Grün, B., Dolnicar, S.: Identifying superfluous survey items. J. Retail. Consum. Serv. **43**(November 2017), 39–45 (2018)
12. Belouali, A.: et al.: Acoustic and language analysis of speech for suicide ideation among US veterans. medRxiv, pp. 1–17 (2020)
13. Barak-Corren, Y.: et al.: Predicting suicidal behavior from longitudinal electronic health records. Am. J. Psychiatry **174**(2), 154–162 (2017)
14. Van Loo, H.M., et al.: Major depressive disorder subtypes to predict long-term course. Depress. Anxiety **31**(9), 765–777 (2014)
15. Chekroud, A.M., et al.: Cross-trial prediction of treatment outcome in depression: a machine learning approach. Lancet Psychiatry 3(3), 243–250 (2016)
16. James, S.L., et al.: Global, regional, and national incidence, prevalence, and years lived with disability for 354 Diseases and Injuries for 195 countries and territories, 1990–2017: a systematic analysis for the Global Burden of Disease Study 2017. Lancet **392**(10159), 1789–1858 (2018)
17. Copeland, B.J.: Artificial intelligence | Definition, Examples, and Applications | Britannica (2021). Available: https://www.britannica.com/technology/artificial-intelligence/Reasoning. Accessed 29 Apr 2021

18. Kolasani, S.V., Assaf, R.: Predicting stock movement using sentiment analysis of Twitter feed with neural networks. J. Data Anal. Inf. Process. **8**(4), 309–319 (2020)
19. Marder, E., Taylor, A.L.: Multiple models to capture the variability in biological neurons and networks. Nat. Neurosci. **14**(2), 133–138 (2011)
20. Hinton, G., Rumelhart, D., Williams, R.: Learning representations by back-propagating errors. Nature **323**, 533–536 (1986)
21. Boudjit, K., Ramzan, N.: Human detection based on deep learning YOLO-v2 for real-time UAV applications. J. Exp. Theor. Artif. Intell. (2021)
22. Dale, R.: GPT-3: what's it good for? Nat. Lang. Eng. **27**(1), 113–118 (2021)
23. He, L., Cao, C.: Automated depression analysis using convolutional neural networks from speech. J. Biomed. Inform. **83**(May), 103–111 (2018)
24. Trotzek, M., Koitka, S., Friedrich, C.M.: Utilizing neural networks and linguistic metadata for early detection of depression indications in text sequences. IEEE Trans. Knowl. Data Eng. **32**(3), 588–601 (2018)
25. Acharya, U.R., Oh, S.L., Hagiwara, Y., Tan, J.H., Adeli, H., Subha, D.P.: Automated EEG-based screening of depression using deep convolutional neural network. Comput. Methods Programs Biomed. **161**, 103–113 (2018)
26. Baghdadi, A., Aribi, Y., Fourati, R., Halouani, N., Siarry, P., Alimi, A.: Psychological stimulation for anxious states detection based on EEG-related features. J. Ambient Intell. Humaniz. Comput. 0123456789 (2020.)
27. Zhu, C., Li, B., Li, A., Zhu, T.: Predicting depression from internet behaviors by time-frequency features. In: Proceedings of the 2016 IEEE/WIC/ACM International Conference Web Intelligence, WI 2016, pp. 383–390 (2017)
28. Li, A., Jiao, D., Zhu, T.: Detecting depression stigma on social media: A linguistic analysis. J. Affect. Disord. **232**(16), 358–362 (2018)
29. Cheng, Q., Li, T.M., Kwokm, C.L., Zhu, T., Yip, P.S.: Assessing suicide risk and emotional distress in Chinese social media: a text mining and machine learning study. J. Med. Internet Res. **19**(7) (2017)
30. Chawla, N.V., Bowyer, K.W., Hall, L.O., Kegelmeyer, W.P.: SMOTE: synthetic minority over-sampling technique. J. Artif. Intell. Res. **16**, 321–357 (2002)
31. Nguyen, Q.H., et al.: Influence of data splitting on performance of machine learning models in prediction of shear strength of soil, vol. 2021 (2021)
32. Marquardt, D.W.: An algorithm for least-squares estimation of nonlinear parameters. J. Soc. Ind. Appl. Math. **11**(2), 431–441 (1963)
33. Pearson, K.: On lines and planes of closest fit to systems of points in space. London Edinburgh Dublin Philos. Mag. J. Sci. **2**(11), 559–572 (1901)
34. Orozco-del-Castillo, M.G., et al.: A texture-based region growing algorithm for volume extraction in seismic data. Geophys. Prospect. **65**(1), 97–105 (2017)
35. Zeng, X., Yeung, D.S., Sun, X.: Sensitivity analysis of multilayer perceptron to input perturbation. In: Proceedings of the IEEE International Conference on System Man Cybernetics, vol. 4, no. 6, pp. 2509–2514 (2000)
36. Holland, J.H.: Adaptation in Natural and Artificial Systems. University of Michigan Press, Michigan (1975)
37. Orozco-del-Castillo, M.G., Ortiz-Aleman, C., Urrutia-Fucugauchi, J., Martin, R., Rodríguez-Castellanos, A., Villaseñor-Rojas, P.E.: A genetic algorithm for filter design to enhance features in seismic images. Geophys. Prospect. **62**(2), 210–222 (2013)

Mexican Edaphology Database

Vladimir Avalos-Bravo[1]([✉]) [iD], Chadwick Carreto Arellano[2] [iD],
Macario Hernández Cruz[3] [iD], Blanca Barragán-Tognola[4] [iD],
and Mónica Fernanda Barragán-Tognola[5] [iD]

[1] Direccion de Educacion Virtual, SEPI-ESIQIE, UPIEM, SARACS Research Group ESIME
Zacatenco, Instituto Politécnico Nacional, Mexico City, Mexico
ravalos@ipn.mx
[2] Direccion de Educacion Virtual, SEPI-ESCOM, Instituto Politécnico Nacional,
Mexico City, Mexico
ccarretoa@ipn.mx
[3] Direccion de Educacion Virtual, Instituto Politécnico Nacional, Mexico City, Mexico
mahernandezc@ipn.mx
[4] SEPI-ESIQIE, Instituto Politécnico Nacional, Mexico City, Mexico
blanca.barragan@upgm.com.mx
[5] Universidad Politécnica del Golfo de México, Paraíso, Tabasco, Mexico
monica.barragan@updelgolfo.mx

Abstract. This paper presents a Mexican Edaphology Database designed and developed to provide essential information about 16 different type of soils in 2457 Mexican municipalities (in percentage %) for a total of 122850 classified values. The database was developed on Java Script Object format in order to exchange data with an open source tool and it is also a subset of the literal notation of JavaScript® objects independent of the language and that has many advantages when is used as a data exchange. Once the application was built, Materialize® Software was used because it was specially conceived for projects that make Material Design their flag and allows this Cascading Style Sheet framework to save time at web project implementation and optimization due a lot of Styles already configured.

Keywords: Mexican soils · Edaphology database · Communication platform

1 Introduction

The care and conservation of the environment is a very complex issue. In the same way that the chemical elements essential for life, for example, oxygen, nitrogen and carbon in the form of various chemical elements or compounds are cyclically exchanged between soil, air and water of the planet to maintain an environmental balance. In México there are extensive areas of soils contaminated by hydrocarbons, due to the tasks of exploration and refining, and from lack of maintenance and fuel theft [1]. Environmental pollution is a cyclical process that encompasses soil, water and air and alters the natural processes that sustain life, being able to break the ecological balance and severely compromise the sustainability of human society. Anthropogenic activities contribute significantly to the pollution of the environment. Industrial processes do it in a significant way, since they

M. F. Mata-Rivera and R. Zagal-Flores (Eds.): WITCOM 2021, CCIS 1430, pp. 14–22, 2021.
https://doi.org/10.1007/978-3-030-89586-0_2

use energy and petrochemicals intensively derived from oil and natural gas, which are extracted from the terrestrial and marine subsoil.

International society has had to accept that global warming and the emission of industrial and municipal waste and waste into the environment are problems that transcend the borders of nations, and must be individually and collectively attacked both within and outside of countries. The consumption of fossil fuels by contemporary societies has been detrimental from an ecological point of view, it has caused backwardness in technological matters, in addition to which is economically expensive and with many practical unnecessary, which implies a challenge and opportunity to improve and clear the way to energy [2].

In 50's decades and until 70's the term Pollution Control was widely used, indicating that economic and social development necessarily resulted in natural environments deterioration. Progressively, Environmental Control evolved into what is now known as the management of environmental pollution and is designated as Environmental Management. From a practical point of view, Environmental Management at the governmental and social level means designing, applying, directing and controlling strategies and actions that are relatively simple in concept: Preventing means doing everything necessary to minimize the probability of an unwanted event (accident, or loss) occurring, Attack and Contain means doing everything necessary so that once the event has occurred, acting on the causes that originate it, either minimizing or eliminating them, and at the same time confining the event to the smallest area possible, preventing it from spreading and affecting nearby sites.

Oil spills deeply affect environment; it is for this reason that oil industry must comply with current legislation on environmental protection. In recent years the increase in clandestine takes has caused many cases of water bodies' contamination, soil pollution, environmental damage, as well as animals, plants and humans affectations [3]. An important affectation happens when these claims damage agricultural soils, causing economic and social damage due to that soils are no longer suitable for crops production [4].

1.1 Mexican Soils

In Mexico there is a great variety of soils due to various factors interaction, such as complex topography caused by the Cenozoic volcanic activity, altitudinal gradient (from zero to 5,600 m above sea level), the presence of four of the Five types of climates and the landscape diversity and rocks type in territory, in Mexico there are 26 of 32 soil groups recognized by International World Reference Base System for Soil Resources (IUSS). Leptosols (28.3% of territory), Regosols (13.7%), Phaeozems (11.7%), Calcisols (10.4%), Luvisols (9%) and Vertisols (8.6%) dominate all over the country, together occupy 81.7% of national surface [5].

Shallow and poorly developed soils predominate in more than a half of national territory, that is, without vegetation such as Leptosols (54.3 million hectare), Regosols (26.3 million) and Calcisols (20 million), which makes their use for agricultural purposes very difficult, besides, increasing their erosion vulnerability. Soils with the highest fertility are: Phaeozems, Luvisols and Vertisols (22.5, 17.3 and 16.5 million hectares respectively) that cover 29.3% of the country together. The rest of the territory (around

35 million hectares) has the other 20 edaphic groups, distributed in a large number of reliefs, microclimates and types of vegetation [6]. Figure 1 shows soils distribution all over the Mexican country.

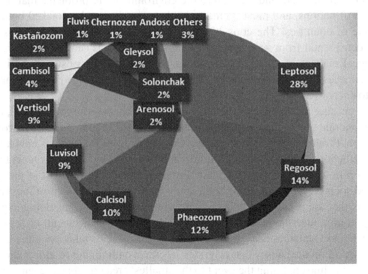

Fig. 1. Relative area of the main soil groups in Mexico.

In recent decades, agricultural sector of the country increase activities, so that soils were more fertile and deep, with a good structure and a high content of nutrients, in addition to organic matter, it had greater demand. For this reason, in the mid 70's and the end of the first decade of 21st century, the percentage of Luvisols, Vertisols and Phaeozems dedicated to agricultural activities increased from 35.8% (24.1% dedicated to agriculture and 11.7% in grasslands for livestock) to 44.4% (29.6% in agriculture and 14.8% in grasslands). To a lesser extent, soils that are considered unsuitable for agriculture or livestock (such as Leptosols, Regosols and Calcisols) have also been used for these purposes. In the middle of 70s, 9.9% of the national surface of this set of soils was dedicated to agricultural activities, while at the end of the first decade of the 21st century, increased to 14% (7.4% in agriculture and 6.6% in grasslands).

1.2 Polluted Soils in Mexico

Soils contaminated with hydrocarbons represent a risk to human health, as well as to flora and fauna. In Mexico, this contamination occurs, in some cases, by clandestine intakes of gasoline or diesel, therefore, the occurrence of this type of unwanted events must be prevented, and if they do happen, the impacted areas should be remedied as soon as possible. possible, this in order to prevent these accidents from generating much greater damage to the environment. Contaminated soil is defined as any soil whose characteristics have been negatively altered by the presence of hazardous chemical components of human origin, in a concentration such that it poses an unacceptable risk to human health or the environment.

Oil spills affect the physical properties of the soil and especially the natural populations of microorganisms. In particular, they cause a decrease in free-living nitrogen-fixing bacteria, responsible for assimilating and recycling nutrients in biogeochemical cycles [7]. In addition to the effects produced by soil contamination, the presence of gasoline, diesel or fuel oil interferes in the determination of parameters such as texture, organic matter, real density and porosity.

For this reason, the introduction of pollutants into the soil can result in damage to the soil or the loss of some of its functions and possible contamination of the water, particularly the groundwater. The concentration of dangerous pollutants in the soil above certain levels entails a large number of negative consequences for the food chain and therefore for human health, as well as for all types of ecosystems and other natural resources. For this reason, contaminated soils constitute the most urgent and important problem still unsolved in environmental matters.

1.3 Complaints for Contaminated Soils

Of the 5,461 complaints received by PROFEPA up to 2018, 1.2% (64/5461) correspond to soils contaminated by spillage of chemical substances, where on many occasions the remediation of contaminated sites is ordered through inspection and surveillance. of those responsible for such emergencies, following up until the total cleaning of the site and its restoration. In 2017 alone, 221 inspection visits were made to companies where effects on the soil derived from contamination by hazardous waste were observed, including hydrocarbons [8]. Figure 2 shows popular complaint received by PROFEPA, and every month and every year the number of received complaints increase, that is the reason why a database that show the type of soil is necessary to plan mitigation action in case of spill or pollution.

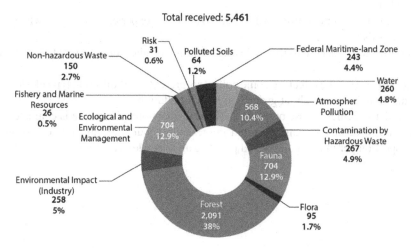

Fig. 2. Popular complaint received, distribution by affected resource 2018 [8].

2   Mexican Edaphology Database Development

A Mexican soils application was developed by SEMARNAT (https://apps1.semarnat.gob.mx:8443/dgeia/informe_resumen/03_suelos/cap3.html#1) [9]. However, the data structure is very different and the plugins like flash are no longer available. The focus of this application is to complement the national Forest and Soil Inventory, a National forest policy instrument that provides comprehensive, updated and periodic information on the location, quantity, characteristics, dynamics and quality of forest resources and associated with them [10] and Forest and soil inventories of the Federal Entities [11]. There are some databases that have undergone different stages with different structures in order to focus on different safety information [12], but no soils database have been developed in Mexico.

But due to the fact that these applications do not contain a description of soils type that exists in Mexico, as well as the use that each one of these has, it was necessary to develop an edaphology database. It is worth mentioning that information in a particular way of each municipality of the Mexican Republic, is information provided on INEGI website [13], but it contains infographics in pdf format with a lot of information that forces readers to waste time, when sometimes only information about soils and its geological composition is required. This is of great help when a soil becomes contaminated, in order to determine affectation due to contaminant composition and its reaction on the type of soil.

Mexican Edaphology Database was designed to become a standard soils information tool that can be able to link to another database like hydrocarbons affectation on soils one. In short term operation edaphology database has been made available to a wide range of users. It was designed to be a collaborative and communicative web-based information platform, aimed at promoting information about Mexican soils in every municipalities and the percentage of total occupied land for each one. specifically, edaphology database is intended to:

Contribute to integration and harmonization of experience and knowledge of Mexican soils.

Improve the understanding of all types of soils over the Mexican republic and their proportion.

Help to prevent the effects of some pollutants present in the different type of Mexican soils due to information about ground effects on pollution.

In order to achieve those objectives, Mexican edaphology database is characterized by significant details, organization and information about Mexican soils composition and proportion per municipalities and per state all over Mexican country.

2.1 Database Construction

The necessary information was obtained for the creation of the database in Excel® software by consulting the different pro-municipal files of INEGI [14]. Because Excel® is a registered trademark of Microsoft®, the use of freeware was considered for database migration, for this reason it was sought to import it with help of simple text format for data exchange JSON. It is important to mention that it is due to this data collection that a non-relational database will be generated.

As a first phase, reports by municipality (2,467) and by state (32) with different characteristics of the region were obtained from INEGI [15], including hydrological information, edaphologic information, geologic information and economic information of every place, production modes among other facts. Only the necessary information that would be required for the database elaboration had to be captured and some fields that help to its exploration in order to obtain desired results, once information had been reviewed, it was then synthesized into State, number of municipalities and soils percentage, classified in an edaphological way by each of them, as well as the use of land in corresponding municipality (urban, agriculture and pasture) as shown in Fig. 3.

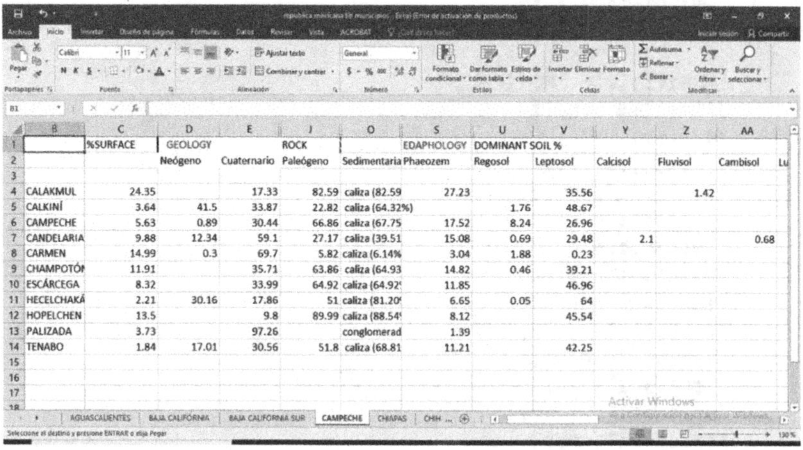

	%SURFACE	GEOLOGY			ROCK	EDAPHOLOGY DOMINANT SOIL %						
		Neógeno	Cuaternario	Paleógeno	Sedimentaria	Phaeozem	Regosol	Leptosol	Calcisol	Fluvisol	Cambisol	Lu
CALAKMUL	24.35		17.33	82.59	caliza (82.59	27.23		35.56			1.42	
CALKINÍ	3.64	41.5	33.87	22.82	caliza (64.32%)		1.76	48.67				
CAMPECHE	5.63	0.89	30.44	66.86	caliza (67.75	17.52	8.24	26.96				
CANDELARIA	9.88	12.34	59.1	27.17	caliza (39.51	15.08	0.69	29.48	2.1		0.68	
CARMEN	14.99	0.3	69.7	5.82	caliza (6.14%	3.04	1.88	0.23				
CHAMPOTÓN	11.91		35.71	63.86	caliza (64.93	14.82	0.46	39.21				
ESCÁRCEGA	8.32		33.99	64.92	caliza (64.92'	11.85		46.96				
HECELCHAKÁ	2.21	30.16	17.86	51	caliza (81.20'	6.65	0.05	64				
HOPELCHEN	13.5		9.8	89.99	caliza (88.54'	8.12		45.54				
PALIZADA	3.73		97.26		conglomerad	1.39						
TENABO	1.84	17.01	30.56	51.8	caliza (68.81	11.21		42.25				

Fig. 3. Municipalities Database created in Excel®.

The first step will be to convert the Excel® database to Java Script Object (JSON), format. JSON is a simple text format that is used for data exchange because it is open source and has no cost, it is also a subset of the independent - language JavaScript object literal notation and has many advantages as it is used as a data exchange format. In order to add the values contained in the Excel® database to the compilation code, it must be carried out through transformation and adaptation to JSON, constructing and referencing the values contained in each cell linearly so that they can be represented in the tool, which implies the construction and declaration of the 122,850 values contained in the database.

It is important to mention that the no relational database or the NoSQL query language, works under the principle that they do not contain an identifier that serves as a data set and others, the information is organized in tables or documents and it is very useful when there is not an exact scheme of what is going to be stored (Fig. 4).

```
[{
        "Municipio": "ENSENADA",
        "Phaeozem": 1.93,
        "durisol": "",
        "regosol": 25.03,
        "leptosol": 51.04,
        "planosol": 2.03,
        "kastanozem": "",
        "calcisol": 5.56,
        "fluvisol": 3.56,
        "cambisol": 1.64,
        "luvisol": 1.03,
        "vertisol": 4.18,
        "arenosol": 1.93,
        "solonetz": 0.42,
        "gleysol": 0.02,
        "solonchak": 1.14
},
{
        "Municipio": "MEXICALI",
        "Phaeozem": null,
        "durisol": "",
        "regosol": 22.2,
        "leptosol": 26.78,
        "planosol": null,
        "kastanozem": "",
        "calcisol": 4.36,
        "fluvisol": 6.72,
        "cambisol": 2.09,
        "luvisol": 0.01,
        "vertisol": 7.11,
        "arenosol": 12.35,
        "solonetz": null,
        "gleysol": null,
        "solonchak": 14.99
},
{
```

Fig. 4. Hierarchical elements of a table in JSON format for a non-relational Database.

Next, the Materialize® Software is used, Materialize® is a modern responsive front-end framework based on Material Design, specially conceived for projects that make Material Design their flag. This CSS framework allows you to save time and effort when implementing and optimizing web projects. Not only does it contain a multitude of CSS classes already configured, but by incorporating JavaScript® code, the values from the database can be added to our interface.

On the one hand, the advantages of Materialize® CSS framework are:

The development time is less, since most of the code is already written. A CSS framework is applied to achieve a beautiful aesthetic in future projects. Design is more robust and the final aesthetic is more homogeneous. Materialize® occupies only 140 KB with its CSS, to which must be added 180 KB with Java Script® for a low space and resources demand. At present, edaphology database is fully operational and is available online via http://148.204.111.72/edafologia2/ web page as shown in Fig. 5.

MEXICAN EDAPHOLOGY

State	Municipalitie	Phaeozem	Durisol	Regosol	Leptosol	Planosol	Kastañozem	Calcisol	Fluvisol	Cambisol	Luvisol
Aguascalientes	AGUASCALIENTES	63.73	8.28	6.89	3.93	2.13	1.97	1.91	0.93	0.24	
Baja California	ASIENTOS	6.48	49.34	6.91	24.22	4.51	1.09	3.57	0.48		
Baja California Sur	CALVILLO	33.23		18.63	28.48	2.88	2.06	5.33	2.57	2.03	6.73
Campeche	COSÍO	14.21	58.26		22.56		2.9				
Coahuila	EL LLANO	24.47	32.18	27.15	12.14		3.09				
Colima	JESÚS MARÍA	51.98	6.52	4.22	32.92	1.03				1.83	
Chiapas	PABELLÓN DE ARTEAGA	12.17	55.13		26.86	3.9					
Chihuahua	RINCÓN DE ROMOS	12.84	36.32	11.41	19.29	0.46	0.83			17.33	
Distrito Federal	SAN FRANCISCO DE LOS ROMO	31.88	35.71		0.04			22.58	7.36		
Durango	SAN JOSÉ DE GRACIA	11.33		0.81	38.41	16.56	9.34			11.02	12.42
Guanajuato	TEPEZALÁ	3.08	54.31		20.12			12.37			
Guerrero											

Fig. 5. Mexican Edaphoplogy Database Web Application.

3 Conclusions

Being a knowledge tool that helps to improve the understanding of all types of soils over the Mexican republic and their proportion will reduce the risk of animals and population affectation due to pollution.

The risk of contamination in food and the constant exposure to hydrocarbon volatiles that can cause damages to the population due polluted soils is real, so a tool with information of soils can help to prevent the effects of some pollutants present in them.

A soils database at the service of specialists, can sample the soils and determine the health risks over their consumption.

Developing a culture of safety and integrating information networks that benefit people using soils information, is required to plan population and settlement of communities, as well as job opportunities, through agriculture or animal husbandry in remote regions.

As a result of lack of soils distribution information, populations or animals impacted by a pollutant on their region, do not have the attention of specialists, doctors or risk engineers.

Information systems usage allow the decision making process to be opportune in order to mitigate undesired events.

This type of information systems will serve as a reference for design of remediation and restoration processes on refineries, gas stations, storage and distribution plants adjacent land, as well as lands where these types of facilities have existed and could have affected the soil, in addition to serving as a reference for the development of standards related to characterization and sanitation of soils in the proximity of gas stations, refineries and storage and distribution terminals.

Acknowledgments. This project was funded under the following grants: SIP-IPN: No-20210303 and the support of DEV-IPN, Instituto Politecnico Nacional.

References

1. Cavazos-Arroyo, J., et al.: Impacts and consequences from hydrocarbon spills on agricultural soils in Acatzingo, Puebla, Mexico (2013)
2. Woynillowicz, D., Severson-Baker, C., Raynolds, M.: Oil Sands Fever. The Environmental Implications of Canada's Oil Sands Rush. The Pembina Institute, Canada (2005)
3. Avalos-Bravo, V., et al.: A preliminary analysis of a clandestine take explosion in Mexico City. In: Proceedings of the 30th European Safety and Reliability and 15th Probabilistic Safety Assessment and Management Conference, Venice Italy (2020)
4. Infante, C.: Biorremediación de derrames de hidrocarburos en ambientes naturales. Memorias del IV Congreso Interamericano sobre el Medio Ambiente. Caracas, Venezuela, (1998)
5. INEGI Carta Edafológica de la República Mexicana (2007)
6. INEGI Compendio de información geográfica municipal 2010 San Martin Texmelucan Puebla (2018)
7. Vázquez-Luna, et al.: Impacto del Petróleo Crudo en Suelo Sobre la Microbiota de Vida Libre Fijadora de Nitrógeno, Tropical and Subtropical Agroecosystems, vol. 13, pp. 511–523 (2011)
8. INFOMEX A través de PROFEPA, solicitud No. 1613100059519, informe sobre los niveles de contaminación en el sitio donde ocurrió la explosión del 18 de enero en Tlahuelilpan en donde se menciona que los límites de hidrocarburos permitidos y establecidos en la NOM-138-SEMARNAT/SSA1-2012 fueron rebasados (2018)
9. INEGI Los suelos de México (2021). https://apps1.semarnat.gob.mx:8443/dgeia/informe_r esumen/03_suelos/cap3.html#1. Accessed 17 May 2021
10. Sistema Nacional de Información y Gestión Forestal Inventario Nacional Forestal y de Suelos (2021). https://leyes-mx.com/ley_general_de_desarrollo_forestal_sustentable/7.htm#:~: text=XXXII.,XXXIII. Accessed 17 May 2021
11. Forest and soil inventories of the Federal Entities (2021). https://leyes-mx.com/ley_gen eral_de_desarrollo_forestal_sustentable/7.htm#:~:text=XXXII.,XXXIII. Accessed 17 May 2021
12. Weiner, S.C., et al.: Lessons learned from safety events. In: 4th International Conference on Hydrogen Safety, USA (2011)
13. Municipios de Mexico (2021). https://www.inegi.org.mx/. Accessed 17 May 2021
14. INEGI edafología de la república mexicana (2021). https://www.inegi.org.mx/temas/edafol ogia/. Accessed 17 May 2021
15. INEGI información sobre suelos de municipios (2021). https://www.inegi.org.mx/datos/. Accessed 17 May 2021

Security Incident Classification Applied to Automated Decisions Using Machine Learning

Eduardo Eloy Loza Pacheco[1]([✉]) [ID], Mayra Lorena Díaz Sosa[1] [ID],
Christian Carlos Delgado Elizondo[1], Miguel Jesús Torres Ruiz[2] [ID],
and Dulce Lourdes Loza Pacheco[3] [ID]

[1] Universidad Nacional Autónoma de México, Acatlán Edomex,
08544 Naucalpan de Juárez, Mexico
{eduardo.loza,mlds,ccdelgado}@acatlan.unam.mx
[2] Instituto Politecnico Nacional, Mexico City, Mexico
mtorres@ipn.mx
[3] Centro de Investigación y de Estudios Avanzados del Instituto Politécnico Nacional,
Mexico City, Mexico
dloza@cinvestav.mx

Abstract. There is an immense number of attacks on the logical infrastructure of an organization. Cybersecurity professionals need tools to help discriminate levels of attacks to design operational plans to prevent, mitigate, and restore without significant damage to an organization's resources. Machine learning helps build valuable models to identify relevant values of a vulnerability vector attack needed to improve our security plan. The following work presents a framework that uses a machine learning model that classifies the level of an incident detection indicator.

Keywords: Cybersecurity · Preparation of security incidents · Machine learning

1 Introduction

Cybersecurity is a relevant topic due to the importance of being protected from cybercrime, security incidents such as zero-day attacks, data breaches, denial of service, social engineering, or phishing [1]. In our days, we witness the professionalization of the attackers. As it is said in [2], we live in the golden age of Hacking. We can see this as it is sawed the data breach to extract Covid19 vaccine information from Pfizer [3, 4], or the ransomware to attack the gas infrastructure is the US [5]. On the other hand, we have that artificial intelligence; specifically, Machine Learning helps to improve defensive security [6] by developing interesting algorithms such as regression logistics, trees, k-means, artificial neuronal networks, etc. that can help to identify and predict vulnerability and risk models which are built with trained and test data. In the field of cybersecurity and machine learning, there are exciting works such as [7], where a machine learning classifier is used to develop a framework that identifies a zero-day attack using decision trees, random forest, among others. In [8], we can see a methodology that uses several malware characteristics as a vector of features to perform an attack. Finally, in

M. F. Mata-Rivera and R. Zagal-Flores (Eds.): WITCOM 2021, CCIS 1430, pp. 23–34, 2021.
https://doi.org/10.1007/978-3-030-89586-0_3

[1], we can see the importance of machine learning in all devices such as the Internet of things to avoid security incidents. This work shows a framework that can help to detect a security incident based on the features of a cybersecurity specialist with the help of a team response, system administrators who collect information from the pool of servers, network infrastructure to detect a vector of features that can be related to a type of a security incident.

2   Framework

As is defined by ITU X.1205 [9], Cybersecurity is the collection of tools, policies, security concepts, security safeguards, etc., that can be used to protect the environment of an organization. One of these is to harden the logical infrastructure by updating software patches, applying good security practices, antivirus, firewalls, for example. Incident response is the mechanism to enforce the infrastructure. One of the main parts of protecting information [10] of the incident response life cycle is Preparation, as is mentioned in the computer security Incident Handling guide of NIST [11]. Preparation helps to plan an adequate response. For that, we need to identify the sources and attack vectors of the most likely security incidents in our organization we have identified. This tool is better if it is automated with the help of machine learning artifacts. In the following figure, we see the lifecycle of the incident response (Fig. 1).

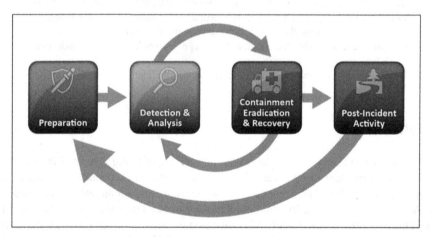

Fig. 1. Incident response life cycle take from [11]

Practical machine learning models require a flexible framework. Then we need to identify the most common signs of security incidents, such as low performance of the equipment, port scanning, memory usage, CPU usage [12], an antivirus alert, change in logs, network intrusion, multiple login attempts, a large number of emails.

The following figure shows the framework that is divided into three main parts. The first stage is Analysis, where the cybersecurity stakeholders can gather previous information of risks, vulnerabilities, and attacks from the technical reports, system logs, and interviews of employees of the response team. The aim is to build a vector of characteristics that synthesizes the most relevant and differentiable elements that are susceptible to represent an incident that can be cluster into a class. After that, the security team maps every vector of characteristics to a security incident to represent every security incident with the respective set of the vector of attributes. Finally, it is possible to build a machine learning model to describe the general rules for the vector of characteristics according to the security incidents to classify most security incidents (Fig. 2).

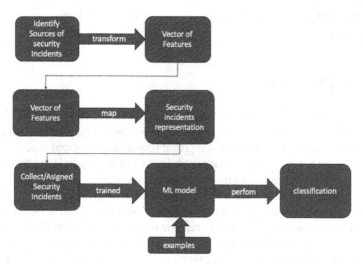

Fig. 2. Security incidents analysis framework

3 Security Incidents Sources

For this reason, the detection of security incidents that can produce an interruption or degradation of the service the organization is offering is fundamental as it is mention in the ITU X.805 recommendation for Security architecture for System providing end-to-end communications [13]. So, it is needed the identification of the security indicators such as low performance of the equipment for example as it is done in [8], detection of new open ports, strange activities in our logs, new folders, change of permissions to system files, significant use of memory, new conventional user, or kernel users, too many processes running [12, 14]. Therefore, a diagnosis matrix of the observed phenomena can be built. The following table shows an incident matrix, where three types of incidents from malicious code, denial of service, and unauthorized access, and their symptoms are presented. The symptoms selected here were obtained to show the framework and according to [12] but can be extended to the necessities of the problem.

Table 1. Symptoms and incidents types.

Syntom	Malicious code	DOS	Unauthorized acces
Port scanning	Low	High	Medium
Server down	High	High	Medium
Modified files	High	Low	High
Unusual network traffic	Medium	High	Medium
Low performace of network	Medium	High	Low
Suspicious mails	High	Low	Medium

4   Vector of Features

Suppose there have been identified three types of incidents. It is observed that there are additional open ports that were supposed to be open. For example, when more ports are open in a security incident, the probability of unauthorized access grows. In contrast, when are fewer open ports, the possibility of a malicious code executing is more probable. On the other hand, the processor usage is too high; also, de memory is used. And finally, the traffic flow is high. For example, the latency is significantly elevated. So, for that, they are classified as malicious code, Denial of service, or unauthorized access. Relevant values can help to differentiate one type of incident from another. As we see in Table 1. we can differentiate the symptoms from different types of incidents. In the following table, we can see a segment of sensed events represented by the rows. The first four columns represent the symptoms, and the final column represents the associated security incident, where 0 denotes malicious code, 1 denial of service, and 2 for unauthorized access (Table 2).

Table 2. Segment of incidents events

Open ports	Processor usage	Memory usage	Traffic	Cybersecurity incident type
11	81	51	115	2
3	84	83	189	0
3	91	95	80	0
6	91	55	75	0
5	90	84	171	0
9	96	63	91	2
6	85	91	188	0
7	97	90	278	1

Suppose the system administrator classifies several different events, for example, 1000, and we storages this information in our knowledge base, then he converted it into a comma-separated values file (csv) to manipulate the information. This work uses Python to show the functionality of the framework and the libraries Pandas, Matplotlib, and Sklearn and methods and functions of Logistic Regression, Trees, Forest, Knn, K-means, etc.; that is provided by this library [15, 16].

5   Generating the Model

The process used to generate the model is conventional that can be found in machine learning that is: load the data set, divide the dataset randomly in the training part, the testing part. The framework also preprocesses the data, escalate, normalize, transforms from conceptual data to quantitative data, etc. Reduction of the dimensionality will be important to add more symptoms or variables. Then the training of the model is based on the classification selection. Finally, it is necessary to test the resulting model and used more information to find whether it is generalizing well. Finally, it is necessary to measure the precision and check if it is not overfitting or is underfitting. The following diagram shows the process (Fig. 3).

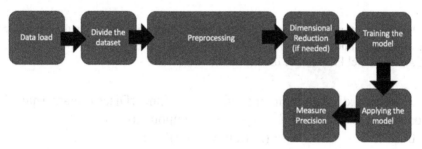

Fig. 3. Process to generating a model.

6   Building the Model

The first activity to perform is to load the data and divide the dataset into training and test sets. As it is shown in Fig. 4.

```
dataset = pd.read_csv("ComputerUse.csv")
X = dataset.iloc[:,:4].values
y = dataset.iloc[:,4].values

from sklearn.model_selection import train_test_split
x_train,x_test,y_train,y_test =
train_test_split(X,y,test_size=.25,random_state=2)
```

Fig. 4. Data set extraction and assigning training and testing sets.

After that, the information need to be escalated to normalize the results (Fig. 5).

```
from sklearn.preprocessing import StandardScaler
escalateX=StandardScaler()
x_train= escalateX.fit_transform(x_train)
x_test =escalateX.fit_transform(x_test)
```

Fig. 5. Scaling training and testing data sets.

It will be common to find several symptoms, so dimensionality reductions is needed. The work uses linear discriminant analysis (LDA), but Principal component analysis (PCA), or Kernel PCA can be used (Fig. 6).

```
from sklearn.discriminant_analysis import LinearDiscriminantAnalysis
Lda = LinearDiscriminantAnalysis(n_components=2)
x_train = lda.fit_transform(x_train,y_train)
x_test = lda.transform(x_test)
```

Fig. 6. Dimensionality reduction.

6.1 Using a Logistic Regression Model

A model is generated that fits the space of the data. In the following figure we see a linear regression model (Fig. 7).

```
from sklearn.linear_model import LogisticRegression
classifier = LogisticRegression(random_state=0)
classifier.fit(x_train,y_train)
```

Fig. 7. Logistic regrassion model.

6.2 Using a Random Forest Classifier Model

Another option es random forest classification (Fig. 8).

```
from sklearn.ensemble import RandomForestClassifier
classifier = RandomForestClassifier(n_estimators=1000,
criterion="entropy",random_state=0)
classifier.fit(x_train,y_train)
```

Fig. 8. Random forest classification model

6.3 Using a K Nearest Neighbor Model

For the Knn algorithm, 5 closest neighbors were selected. Choosing k is crucial for the algorithm, for large datasets k can be larger to reduce error. The number of k is often determined by experimentation [19].

```
from sklearn.neighbors import KNeighborsClassifier
classifier = KNeighborsClassifier(n_neighbors=5,
metric="minkowski", p=2)
classifier.fit(x_train,y_train)
```

Fig. 9. KNN models classification

6.4 Using Bayes Model

The final model showed in Fig. 9 is the Bayes Model implementation (Fig. 10).

```
from sklearn.naive_bayes import GaussianNB
classifier = GaussianNB()
classifier.fit(x_train,y_train)
```

(a)

```
y_predice = classifier.predict(x_test)
```

(b)

Fig. 10. a) Bayes classification. b) Bayes classification.

Finally, once a model is obtained, A predictions can be perfoms using Sklearn to produce an automated result. The figure shows the result from the testing stage and the comparison with the test using Bayes (Fig. 11).

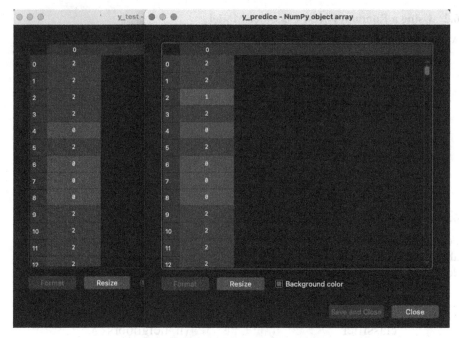

Fig. 11. Prediction test versus prediction set

6.5 Confusion Matrix

The confusion matrix measures the precision of the model. As seen in the table for the logistic regression [17] (Fig. 12, Tables 3 and 4).

from **sklearn.metrics** import **confusion_matrix**
cm = confusion_matrix(**y_test,y_predice**)

Fig. 12. Building the confusion matrix

Table 3. Confusion matrix of the Random Forest

144	5	0
0	11	3
0	5	87

We can calculate the accuracy by adding the result in the diagonal [18], as it is showed in the following equation. For each class the true positives (TP), True Negatives (TN), False Positives (FP), and False Negatives (FN) are required.

$$Accuracy = \frac{TP + FP}{TP + FP + TN + FN} \qquad (1)$$

Table 4. Confusion matrix of the KNN

147	2	0
0	12	1
0	1	86

$$Accuracy = \frac{242 + 8}{242 + 5 + 3 + 5} = .98 \qquad (2)$$

Additionally, can be calculated, sensitivity, specificity, precision, recall and the, F1 measure.

6.6 Results

Since the example has two components, after the dimensionality reduction, we can see the result in the cartesian plane. Additionally, for this purpose, only three classes, as it was mentioned before, DOS, Malicious Code, and Unauthorized access, were used. It is possible to add more classes. The following image shows the example of using Bayes, where the boundaries describe the problem better after the dimensional reduction (Fig. 13).

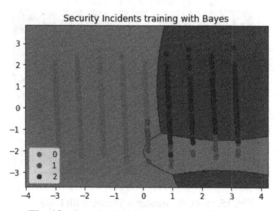

Fig. 13. Security incidents training with Bayes

Therefore can be compared the results with the Knn algorithm, where the boundaries help us to map more elements to their appropriate class (Fig. 14).

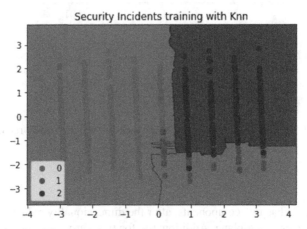

Fig. 14. Security incidents training with KNN

Finally see the next figure the testing phase with Bayes (Fig. 15).

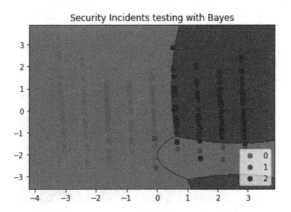

Fig. 15. Security incidents Testing with Bayes.

7   Conclusion

The aim of a cybersecurity specialist is to be prepared in the event of any security incident by applying the elements of the Incident Response Life Cycle. The first stage of this cycle is preparation. The response team can gather previous information of attacks, suggest possible vulnerability vectors, and integrate them into the analysis. Machine learning is a powerful tool that can synthesize a large volume of information into relevant and significant knowledge that allows us to plan better the response in the event of an incident. Also, allow us to classify the type and severity. So, in the future can be processed in real-time. The models used in this work were Bayes, Logistic Regression, Random Forest, and KNN algorithm. The models used in this work were Bayes, Logistic Regression, Random Forest, and KNN algorithm. The models used in this work were Bayes, Logistic Regression, Random Forest, and KNN algorithm. An ANN model comparative respect ML conventional models can be useful to reduce error in the confusion matrix. An ANN can be tested with 50 epochs with RELU to test. The framework proposed here permits the identification of security incidents according to an ad hoc scenario in which the specialist must identify problems in the organization. To build a functional representation to build a series of Machine Models that help to interpret the situation and can classify the type of incident.

Acknowledgements. The authors would like to thank to Universidad Nacional Autónoma de México, Facultad de Estudios Superiores Acatlán and DGAPA-UNAM (PAPIME PE 301521) for the funds to support this work.

References

1. Sarker, I.H., Kayes, A.S.M., Badsha, S., Alqahtani, H., Watters, P., Ng, A.: Cybersecurity data science: an overview from machine learning perspective. J. Big Data **7**(1) (2020)
2. Rankin, K.: Linux Hardening in Hostile Networks: Server Security from TLS to Tor. Addison-Wesley Professional (2017)
3. M. from S. S. Marketing, S. S. Marketing, Adam Strange | 2 days ago, Kyle Marchini | 3 days ago, Mike Nelson | 3 days ago, Richi Jennings | 2 days ago, Richi Jennings | 4 days ago, and R. J. | J. 07, "Pfizer Suffers Huge Data Breach on Unsecured Cloud Storage," Security Boulevard, 22 October 2020. https://securityboulevard.com/2020/10/pfizer-suffers-huge-data-breach-on-unsecured-cloud-storage/. Accessed 13 June 2021
4. Pfizer COVID-19 vaccine data leaked by hackers: Healthcare IT News, 14 January 2021. https://www.healthcareitnews.com/news/emea/pfizer-covid-19-vaccine-data-leaked-hackers. Accessed 13 June 2021
5. Ellen Nakashima, Y.T.: Ransomware attack leads to shutdown of major U.S. pipeline system. The Washington Post, 08 May 2021. https://www.washingtonpost.com/business/2021/05/08/cyber-attack-colonial-pipeline/. Accessed 13 June 2021
6. Kamoun, F., Iqbal, F., Esseghir, M.A., Baker, T.: AI and machine learning: a mixed blessing for cybersecurity. In: 2020 International Symposium on Networks, Computers and Communications (ISNCC) (2020)
7. He, Z., Miari, T., Makrani, H.M., Aliasgari, M., Homayoun, H., Sayadi, H.: When machine learning meets hardware cybersecurity: delving into accurate zero-day malware detection. In: 2021 22nd International Symposium on Quality Electronic Design (ISQED) (2021)
8. Zhang, S., Xie, X., Xu, Y.: A brute-force black-box method to attack machine learning-based systems in cybersecurity. IEEE Access **8**, 128250–128263 (2020)
9. Series X: Data Networks, Open System Communications and Security: Data networks, open system communications and security. https://www.itu.int/rec/T-REC-X/en. Accessed 13 June 2021
10. NIST Editor: Computer Security Incident – Glossary, CSRC. https://csrc.nist.gov/glossary/term/Computer_Security_Incident. Accessed 13 June 2021

11. Computer Security Incident Handling Guide. https://nvlpubs.nist.gov/nistpubs/SpecialPubli cations/NIST.SP.800-61r2.pdf. Accessed 13 June 2021

12. Vieites, A.: Enciclopedia de la Seguridad Informatica, RAMA, Mexico (2011)

13. ITU: Security architecture for System providing end to end communications. X.805: Security architecture for systems providing end-to-end communications. https://www.itu.int/rec/ T-REC-X.805-200310-I/en. Accessed 13 June 2021

14. Action List for Developing a Computer Security Incident Response Team (CSIRT), 02 November 2006. https://resources.sei.cmu.edu/library/asset-view.cfm?assetid=53102. Accessed 13 June 2021

15. Albon, C.: Machine Learning with Python Cookbook: Practical Solutions from Preprocessing to Deep Learning. OReilly Media, Sebastopol (2018)

16. Learn: machine learning in Python - scikit-learn 0.16.1 documentation. scikit. https://scikit-learn.org/. Accessed 13 June 2021

17. Marsland, S.: Machine Learning: An Algorithmic Perspective. CRC Press, Taylor & Francis Group, Boca Raton (2015)

18. Mohajon, J.: Confusion Matrix for Your Multi-Class Machine Learning Model, Medium, 09 September 2020. https://towardsdatascience.com/confusion-matrix-for-your-multi-class-machine-learning-model-ff9aa3bf7826. Accessed 13 June 2021

19. Narasimba, M., Susheela, D.: Pattern Recognition an Algorithmic Approach. Springer, Universities Press, UTiCS

Integration of Rural and Urban Training in Teachers, Students and Older Adults in Computer Security Mediated by Technology

Jose Luiyi Plaza Arias[1]([📧]) [iD] and Clara Lucía Burbano González[2]([📧]) [iD]

[1] Corporación Universitaria Comfacauca-Unicomfacauca, Popayán, Colombia
luiyiplaza98@gmail.com
[2] Universidaad Mayor, Santiago, Chile
claritaluciab@gmail.com

Abstract. The transmission of knowledge in areas such as Computer Security is a primary factor in the acquisition of skills in the knowledge and use of technologies, allowing to improve Human-Computer Interaction (HCI) in society through a segmented knowledge base for the training of individuals., where technological mediation is a factor to take into account to guarantee learning, acquisition of competences and adaptability to the change that contemporary society requires through Stages in Cognitive Development. This article presents results of the intervention carried out by the Virtual Learning Environment Think Safe App (2020-Urban/Students) and Virtual Learning Objects, Rural App (2021 Rural/Teachers) and SIMPA App (2021 Urban/Older Adults), focused on training in computer security and the development of technological and cognitive skills, necessary for daily life from the professional, educational and individual perspective, prepared for the change that contemporary society in the new virtuality, due to the state of pandemic generated by COVID-19, affecting the normality of intelligent learning and exposing the existing gap in relation to the way in which learning is acquired and accessed.

Keywords: Learning and Knowledge Technologies (TAC) · Virtual Learning Environment (AVA) · Human-Computer Interaction (HCI) · Information security · Intelligent learning

1 Introduction

Technology has currently taken on great value, because it allows interconnecting a society that seeks to define new paradigms and knowledge about the world that surrounds it, from this perspective the concept of Network Society arises raised by Manuel Castells understood as: "The set of scientific, social and humanistic branches, which postulate a style of organization that revolves around information" [1]. It is important to understand that technology is considered as the basis for developing knowledge in various areas, allowing the interconnection of society through the adoption of Critical-Reflective Thinking (CRP) and Teaching Competences/Soft Competences (a. Communication; b. Teamwork; c. Motivation; d. Affective Listening).

© Springer Nature Switzerland AG 2021
M. F. Mata-Rivera and R. Zagal-Flores (Eds.): WITCOM 2021, CCIS 1430, pp. 35–61, 2021.
https://doi.org/10.1007/978-3-030-89586-0_4

The virtual training of the XXI century, has allowed to transform the unidirectional strategies (Teacher/Student) used to transmit knowledge (Board, notebook and pencil), towards an environment conducive to generating collaboration and experimentation (Teacher/Student/Technology) in the group through virtualization and gamification. The reason for inter-cognitive research was the design, development and implementation of virtual training resources, aimed at obtaining both cognitive and communicative skills on the contemporary environment generated by the evolution of technology, reducing the existing gap on the subject of computer security and electronic means of payment where the National Council of Economic and Social Policy (Conpes) mentions that:

"The growing participation of citizens in the digital environment, the high dependence on digital infrastructure and the increase in the use and adoption of new Information and Communication Technologies (ICT) bring with them a series of risks and uncertainties related to security digital, which requires the country to have sufficient capacities for its proper and timely management." [2].

The study carried out with students of Systems Engineering, VI Semester of the Comfacauca-Unicomfacauca University Corporation Popayán Cauca-Colombia, teachers from the rural area of Hualaihue (Chile) and older adults from the compensation fund Los Andes-Chile, allowed to establish the impact obtained, by integrating the specific knowledge of Computer Security/Network Security (SI/SR) and security in electronic means of payment, through the appropriation of Technological Mediations (MT), in search of impacting the appropriation of knowledge and use correct technology, by transmitting soft skills (critical-reflective thinking) and strong skills (mastery of technology), necessary in the 21st century to develop most daily activities where devices such as computers, telephones, smart televisions are the door to the world. Consequently, it was obtained as a result/solution, the development of three Information and Communication Resources (RIC) to promote Learning Mediated by Mobile Devices (Think Safe App) and decentralization of knowledge (Rural App and SIMPA App) in the stage of cognitive development corresponding to Formal Operations [3] and that take shape from Heutagogy (Adult Training) [4] and Andragogy (Senior Adult Training) [5].

"The threats, attacks, and incidents of digital security, day by day are more sophisticated and complex, involving serious economic or social consequences. For example, according to Accenture estimates, the cost to businesses derived from the impact of cybercrime has increased by 72% between 2014 and 2019" [6].

"This leads to a deterioration in digital confidence and a slowdown in the development of countries in the digital future. Consequently, governments around the world have joined forces to address the new challenges in detecting and managing cyber threats, attacks, and incidents by formulating and updating strategies or policies related to digital security." [7].

The main problem on which the research project was worked, lies in the lack of Information and Communication Resources that do not focus on the delivery of content, on the contrary, allow the student to experience, appropriate and interact with the technological environment freely, where it generates a solid knowledge base through the use of virtual tools and content focused on the development of skills and competencies for life; Currently, the topic of Computer Security and Electronic Payment Means has gained strength due to the presentation of increasingly complex technology, therefore, society must understand how to protect, avoid and act in the face of risks, threats or vulnerabilities, promoting thus optimal and safe cyberculture.

"In Colombia, according to the 2019–2020 Cybercrime Trends Report, carried out jointly by a team of private investigators, a team from the National Police and allied technology companies, a total of 15,948 complaints were reported in 2019, this being 5.8% less than the year 2018, which had 22,524, 2 these figures suggest whether the security measures adopted are being sufficient or the level of awareness of the problem has not yet been adequate" [2].

The present research allowed a descriptive analysis of the information collected regarding Critical-Reflective Thinking Skills, Teaching Competencies and knowledge, achieved by the study groups a priori/posterior to the intervention mediated by technology, articulated under the Specific Knowledge of Computer Security/Network Security (SI/SR) and electronic payment methods, determined comparatively, the evolution obtained thanks to the intervention and training modality used for each case study, providing an iterative-incremental diagnosis between strategies and possible future improvements to ensure an optimal ICT-mediated learning experience.

2 Digital Transposition in the Computer Age

The computer age and the New Contemporary Society assume the role of builder for a prosperous future, full of new mixtures between technology and human resources, the Digital Transformation required for the solution of new paradigms that affect the needs of the environment through proposed solutions to cushion the accelerated technological advance that has turned normality into an opportunity for literacy; It is possible to identify in the educational field from the training of students and apprentices in higher education the critical-reflective thinking necessary to face new training modalities, generating competent graduates with mastery of knowledge in a dynamic and non-repetitive way, there is the development of Teacher Competencies, structured in the conceptual framework relating training styles, virtuality and tools, generating impact on the strategy used by the teacher, migrating from flat training to dynamic/diversified by Emerging Technologies, the above from the framework of urban/rural training in Colombia (Popayán, department of Cauca) and Chile (Hualaihué, province of Palena). It is important to observe how learning has evolved in older adults, who are part of the New Contemporary Society, on issues that guarantee the safe mastery of technology in the 21st century. Despite being different contexts (Urban/Rural), they focus directly on experiences, having as a fundamental pillar the appropriation of computer security concepts that converge in the use of information and communication resources from learning and knowledge technologies (Mobile App and Information and Communication Resource), generating significant results to the discovery of improvements in educational-communicative processes mediated by ICT.

Next, through the development of the state of the art, the relationship between skills and competencies for the training of students in higher education, teachers and older adults, in the urban/rural area, additionally the types of training and results compared to the new challenges posed by the technological revolution of the XXI century to finally guarantee the identification of the existing need in the appropriation of Emerging Technologies, as a strategy to strengthen virtual education in cutting-edge topics, which in our case are Computer Security and Security in Payment Methods Electronic Insurance.

2.1 Training and Development of Critical-Reflective Thinking Skills in Higher Education

Teaching innovation represents an area for the training and development of skills that allow the adaptation of knowledge to the needs of the 21st century; the acquisition of Soft Skills (S-Skills), seeks to strengthen day by day, the ability to interact and communicate collaboratively the ideas that will later be the activation mechanism to guarantee an optimal interaction between the individual/learner and the technology used, as a channel to transmit knowledge within the classroom; Teachers promote the incorporation of technology through the design and implementation of virtual courses, obtaining as a result, an improvement in the domain of topics, decentralization of computer content and appropriate use of emerging technology, favoring the construction of knowledge and the development of skills necessary to the transformation of the environment [8]. Consequently, the transformation of the teacher/promoter of learning within the classroom presents information to students/learners through mechanisms such as Contemporary Pedagogical Models (MPC) from which constructivism and instructional design stand out, as support to the themes inserted within the Learning Object or Personal Learning Environment (PLE): a. M-Learning: Learning through mobile devices; b. B-Learning: Mixed learning, uses face-to-face and virtuality to transform the classroom into a collaborative classroom; c. E-Learning: Totally virtual learning, interaction, collaboration, and appropriation of knowledge through an autonomous training sequence (Fig. 1).

The need to transmit knowledge to guarantee a prosperous future, especially without losing sight of the transformation of the technological environment, is one of the challenges worldwide, the adoption of Critical-Reflective Thinking becomes visible, as an element to impact on experiences and expectations of the student/apprentice, allowing to generate a high index of significance (Acceptance and relationship with the individual's reality) later, it transforms knowledge, improving contributions in the labor, social and economic field.

Over time, the New Knowledge Society (NSC) of which Higher Education institutions are part, require Soft Skills (S-Skills), teamwork, learning to learn, time management, and information, essential for mastering and adapting to the evolution of companies/organizations [8]; Teaching Innovation, identifies the existing link between Soft Skills (S-Skill), provided from the perspective of the Constructivist Pedagogical model and Personal Learning Environments (PLE) from M-Learning, the investigative contribution of Jean Piaget and Lev Vigotsky, places the Pedagogical Model Constructivist, as an element focused on the construction of knowledge and a social channel for the internal restructuring of thought, respectively [9]. Learning instruction is born from applications of Behavioral Psychology, delimiting the mechanisms (Channels) necessary in the

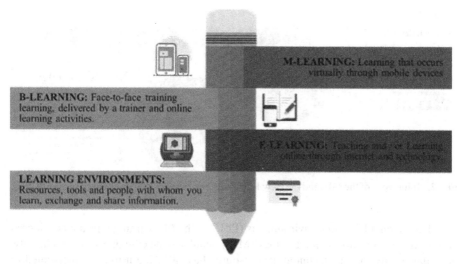

Fig. 1. Personal learning environments towards the transformation of the computer age.

transmission of knowledge, when planning and designing a Virtual Environment (AV) mediated by ICT [8]. Personal Learning Environments (PLE) in Higher Education are popular due to the added value they provide towards the transmission of information, regardless of the Pedagogical Modality used, the constant use of ICT in the adoption of knowledge, serves as support to the needs obtained by society, which is classified as a Volatile, Uncertain, Complex and Ambiguous society (VUCA Environment), forming an ideology about the need to learn for life, postulating that knowledge is the central axis for production value, where quality prevails over quantity, through productivity [10].

> *"When defining M-Learning, as a mediator of knowledge, it was found that:" Any activity mediated by mobile technology "[...]" Within this conception, M-Learning was defined as any type of learning that occurs when the student does not it is in a predetermined fixed location, or what happens when the student takes advantage of the learning opportunities offered by mobile technologies. " According to Susana I. Herrera and Marta C. Fennema [11].*

The above breaks down the New Contemporary Society, a Network Society optimized daily through the acquisition of knowledge that promotes decentralized, ubiquitous, and strongly collaborative learning, where this last characteristic allows Contemporary Pedagogical Models (MPC) to migrate towards education. a distance and make the most of the range of tools available on the network, intercommunicating thoughts, opinions, and the Knowledge Society in general. Learning Mediated by Mobile Devices (M-Learning), is Media and Informational Literacy (MIL), made up of two important aspects for literacy, considered as the media and the informational segment; They were considered separate and distinct, but UNESCO rebuilt them, by combining competencies (knowledge, skills, and attitudes) and work in the contemporary era, encompassing the media and other elements that provide information regardless of the Technological Mediation used [12] (Fig. 2).

Media and Information Literacy (MIL)

They constitute tools, methods and mechanisms used to transmit cutting-edge knowledge in informational channels such as mobile devices, computers, tablets, among others, significantly impacting traditional static training strategies, through contemporary strategies that are dynamic and adaptive to needs.

New Knowledge Society (NKS)

It is the one who largely absorbs the decisions that are made in educational settings, therefore, the responsibility falls clearly on the training styles used in these sites, therefore, quality education must be guaranteed and with the best mechanisms, to build a New Adaptive and dynamic Knowledge Society from the points raised by MIL

Fig. 2. Joint work of the MIL and the New Knowledge Society to achieve Digital Transformation.

The Personal Learning Environments (PLE) of the M-Learning type are considered part of Media and Information Literacy (MIL), thanks to the ease of access, availability, and adaptability that the technological resource has, allowing it to be implemented in diverse branches of knowledge and intercommunicating a Network Society increasingly submerged in virtuality, transforming the virtual training environment into a conducive environment where effective communication and the development of meaningful experiences are the methods to achieve an adaptive, avant-garde and with a commitment to sustainable development.

2.2 Development of Teaching Skills for the Appropriation of New Technological Horizons

Digital Competences are a strategy that has become a trend for the teaching context in Technological Mediations defined as "the existence of complex competencies based on the development of a technological culture, away from technophilia, conceived as the ability to capture and take advantage of opportunities to transform reality" [13]; the concept of assimilation, where the 21st-century student has various needs, such as gaining access to information freely and indiscriminately, where in retrospect with previous decades, most individuals focused on memorizing information, while today, They focus on developing lifelong competencies/skills, allowing knowledge to be assimilated with learning experiences that turn the classroom into a space for interaction and information correlation.

"The need for teachers to know and understand the benefits of collaboration, because this will mean knowing the interactions between their students to enhance shared learning between them" [14].

The need to train teachers and their skills is due to the transformation from a traditional era, where the student was oriented with the contents of a book or laboratory guides are followed, to a completely digital era, where supporting documents such as books, podcasts and videos are found online, allowing teachers to access documentation to transform and innovate the strategies used to transmit knowledge to their students/learners through didactics and empathy (Connectivism).

"Teachers need to understand the practices, designs, and results of collabora-tive strategies, since this implies improvement of learning from inside and out-side schools, including families as fundamental components in the educational community, especially at the levels initial training courses" [15].

The 21st-century teacher must be aware of their role in the classroom, as responsible for the knowledge presented to their students, being prepared for any setback such as the hasty arrival of virtuality due to the state of pandemic declared in 2019 by the COVID-19 virus, evidencing the need to train teachers in the use of technology, especially in the implementation of Virtual Objects that allow the replacement of the board, pencil, and notebook, by didactic activities, training dynamics, synchronous or asynchronous tuto-rials to the process of training and encouraging the teacher to adapt to change, reaching the second competence which is the use of Technological Mediations, giving the teacher a channel to transmit knowledge, but it is not a matter of simply making PowerPoint presentations or the use of office automation tools to insert content on a platform. To achieve this objective, cutting-edge tools must be used to facilitate the interaction and increase of new didactic resources, allowing the topics previously considered difficult by the student/learner to be easy and understandable, to the point that they can remember what learned just by looking at the context (Fig. 3).

"Teachers who work in collaborative cultures acquire and develop positive attitudes towards teaching" [16].

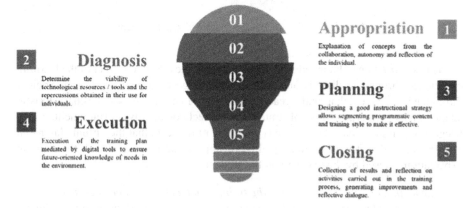

Fig. 3. Five stages for the application of teaching skills in the classroom.

Collaboration as a method for the transmission of knowledge, takes power due to the proposals obtained from the educational ecosystem, where students interact and the teacher becomes a promoter of knowledge; "It is necessary to train teachers to generate a professional culture of constructive relationships in this way to create strong and intelligent learning networks to achieve joint purposes." [17].

The use of Technological Mediations are considered fundamental to achieve Digital Transformation, starting from the knowledge, experience and interaction of individuals, as a primary factor to Literacy the New Contemporary Society, research in the area of training/education, evolved to integrate mechanisms that support existing information, modifying educational paradigms and improving the responsible use of technology. Generating in the teacher competencies for the use of technology, knowledge and content design within a tool, optimizes the interaction between tutor, apprentice and technology, where the teacher as an instructor, analyzes, organizes and proposes evaluation/training strategies appropriate, allowing learners to analyze, interpret and transform a significant experience of what they have learned through the technological tool as a container for the training process, simplifying the learning chain, in a virtual environment (Fig. 4).

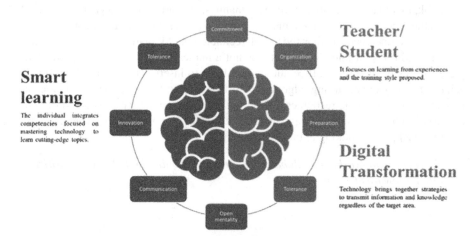

Fig. 4. Individuo, Tecnología y Aprendizaje Inteligente.

The construction of knowledge from the vision of the user or designer of the learning experience, through the digital transformation that suggests the New Knowledge Society through new ICTs and that finally reaches Intelligent Learning, makes the characteristic adaptability of this type visible. of strategy for the techno/cognitive development, which triggers a series of strategies and the typification of the level that the virtual classroom must-have, so that it is of optimal quality, of impact and associated with the training expectations, raised by the teacher and the student.

"The methodological approach for the training of teaching competencies must be accompanied by strategies that favor the search for solutions to the problems that are experienced in the real world." [18].

2.3 The Elderly and Their Perception of the Technological Environment in the 21st Century

In the Theory of Education, the social context is mainly highlighted, which segments the main objective of education [5], proposing three conceptual axes that will guarantee efficiency and the successful completion of the strategy as evidenced below (Fig. 5):

Learning

Acquisition of knowledge mediated by study, exercise or experience support, of the knowledge necessary to learn an art or trade.

Self-directed learning

Taking initiative with or without accompaniment, on topics of interest.

Individualism / Communitarianism

Ability to associate problems and generate a solution that increases the efficiency of the final product.

Cosmopolisism

Ability to work under the principles of morality and teamwork, promoting knowledge decentralization in an inclusive way and without limitations.

Fig. 5. Learning and it is three conceptual axes to guarantee its effectiveness from the theory of education.

Making use of fundamental concepts in contemporary education allows the creation of Meaningful Learning that directly impacts the needs of individuals whom it is desired to train, guaranteeing the vanguard of knowledge and management of techniques regardless of the strategy and tools for the transmission of information used.; understands that one of the main behavioral objectives of education, evidenced in the society of the twentieth century, understood as the era of learning "Self Directed Throughout Life", the term "Self Directed" obtains the psychological need of the adult, by feeling the owner of his life and the directly proportional relationship between the advancement of his studies carried out (Knowledge) and the increase of the independence required on his learning experience (Experimentation). The term "Throughout Life" is generated thanks to the acceleration of the obsolescence of the human being (the passing of the years) decreasing the capacity of attention, concentration, retention, and disposition to understand and face the technological world, forcing a change in the continuous training process, developing skills and abilities necessary to evolve with the world [19]. In the particular case of training for the elderly, the main objective is to promote learning throughout life as mentioned, however, within companies and government institutions, it does not seem that The intention is to prevent the inability to understand and participate in today's globalized world or to ensure the right to self-realization and the maximum development of potential that comes from humanism; on the contrary, the "workforce" is durable and productive, seeking to promote "active aging".

Lifelong learning ceases to be a matter of "Learning to Be" to become "Learning to Be Productive and Employable" [20], resulting in demotivating for those who are just beginning their process of acquiring experiences, due to the long line of unemployed and considerations for acquiring a stable and reliable job. The "adults" are understood as "subjects" of education, it is necessary to inquire about the concept of "subject" and "adult", adding a stabilizing component, determined as the concept of "maturity", which allows both the "Subject" as the "adult", can exist at the same time without creating a retrograde malformation to the prevailing need to "learn for life"; The above defines the "subject", made up of knowledge, knowledge, and discipline, as the orientation of education towards students (entities of action and responsibility) towards the continuous evolution of knowledge and science [21]; The "adult" is considered as the being to be transformed both cognitively and procedurally, providing the necessary aids to achieve said objective, but not without first evaluating their potentials and abilities where tools can be built that transmit knowledge in an accessible, clear and appropriate way. according to the kind of individual you want to train.

The concept of "Andragogy" is related to socio-cultural aspects and is based on ensuring that the elderly are integrated into the environment where they work, making effective use of what they have learned [22], it is possible to affirm that this theory seeks to simplify the process cognitive and the acquisition of skills related to life and vocational training [23]. The foregoing states that the theory of "Andragogy" aims to train/prepare older adults in specific knowledge related to their daily lives in the use of technological tools, structures from knowledge or face-to-face classes, independent of the channel, making the individual take the maximum benefit and in the same way digest the greatest amount of content sequentially, constantly and effectively; the way of acquiring knowledge by the elderly, were identified in 3 postulates according to [24] for learning in the elderly population (Fig. 6).

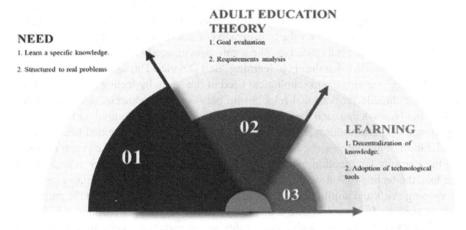

Fig. 6. Fundamental pillars for adult learning from Knowles's Andragogy theory [19].

The above clearly shows the needs of the elderly, which are fundamental in the theory of "Adult Education" to reach meaningful learning, ordering it in a stepped and joint process, to include the elderly and technology, who converge in a new class as an adult that we will call "Super Adult", in the capacity of appropriating, adapting, shaping and promulgating the knowledge from their expertise and learning acquired over time and the creation of a favorable training environment, allows an atmosphere of trust around of process. The author Knowles mentions that the first step in the formation of the elderly is to improve virtuality and presence through constructivist and behavioral pedagogical models, mediated by ICT and adapted to the end-user [19]; The use of collaboration allows students to not only work with the tutor/facilitator, they include collaboration between group members (study partners), to improve communication skills, leadership, and participation, reducing the fear of mistakes and increasing participation within the study group.

> "The education of the human being, in its nature and freedom, remains a prisoner of this new order; the classic is outdated because in its place it will no longer be a question of behavior but of disposition and capacities - disposition and capacity to learn - to this is added the insatiable demand for innovation. The new is trapped in the limit of time and the succession of events becomes an awakening of the mind" [25].

The factions that the teacher must consider when imparting the training in a study group, being aware of the actions, deficiencies, and shortcomings they incur, producing frustration and demotivation of their learners, recommending the following considerations to virtual teachers [26] (Fig. 7):

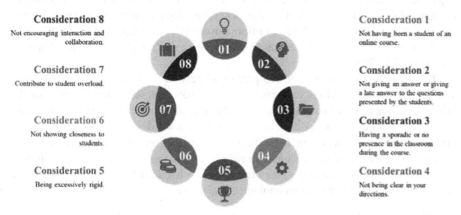

Consideration 8
Not encouraging interaction and collaboration.

Consideration 7
Contribute to student overload.

Consideration 6
Not showing closeness to students.

Consideration 5
Being excessively rigid.

Consideration 1
Not having been a student of an online course.

Consideration 2
Not giving an answer or giving a late answer to the questions presented by the students.

Consideration 3
Having a sporadic or no presence in the classroom during the course.

Consideration 4
Not being clear in your directions.

Fig. 7. Eight considerations to take into account by virtual teachers of the 21st century

Virtual tutors must be objective and purposeful to provide alternatives to their students' learning, modeling a structure that is clear and diversified, to optimize how knowledge is acquired in the study group, who will give the necessary clues to identify, plan and design the construction of a resource that responds to the needs of the public, knowledge and the market.

2.4 Need to Transform the Educational Environment of the Student, Teacher and Older Adult Through Emerging Technology

In the case of the training of students in the urban area of Colombia, the creation of an Information and Communication Resource (RIC) permeates, which contributes to the adoption of knowledge in the specific knowledge of Computer Security/Network Security (SI/SR) being necessary, due to the absence of educational technologies that function as practical support and allow the appropriate appropriation of knowledge interactively, Technological Mediations (MT) in the training of Systems Engineers and the current pandemic situation declared by COVID-19, exposes the existence of an important level of maturity in terms of Computer Security, but concerning the organizational technological infrastructure, the same does not happen, especially with the use of mobile applications, reducing its effectiveness and impact on the generation of Meaningful Learning.

On the other hand, Chile is one of the countries that has a legal framework focused on the issue of computer crimes and the protection of personal data. In particular, there are computer crime laws, such as Law No. 19,223 of 1993 (which penalizes those who carry out illicit information systems) and, additionally, Law No. 19,628. 116, in charge of data protection; In 2018, it approved an amendment to numeral 4 of article 19 in the Political Constitution of the Republic of Chile, where it recognizes the right to honor and private life, introducing the protection of personal data; Currently, two bills are being processed in Congress, the first modifies the regulations on the protection of personal data (Bulletin No. 11.144-07 118) the second, adapts the Chilean regulations to the Budapest Convention on Cybercrime and additionally, it provides modifications in legal bodies (Bulletin N°12.192-25 119). Along the same lines, there are legal initiatives in financial matters (modifications to the General Banking Law on operational risk and incorporation of specific standards for Information on Operational Incidents (RAN 20-8) and Business Continuity Management (RAN 20-9).) of the Commission for the Financial Market (CMF) [27].

The panorama shows the need to prepare society in favor of improving cognitive and technological capacities to prevent security risks that affect the integrity of the information that travels through the network, Intelligent Learning as a means to integrate technology towards the acquisition of cutting-edge knowledge, They are an alternative to process information that guarantees the promulgation of security in technological ecosystems for the training of skills and knowledge in the use of emerging technologies, the intervention of the training style in teachers who live in rural areas of Chile are the beginning towards change and technological inclusion.

"The risk of cyberattacks on critical infrastructure and fraud or data theft has always been a priority for business leaders globally. According to the Global Risks Report 2020 of the World Economic Forum, 17 the risk of cyberattacks to critical infrastructure and fraud or data theft were ranked among the top 10 risks most likely to occur" [27].

In the context of training for older adults, practical and viable solutions are proposed, which allow enhancing the concept of continuous learning, that is, the older adult can improve their skills on elements that they use in their daily lives [28]. When generating Virtual Learning Objects (OVA) that contribute to the training of different types of learners, it takes high importance, by encouraging and including older adults towards participation directed to the well-being proposed by the inclusion of ICT. Sometimes a low-reliability rate in electronic devices, due to little familiarity, cultural aspects, or perceived lack of interest in older adults, are a reflection of the little acceptance of the use of this type of tools, prevailing the tradition of handling physical money and go to the collection sites in a personal way, opening the digital divide in this area of the knowledge society day by day.

Technology has become an ally for the subsistence of companies and SMEs, demonstrating once again the potential and scope that technology has on contemporary society, especially in carrying out online procedures and payments. This stems from the speed of attention and comfort in preventing individuals from having to travel to collection sites and therefore being exposed to crowds. The advantages and proposals made by New ICTs, where a segment of the population (older adults), will be able to analyze, identify and understand the main difficulties that they claim to have in Santiago de Chile, who, according to the AMUCH (Association of Senior Citizens) Characterization survey Municipalities of Chile) of the year 2020, indicates ICT access at home, presents a technology accessibility rate of a) It does not have technological resources (Desktop, Tablet or Notebook): 78.4%; b) They do not have access to the written press: 63.5%; c) Does not have internet: 57.3%.

"93.7% of the elderly in rural areas do not have a computer or Tablet or Notebook, a figure that reaches 76.2% in urban areas. Internet access also presents gaps based on territoriality, which is part of the country's technological infrastructure and the territorial dispersion of the population, and f) 84.1% of this segment does not have internet access in rural areas, a figure that drops to g) 53.6% in urban áreas" [29].

The barriers that hinder the use of ICT in older adults, the pre-existing gaps are positioned as the main aspect in studies by several authors, that is, those that are generated especially from the educational level [30], in second place is the previous contact/familiarization with ICT in the last working years, called the "gray gap" [31] which is understood as the exclusion and barriers of access to the internet of the elderly [32] and [33]. Consequently, the knowledge society considers the New ICTs as a means to develop autonomy, plurality, and respect for human rights on equality, and in a parallel way, it gains importance in this context described as the "learning society" were to "learn for life"; "Learning society" and refers to a new type of society where knowledge is built outside educational institutions and is not limited to initial training, where "learning for life" means that people are currently obliged to perform in different activities throughout his life [29], therefore it is essential to train constantly [34].

3   Methodology

The orientation of experiences through Technological Mediations in search of generating Critical-Reflective Thinking Skills (Think Safe App), Teaching Competences (Rural App) and Knowledge in Safe Payment Means (SIMPA APP) in systems engineers, basic teachers primary school and older adults respectively, mark a strong trend for educational work in general in search of improving the connectivity between productivity, need and training processes for life. The Alternative Research method and an apprehensive level methodology oriented in the comparative/analytical holotype, allowed the performance of three diagnostic tests through which it was possible: a. Identify the development obtained in the thinking skills corresponding to Analysis and Interpretation in a group of 23 students from the Comfacauca University Corporation (Popayán); b. Identify the development of Teacher Competencies with a population of 20 teachers, inhabitants of the rural area of Hualaihué under a sample of 11 individuals; c. Identify the level of adoption of knowledge regarding electronic means of payment in a population of 40 older adults recognized in the compensation fund of the Andes Chile, with a sample of 12 individuals; From the previous samples, it was possible to establish initial and final state mediated by ICT in virtual training.

3.1 Technique and Instruments

Regarding the use of techniques and instruments that allow evaluating the state of knowledge and satisfaction about the formation of Critical-Reflective Thinking Skills, Teaching Competencies and knowledge in electronic payment means, it was chosen to use test (Pre/Post) validated by "Alpha Cronbach's" to establish the level of reliability of the instrument, document analysis and use/selection of a sample to allow centralizing and guaranteeing the respective quality of the research carried out; In addition, three Information and Communication Resources of the Mobile and Web App type were carried out, validated in the principles of Pedagogical Usability to guarantee an effective experience and impact on the population/work group, finally a satisfaction survey was carried out to to identify how effective the strategy was against the level of comfort, acceptability and comprehension capacity.

3.2 Analysis Technique

The technique to being used in the research project was carried out through the analysis of quantitative data, where the specific knowledge of Computer Security is integrated into the training of Students/Apprentices, Teachers, and older adults in the Technological mediations PIENSA SEGURO APP, RURAL APP, and SIMPA APP in the work of collecting data on the state a priori and after the implementation of said mediation, allowing to analyze the state of knowledge of the intervention group, pedagogical usability through the statistical tool "SPSS" version 25 for data analysis.

4 Results

4.1 Acquisition of Critical-Reflective Thinking Skills in Higher Education

In the descriptive analysis carried out to establish the level of appropriation of HPCR, a study group with twenty-three (23) students of Systems Engineering, VI Semester of the Corporación Universitaria Comfacauca-Unicomfacauca Popayán Cauca-Colombia, where a test divided into Pre Test and Post Test, which were applied in week four corresponding to the first cut of the semester and week ten, equivalent to the third academic cut respectively; The tests carried out allowed to measure Critical-Reflective Thinking Skills (HPCR) through the Pre-Test and Post-Test, about the Interpretation, Analysis, Inference, Evaluation, and Explanation, from the mediation of the Information and Communication Resource-Think Safe App, consolidating the results based on scores obtained by the Study Group as shown below (Tables 1 and 2):

Regarding the evolution of each skill evaluated from the pre (Blue Bar) and post (Red Bar) test, they express that in the ability of: a) Interpretation: An average increase

Table 1. Results Cronbach's Alpha Test.

Result Analysis of Cronbach's Alpha test		
Ability	Cronbach's alpha	Decision
Analysis	0,827	Good
Interpretation	0,929	Excellent
Evaluation	0,904	Excellent
Inference	0,938	Excellent
Explicación	0,908	Excelente

Table 2. Results A Priori/A Posteriori Analysis.

Results A Priori/A Posteriori Analysis					
	Interpreta	Analyze	Inference	Evaluate	Explain
Pre	0,6261	0,413	0,613	0,613	0,5087
Pos	0,7261	0,6	0,7217	0,7217	0,6565

of 0.10 is observed in favor of the post-test. b) Analysis: An average increase of 0.21 is observed in the post-test evaluation. c) Inference: An average increase of 0.11 is observed in the post-test evaluation. d) Evaluation: An average increase of 0.11 is observed in the post-test evaluation. e) Explanation: An average increase of 0.15 is observed in the post-test evaluation. The results show that, on average, the ability that presented the greatest increase in favor of the post-test was Analysis, followed by Explanation, then Inference, Evaluation, and with a lower average in favor of the post-test, the Interpretation skill (Fig. 8).

In this order of ideas, through Fig. 9 and Fig. 10, it is possible to appreciate the results obtained in relation to the average percentage of variation, allowing, through this calculation, to determine the differences in relation to the skills evaluated. Next, the percentages of variation of the skills are shown from lowest to highest: Interpretation 20.34%; Evaluation 37.46%; Explanation 41.73%; Analysis 55.07%; Inference 67.94%.

As can be seen in the results, all the evaluated skills presented a favorable percentage of variation in the application of the Post-Test, that is to say, that the Information and Communication Resource Think Safe App if it contributes to the formation of Critical-Reflective Thinking Skills (HPCR).

4.2 Acquisition of Teaching Competencies in Computer Security

It is necessary to understand how competencies were embedded in the training of teachers, thanks to the development of a mixed training strategy where training content is included with aspects taken from the individual's environment, allowing the understanding of the subject in a practical way; To identify the evolution of the knowledge

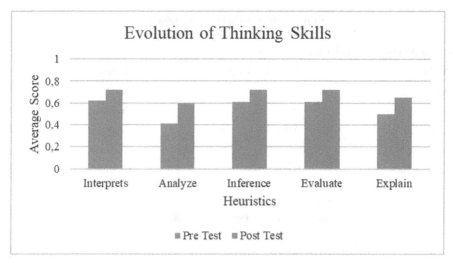

Fig. 8. Evolution of Thinking Skills (Pre-Post Test).

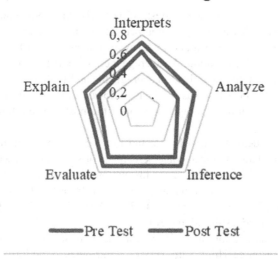

Fig. 9. Pre Test/Post Test averages in the HPCR.

obtained through the Virtual Rural App Object, two tests were carried out where, in the first instance, the initial state of knowledge was determined, to adjust the training structure according to previous knowledge of the group and later the resource is implemented Carrying out the post-test, in charge of evaluating the state of knowledge of individuals

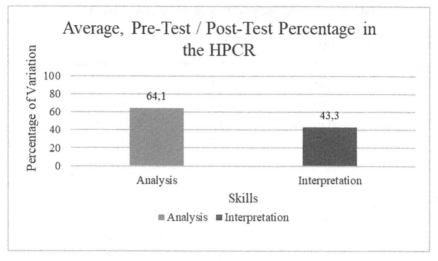

Fig. 10. Average, Pre-Test/Post-Test Percentage in the HPCR.

again, validating the existence of changes in the group. The above obtained the following results:

Table 3 exposes the appropriation of knowledge in computer security by teachers, with a transformation into Mediatization of Learning for Technology, guarantees that teachers in the rural area of Hualaihué, had tools to update knowledge and promote virtual learning; consequently, the teachers in their first intervention measured by the pre-test, had an average rating of 69.5% of effectiveness and use of the subject; The second intervention had a training mediated by the Virtual Rural App Object, obtained an average score of 79% where it is determined that the total evolution of teachers was 1.9 points equivalent to 9.5% compared to the acquisition and mastery of the subject, showing that knowledge in this area was reinforced and understood (Fig. 11).

The exposed data indicate the Teaching Competencies, in knowledge reinforced through the Rural Virtual Object App with acceptance among participants and indirectly the use of technology was optimized, increasing the interest of teachers in rural areas, deepening about technology and its scope.

4.3 Acquisition of Knowledge in Safe Means of Payment in Older Adults

The descriptive analysis that accompanies the results obtained in the measurement in two times (Pre/Post Test), to establish the level of appropriation of knowledge in the specific knowledge of electronic payment means safely in older adults, selecting a focal group of twelve (12) older adults as a unit of analysis belonging to the Los Andes-Chile compensation fund with estimated ages between 45 to 58 years of age, residents in the city of Santiago de Chile-Chile (Analysis Variable) and for those who structured and developed a test with two intervention times: a. Pre-test (Before); b. Post-test (After), applied to the group mentioned above. In this sense, through Table 4, the results were consolidated based on the scores obtained by each older adult, in short, the Value of

Table 3. Percentage analysis of variation in teachers pre/post test.

Variation percentage analysis			
Surveyed	Moment	Outcome	% variation
1	Pre	13	30,8
	Pos	17	
2	Pre	17	11,8
	Pos	19	
3	Pre	15	13,3
	Pos	17	
4	Pre	16	12,5
	Pos	18	
5	Pre	12	33,3
	Pos	16	
6	Pre	14	28,6
	Pos	18	
7	Pre	14	14,3
	Pos	16	
8	Pre	14	28,6
	Pos	18	
9	Pre	12	33,3
	Pos	16	
10	Pre	12	41,7
	Pos	17	
11	Pre	14	28,6
	Pos	18	
Average			25,2

the Percentage of Variation is presented, which described the relationship between the a priori value of the test and test posterior.

Table 4 shows the transformation and impact of technological mediation that contributed to achieving an optimal development of knowledge with a 218.1% improvement. an OVA on electronic means of payment in a secure way. Figure 12 shows the results obtained from the calculation of the mean about the pre/post-test interventions, where a positive impact of technological mediation towards the formation of knowledge can be evidenced:

From the previous figure, it is possible to quantitatively determine that the evolution of knowledge regarding electronic means of payment in a secure way and mediated by

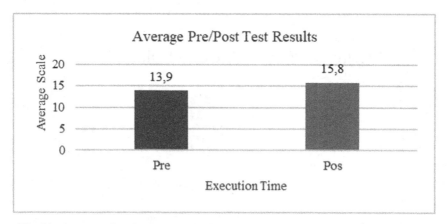

Fig. 11. Average of pre/post test results in teachers in the rural area of Hualaihué-Chile.

Table 4. Pre/Post test variation percentage analysis.

Subject	% Variation	Average % variation
A1	250	*218.1*
A2	0	
A3	33.3	
A4	50	
A5	600	
A6	250	
A7	33.3	
A8	0	
A9	400	
A10	350	
A11	300	
A12	350	

the OVA SIMPA-APP, was 3.8 on average, which shows that ICT-mediated learning is possible and effective. As long as strict guidelines are met to perfect the final product.

4.4   Virtual Objects and Pedagogical Usability

The RIC proposals, before the intervention in reality with end-users, were evaluated using the usability criteria from the elements provided by the tool, as it is a RIC aimed at undergraduate students from Colombia and teachers/adults from Chile who will train in the specific knowledge of Information Security and secure means of payment. It is essential to establish from pedagogy how to create skills, competencies, and knowledge

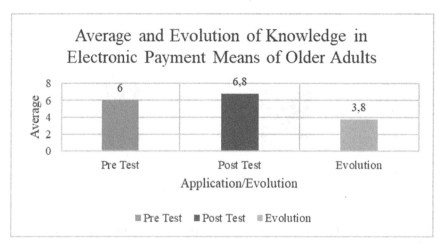

Fig. 12. Average and Evolution of Knowledge in Electronic Payment Means of Older Adults

of impact. Usability according to ISO 9241-11 refers to: "the extent to which a product can be used by specific users to achieve specific goals with effectiveness, efficiency, and satisfaction in a specific context of use" [35]. Now, following the previous premise, a group of RICs is proposed that complies with the parameters offered by the ISO 9241-11 standard and for this, the Think Safe App, Rural App, and Simpa App were created (Fig. 13).

During the inspection, each of the usability criteria considered by the evaluation tool for web and mobile applications in education was taken into account, which in turn are associated with heuristics specifically proposed for each of the tools. The evaluation was carried out by a group of experts on user experience, usability, and pedagogy, inspecting each heuristic, as shown below (Table 5):

Once the inspection on the RICs is completed and taking into account the different evaluation criteria, the results obtained in the pedagogical usability evaluation are presented below, which shows the average of the evaluations obtained by each of the heuristics raised.

In Fig. 14 it is observed that most of the evaluated heuristics stand out with an average greater than four on a scale of one to five; By translating this information into mathematical terms, the Piensa Seguro App Information and Communication Resource (RIC) reached a value greater than or equal to 80% compliance. In the same way, the heuristics that have a lower percentage of compliance are Social Interaction and Personalization with a percentage of 72%, which propose future improvements within the Information and Communication Resource (RIC) to guarantee a better experience and interaction.

It is possible to show in Fig. 15 that the heuristics proposed for the evaluation were accepted globally, with "Aesthetics and Design" being the heuristic with the highest level and "Control and Freedom" the lowest level; the interpretation of results generates an improvement in technology and usability, bringing users an updated proposal with quality. To conclude, the total usability value obtained by the Virtual Rural App Object was 4.1 points, equivalent to 82% concerning content, aesthetics, relationship with the

Preview Piensa Seguro App

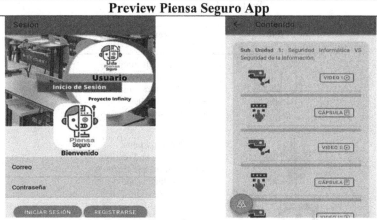

Link: https://ava-piensa-seguro.web.app/

Preview RURAL App

Link: https://ruralapp2021.000webhostapp.com/acerca_de_rural_app.html

Prevew SIMPA App

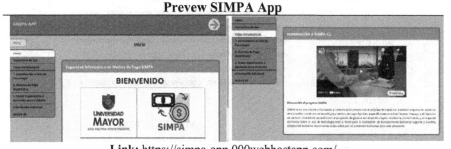

Link: https://simpa-app.000webhostapp.com/

Fig. 13. Information and Communication Resource Captures.

environment, technological medium and the management of the group integrated into the platform (Fig. 16).

From the previous graph, it is possible to determine that the final percentage obtained by the heuristic evaluation carried out is 86% of compliance with the requirements established in the expert evaluation, therefore, it is possible to conclude that the SIMPA Tool- APP is interactive, understandable, impactful and with a good academic level to carry out the process of training older adults in the specific knowledge of secure electronic means of payment.

Table 5. Evaluation heuristics.

Tool	Heuristics
Piensa Seguro	- Personalization. - Social interaction. - Activities and tasks. - Multimedia. - Contents.
RAL	- System Status. - System and reality. - Control and freedom. - Aesthetics and design.
SIMPA	- Interactivity. - Academic level. - Contents. - Understandability.

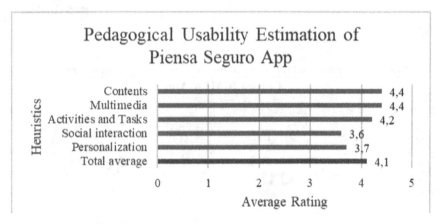

Fig. 14. Result Usability Pedagogical Think Safe App.

5   Conclusions

Regarding the results obtained by the a priori and a posteriori measurement of Critical-Reflective Thinking Skills (Analysis and Interpretation), the students obtained a positive balance, evolving from an initial state (Basic) to a final state (Optimal) thanks to the use of the Information and Communication Resource (RIC) Piensa Seguro App; The proposed resource met the proposed expectations towards the improvement of knowledge and adoption of necessary competencies for work and personal life in computer security and in the same way, an appropriate usability experience was generated, thus allowing, in this

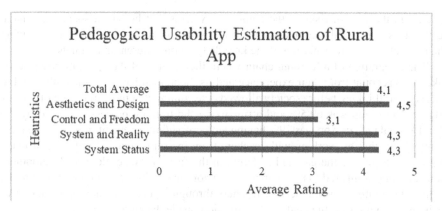

Fig. 15. Pedagogical usability estimation of the Rural Virtual Object App.

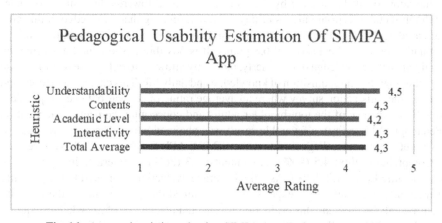

Fig. 16. Average heuristic evaluation SIMPA App (Pedagogical Usability).

way, to reach meaningful learning necessary for the ICT Revolution; From the above, the following aspects before the implementation of the resource are taken into account: a. Pedagogical model of the institution; b. Pedagogical design to be used; c. Technological mediation with which greater affinity is found in the classroom; d. Type of population. The previous aspects allowed to form an appropriate knowledge base to correctly direct the training of students, who in their words defined the experience as "Innovative and appropriate for the formation of knowledge" which motivates to continue improving the Information and Communication Resource (RIC).

For the RIC Rural App in the training of teaching skills, it was possible to connect with the knowledge society, enriching culture and science, by allowing the acquisition of skills to evolve and innovate with the training environment, achieving the appropriation and application of teaching skills, established from knowledge, communication, technology, interaction and culture, obtaining as a result, the appropriation of specific knowledge in Computer Security. The apprentice/teacher identified and adopted the risk prevention strategies, security failures, and computer security pillars, necessary to avoid and act quickly in the face of risks to the computer systems that he has, associating content related to security and safe management of systems with their environment, allowing the interaction and transmission of the knowledge with different individuals.

The integration of a learning chain where the opinion of the apprentice/teacher is taken into account from their experience and its theoretical base is sufficiently valid to defend their thinking before society allowed determining that the initial state of knowledge of the group was 69.5% and at finalizing the training process mediated by the Rural Virtual Object App was 79% having an increase/improvement of 9.5%; The foregoing shows that by working with teachers from the rural area of Hualaihué, it made it possible to reduce the gap and isolation in the face of the accelerated development of technology compared to urban areas, it can continue to improve with motivation, the technical/cognitive development of teachers through Heutagogy and appropriation of technology to improve the quality of instruction inside the classrooms.

Finally, the use of the RIC SIMPA App made it possible to show a great advance in the adoption of knowledge by the strategy proposed towards the training of older adults in secure electronic means of payment, determining that knowledge in this area increased by 218.1% (Pre/Post Test Variation Percentage) going from an initial average evaluation of 3 to a final score of 6.8 points; It is possible to show the transformation obtained on the knowledge of the elderly, indirectly allowing to reduce the fear of the use of technology for the acquisition of knowledge and daily life. This data was corroborated through the satisfaction survey where an average rating of 4.3 was obtained, equivalent to 86% acceptance of the tool by older adults and concerning the heuristic evaluation (Pedagogical Usability), a favorable result was obtained where The 5 experts cited to carry out the process, diagnosed that the SIMPA-APP tool had the following results: a. Comprehensibility: 4.5 (90%); b. Contents: 4.3 (86%); c. Interactivity: 4.3 (86%); d. Academic Level: 4.2 (84%). As a final average evaluation compared to the usability evaluation carried out by the experts, it was obtained that the tool meets the usability requirements by 86% and this evaluation is reflected in the level of knowledge acquired by older adults, as well as the effective management of the OVA SIMPA-APP.

The investigative experience allowed to know training strategies aimed at the student, teacher and elderly of the XXI century through Technological Mediations, to reduce the cognitive and technological gap, oriented to the topic of computer security; consequently, the motivation to learn to improve their quality of life and encourage the adoption of Critical-Reflective Thinking Skills, Teaching Competencies and Knowledge in Secure Digital Payment Means; This was an arduous process, however, the reward is reflected in the increase and management of knowledge to continue innovating in the use of adoption of new technologies that intervene daily in the daily life of citizens and that thanks to them make information accessible to all public regardless of being a native or digital nomad. From the above results, it is also possible to show that learning for students, teachers, and older adults are not isolated, therefore the creation of unified strategies focused on the development and appropriation of competencies-skills where the learner is the epicenter for the mobilization of technology and knowledge broadens the training panorama where the classroom already takes second place and virtualization and interaction take priority within the Higher Education Institutions (HEI), decentralizing the face-to-face modality and moving to a modality hybrid (B-learning) or virtual (E-learning).

As future work, it is reflected to integrate artificial intelligence to make the appropriation of knowledge much more interactive and personalized, adjusting to the level of knowledge of each individual and permeating an experience where the same learner can choose if he wishes to learn in an associative, observational, by discovery, experimental or emotional, which allows the future to have a knowledge base that day by day will transform the way of thinking and interacting with technology. Additionally, the type of content that is presented to the apprentices must be taken into account, being necessary to update and present new topics related to computer security, technology management, and life skills, which will generate interest as the fundamental key to a learning experience with significant impact on the expectations of learners.

References

1. Castells, M., Andrade, J.A.: Reseña: La Sociedad red: una visión global por Manuel Castells. Enl@ce Rev. Venez. Inf. Tecnol. y Conoc. **1**, 139–141 (2010). http://ccuc.cbuc.cat/record= b3600252~S23*cat
2. Africa, S., et al.: Estudio Del Estado Actual De La Seguridad Informática En Las Organizaciones De Colombia. Hum. Relations **3**(1), 1–8 (2020). http://search.ebscohost. com/login.aspx?direct=true&AuthType=ip,shib&db=bth&AN=92948285&site=eds-live& scope=site%0Ahttp://bimpactassessment.net/sites/all/themes/bcorp_impact/pdfs/em_stakeh older_engagement.pdf%0Ahttps://www.glo-bus.com/help/helpFiles/CDJ-Page3b
3. Rafael Linares, A.: Desarrollo Cognitivo: Las Teorías de Piaget y Vygotsky. Univ. Autónoma Barcelona, **1**, 1–29 (2008). http://www.paidopsiquiatria.cat/files/teorias_desarrollo_cognit ivo_0.pdf
4. Koideas: Koideas.com. Heutagogía: La autonomía del aprendiz (2020). https://www.koideas. com/post/heutagogia-la-autonomia-del-aprendiz. Accessed 04 May 2021
5. Sánchez-Domenech, I., Rubia-Avi, M.: ¿Es posible la reconstrucción de la teoría de la educación de personas adultas integrando las perspectivas humanistas, críticas y postmodernas? Rev. Electrónica Educ. **21**(2), 1–26 (2017). https://doi.org/10.15359/ree.21-2.23
6. Abbosh, O., Bissell, K.: Securing the digital economy: reinventing the internet for trust. Accenture, pp. 1–59 (2019). https://www.accenture.com/us-en/insights/cybersecurity/reinve nting-the-internet-digital-economy
7. Departamento Nacional de Planeación: CONPES 3995, Política Nacional de Confianza y Seguridad Digital. Dep. Nac. Planeación, Minist. Tecnol. la Inf. y las Comun. Dep. Adm. la Pres. la República, p. 51 (2020). https://colaboracion.dnp.gov.co/CDT/Conpes/Económicos/ 3995.pdf
8. Hazim, N.G., Sentí, V.E.: Experiencias globales en innovación, evaluación y acreditación en la educación superior a distancia. J. Chem. Inf. Model. **110**(9), pp. 1689– 1699 (2017). http://rai.uapa.edu.do:8080/xmlui/bitstream/handle/123456789/180/LaED-dis eñoyevaluacióndecursosvirtuaes-NGonzález-CITICED-v5.pdf?sequence=1&isAllowed=y
9. Guerrero, N.C.H.: Applications of Vygotskyan Concept of Mediation in SLA. Colomb. Appl. Linguist. J. **9**, 213–228 (2007). http://revistas.udistrital.edu.co/ojs/index.php/calj/art icle/view/3152/4535
10. Reinoso, G.G.L., Barzola, K.M., Caguana, D.M., Lopez, R.P., Lopez, J.C.P.: M-learning, a path to ubiquitous learning in higher education in Ecuador. RISTI - Rev Iber. Sist. e Tecnol. Inf. **2019**(E18), 47–59 (2019)
11. Herrera, S., Fennema, M.: Tecnologías móviles aplicadas a la educación superior. Congr. Argentino Ciencias la, pp. 620–630 (2011). http://sedici.unlp.edu.ar/handle/10915/18718

12. Wilson, C.: Alfabetización mediática e informacional: proyecciones didácticas. Comunicar (2012). http://www.unesco.org/new/es/communication-and-information/media-development/media-literacy/mil-as-composite-concept/#:~:text=Laalfabetizaciónmediáticaeinformacionalreconoceelpapelfundamentalde,ydeinformación%2Caevaluar

13. Avogadro Thomé, M.E., Quiroga Macleimon, S.R.: La mediación tecnológica y las TIC: fenómenos y objetos técnicos. RAZÓN Y PALABRA Prim. Rev. Electrónica en Iberoamérica Espec. en Comun, **92**, 1–18 (2015). https://www.redalyc.org/pdf/1995/199543036052.pdf

14. Roth, R.: The Role of the University in the Preparation of Teachers, 1st edn. Routledge, London (1998)

15. Iglesias, M., Lozano, M., Martínez, I.: The use of digital tools in the development of collaborative learning : analysis of experience in Higher Education. Rev. Docencia Univ. 11(2), 333–351 (2013). https://doi.org/10.4995/redu

16. Flores, M., Day, C.: Contexts which shape and reshape new teachers' identities: a multiperspective study. Teach. Teach. Educ. **22**, 219–232 (2006). https://doi.org/10.1016/j.tate.2005.09.002

17. Hargreaves, S., Earl, A., Moore, L., Manning, S.: Learning to Change: Teaching Beyond Subjects and Standards. Wiley, San Francisco (2001)

18. Molina Torres, M.P., Ortiz Urbano, R.: Educación sostenible y conservación del patrimonio cultural en la formación del profesorado universitario. Form. Univ. **14**, 207–216 (2021). http://www.scielo.cl/scielo.php?script=sci_arttext&pid=S0718-50062021000100207&nrm=iso

19. Knowles, M.: Self-directed learning: a guide for learners and teachers. SELF-DIRECTED Learn. A Guid. Learn. Teach. Malcol m Knowles New York Assoc. Press (1975). 135 pp., Pap. First Publ. June 1, 1977 Other. Artic. Inf. No Access Artic. Inf. **2**(2), 256–257 (1977). https://doi.org/10.1177/105960117700200220

20. Biesta, G.: What's the point of lifelong learning if lifelong learning has no point? On the democratic deficit of policies for lifelong learning. Eur. Educ. Res. Journa **5**(3–4), 169–180 (2006). https://doi.org/10.2304/eerj.2006.5.3.169

21. Biesta, G.: Giving teaching back to education: responding to the disappearance of the teacher. Phenomenol. Pract. **6**(2), 1–16 (2017). https://doi.org/10.29173/pandpr19860

22. Román-González, M.: Codigoalfabetización y pensamiento computacional en educación primaria y secundaria: validación de un instrumento y evaluación de programas [Code-literacy and Computational Thinking in Primary and Secondary Education:.. (2016)

23. Alonso Chacón, P.: La Andragogía como disciplina propulsora de conocimiento en la educación superior. Rev. Electrónica Educ. **16**, 15–26 (2012). https://dialnet.unirioja.es/servlet/articulo?codigo=3975631

24. Torres, M., Fermín, I., Arroyo, C., Piñero, M.: La horizontalidad y la participación en la andragogía. Educere: Artículos **10**, 1–10 (2000). http://www.saber.ula.ve/bitstream/handle/123456789/19444/articulo;jsessionid=24C27110194F07AC941C9F24E3330A00?sequence=1

25. Zambrano Leal, A.: Pedagogía y didáctica: Esbozo de las diferencias, tensiones y relaciones de dos. Rev. Investig. y Pedagog. Maest. en Educ. Uptc **7**(13), 45–61 (2015). https://revistas.uptc.edu.co/index.php/praxis_saber/article/view/4159/3591

26. Borges, F.: La frustración del estudiante en línea . Causas y acciones preventivas. UOC, **7**(7) (2005). https://doi.org/10.7238/d.v0i7.536

27. BID and OEA: Ciberseguridad, riesgos, avances y el camino a seguir en America Latina y El Caribe. Bid- Oea, **1** 204 (2020). https://publications.iadb.org/es/reporte-ciberseguridad-2020-riesgos-avances-y-el-camino-a-seguir-en-america-latina-y-el-caribe

28. Martín Retortillo, T.: Insights: knowledge driven content. El aprendizaje continuo, factor crítico de supervivencia (2017). https://www.ie.edu/insights/es/articulos/aprendizaje-continuo-factor-critico-supervivencia/. Accessed 09 Feb 2021

29. AMUCH: Encuesta de caracterización de la percepción de la población adulto mayor ante la crisis sanitaria derivada del covid-19 2020. Asoc. Munic. Chile, pp. 1–21 (2020). https://www.amuch.cl/wp-content/uploads/2020/04/Encuesta-de-caracterizacion-de-la-percepción-de-la-poblacion-adulto-mayor-por-Covid-19.pdf.pdf

30. Agudo Prado, S., Fombona Cadavieco, J., Pascual Sevillano, M.: Ventajas de la incorporación de las TIC en el envejecimiento. RELATEC Rev. Latinoam. Tecnol. Educ 12(2), 131–142 (2013). https://dialnet.unirioja.es/descarga/articulo/4527180.pdf

31. Barrantes Cáceres, R., Cozzubo Chaparro, A.: Edad para aprender, edad para enseñar: el rol del aprendizaje intergeneracional intrahogar en el uso de la internet por parte de los adultos mayores en latinoamérica. Dep. Econ. Pontif. Univ. católica del Perú, vol. 411, pp. 1–84 (2015). https://files.pucp.education/departamento/economia/DDD411.pdf

32. Millward, P.: The 'grey digital divide': perception, exclusion and barriers of access to the internet for older people, 8(7), 1 (2003). https://doi.org/10.5210/fm.v8i7.1066

33. Morris, A., Brading, H.: E-literacy and the grey digital divide: a review with recommendations. J. Inf. Lit. 1(3), 1–17 (2007). https://doi.org/10.11645/1.3.14

34. UNESCO: Tecnologías de la Información y la Comunicación para la Inclusión – Avances y oportunidades en los países europeos. European A. Odence: European Agency for Development in Special Needs Education 2013 (2013)

35. Myers, B., et al.: Strategic directions in human-computer interaction. ACM Comput. Surv. 28(4), 794–809 (1996). https://doi.org/10.1145/242223.246855

Accuracy Comparison Between Deep Learning Models for Mexican Lemon Classification

Angel Hernández[✉], Francisco Javier Ornelas-Rodríguez,
Juan B. Hurtado-Ramos, and José Joel González-Barbosa

CICATA Querétaro, Instituto Politécnico Nacional, Colinas del Cimatario,
76090 Queréataro, Queréataro, Mexico

Abstract. This paper presents a performance comparison between 8 deep learning models trained to classify Mexican lemons by their visual appearance. The models were trained using 913 lemon images. These images were divided into two classes: faulty and healthy. Half of the models were designed to take color images as input. The other half will take grayscale images. Also, two distributions were used for the training stage. The models were tested against new data, and their performance was acceptable. The best model achieved an accuracy of 92% for the training stage and, for the new data, it was able to classify all the new images correctly.

Keywords: Deep learning · Citrus quality classification · Computer vision system · Mexican lemon quality

1 Introduction

Mexico is one of the significant citrus producers in the world, and it is expected to improve such production in 2021 [1]. The primary citrus fruit produced is lemon. Mexico has over 6.8 million tons of this citrus fruit annually. Despite this fact, some diseases like greening and HLB could affect the production rate [2].

Because of this, they are detecting defects at earlier stages of harvest, and packaging is crucial for producers. In some cases, citrus diseases, when detected, can be put in complete quarantine harvest [9]. Reinforces the idea of having a system that can distinguish between healthy and defective fruits. Because many types of diseases and defects can affect citrus fruits, detecting these problems early and separating healthy from faulty fruits is a good start. Today's systems can separate fruits based on criteria such as color, size, and shape. These systems, while fast, focus on one or two of these criteria. Today, there is a trend to implement vision systems within sorting machines. Machine and deep learning approaches use training samples to discover different patterns and accurate predictions on future data or samples [13]. With technological advances, these models have become more powerful and are capable of processing more complex

© Springer Nature Switzerland AG 2021
M. F. Mata-Rivera and R. Zagal-Flores (Eds.): WITCOM 2021, CCIS 1430, pp. 62–73, 2021.
https://doi.org/10.1007/978-3-030-89586-0_5

data. As a result, deep learning methods with more prominent architectures have been developed to work the data.

Deep learning algorithms are based on representational learning of data. In this case, the observations can be expressed in various ways, such as pixel value, vectors, or more *deep* features such as edges, textures, shapes. Convolutional Neural Networks (CNN) and Recurrent Neural Networks (RNN) frameworks have been implemented in computer vision tasks, speech recognition, pattern recognition, natural language processing. Because of this, deep learning has entered the domain of agriculture [6]. Popular implementations in this field include weed identification, land cover classification, fruits counting, crop type, and plant classification. Plant and fruit classification uses his methods to detect diseases and defects on their peel using visual aspects because it is essential for producers and consumers. Another reason to use deep learning is that the models can improve classification speed and accuracy. Moreover, deep learning models seem to generalize well and can adapt to new data with relatively low work [6].

This paper presents a comparison between deep learning models trained to distinguish healthy lemons from defective lemons. The models used images as inputs that were processed in different forms, and data augmentation was used. The structure is as follows: on Sect. 2 gives a brief description of the problem and a short review of the previous works found; Sect. 3 describes the process followed to generate the datasets, the image processing, how the models were created and trained to make the classification; on Sect. 4, the results obtained from the training process and how the models were able to make predictions are presented; Sect. 5 presents the discussion of the results and the work needed to improve such results.

2 Literature Review

Fruit and vegetable classification involves assigning a qualitative fruit or vegetable class to an observed input. The techniques used for this purpose are kNN, SVM, decision trees and neural networks (with all its variants) [5]. RGB images have been studied to exploit significant characteristics of fruit and vegetable like color, shape, texture, and size for conventional computer vision systems. Robot-aided harvesting, quality analysis, disease identification, and damage analysis are among the leading vision-based fruit classification applications.

Reference [11] presents a comparison between machine and deep learning models for plant leaf disease detection. The aim was to classify citrus leaf disease using both approaches. The machine learning models used were Stochastic Gradient Descent (SGD), Random Forests (RF), and Support Vector Machine (SVM). For deep learning models, architectures Inception-v3, VGG-16, and VGG-19 were used. A total of 609 images were used as a dataset. These images are divided into five classes, four of them being the leaf diseases and the last one, healthy leaves. In the end, deep learning models had a greater accuracy value than machine learning models.

In [10], it is described a deep learning approach to recognize orange fruit diseases at the initial production stage. This research aims to give proper treatment to orange trees, helping them improve the harvest quality. The diseases detected are brown spot, citrus canker, and melanose. For the data distribution, four classes were defined: the diseases mentioned before and healthy oranges. There are 68 images of oranges in the whole dataset.

In [12] describes a computer vision system to detect defects on apple peels. The author used a deep learning object detection based on the architecture YOLO3. The main objective of this work is to help farmers improve their post-harvest quality. Similarly, the author of reference [8] made a comparison between machine learning algorithms. The main task of these algorithms was to classify apples into two classes: healthy or defected. The author used SVM, kNN, and multi-layer perceptrons (MLP). The SVM algorithm was the best one.

Another popular approach to classify fruits is hyperspectral and multispectral imaging [4]. In [3] a computer vision system with multispectral images is presented to detect external defects on oranges. The authors also used other features like color, size, height, and width of the oranges to have more information. However, these approaches tend to have a higher cost and are slow when processing the information.

Although, most of the previous works focus on one or two aspects. The data is relatively low, with datasets having less than 1000 images. For example, the authors of [7] used 150 orange images to detect various defects. Their classification accuracy was 89.1%.

3   Methodology

The main objective of the model developed is to classify a lemon between the classes proposed correctly using convolutional neural networks. Therefore, the model needs to be trained with lemon images provided by one or various datasets. Another important aspect is the model's architecture.

3.1   Image Database

Having a high-quality dataset is essential for obtaining a good result in the classification task. Most of the existing datasets with images contain several examples for each class and objects in different positions or scenarios. Therefore, to train the whole model, data is needed. Because the model will take images as inputs, the dataset must have lemon images, see Fig. 1 which shows some lemons that are present in the dataset. There are 913 images in the dataset. These images are divided into two classes: healthy and faulty. To tell if a lemon belongs to one class or the other, the Mexican norm NMX-FF-077 was used; this norm has specific information and criteria for the ideal values that a lemon must have; also, lemon producers from Colima, Mexico helped with this task. The images contained in the dataset are in RGB. The dimensions for the images are 640×480 pixels. Also, the background of the image was removed using image thresholding techniques. After the classification process, 460 images were tagged as healthy, and 453 were tagged as faulty lemons. The distribution of the classes is pretty balanced, nearly 50%, so there is no problem with an unbalanced classification.

3.2   Creating Various Datasets for Training

Various datasets were created using the images described before. Every dataset was created with Tensorflow and Keras tools, which allow fast setup and prototyping. The datasets have different configurations and features to test the

Fig. 1. Four lemons present in the image dataset.

performance of the models. Tensorflow and Keras offer powerful features such as fast computation mapping, processing the data without additional software. They have built-in support for automatic gradient computation. Tensorflow is used in several projects, such as the Inception Classification Model. Also, it is used in the DeepSpeech developed by Mozilla. So far, the wide purposes of the projects developed with Tensorflow make this tool a good choice for our problem.

Because we want to compare the model's performance upon image size, color and, data distribution, a nomenclature for the datasets was established. The first position refers to the image being in color or grayscale; the second informs the image size in pixels; the last position tells how the data will be distributed. For example, if the name of the dataset is **Color-250-6040**, then color images are used with size 250 × 250 pixels and, 60% of the images are used for training and 40% for validation. For this paper, a total of 8 datasets will be used to train the classification model. See Table 1, where it is shown the names and features for each dataset.

Table 1. The names given to the different datasets generated to test the classification model. When using a 7030 distribution, all the datasets have 640 images for training and 273 images for validation; the 8020 distribution uses 731 for training and 182 for validation.

Dataset	Image type	Size in pixels	Distribution
Color-100-7030	RGB	100 × 100	70% for training
Color-200-7030		200 × 200	30% for validation
Color-100-8020		100 × 100	80% for training
Color-200-8020		200 × 200	20% for validation
Grayscale-100-7030	Grayscale	100 × 100	70% for training
Grayscale-200-7030		200 × 200	30% for training
Grayscale-100-8020		100 × 100	80% for training
Grayscale-200-8020		200 × 200	20% for training

3.3 The Classification Model

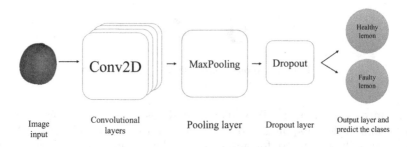

Fig. 2. Conceptual representation of the classification model based on the Xception architecture. The model takes an image as input, then it goes through convolutional, pooling and dropout layers, at last, it predicts the label for the given image.

For the classification task, a designed model can take images as inputs. In particular, convolutional neural networks (CNN) have shown optimal performance for image classification and pattern recognition. The structure of a neural network is known as architecture. There isn't a correct way to create a network. In many cases, it entirely depends on the problem to solve and the data available. A conceptual representation of the model's architecture is shown in Fig. 2.

- The first layer is the input layer. This layer takes an image as input (as we mentioned before) which size may vary depending on the dataset selected. The images are squared, i.e., they have the same width and height.
- Although it is not present in Fig. 2, a preprocessing stage is done after the image is loaded and before entering the convolutional layers. This process is described in the next paragraphs.
- The second and third layers are convolutional layers. They owe their name to the mathematical operator convolution that can filter two signals into one.
- After each convolutional layer, a batch normalization layer was placed. The layer normalizes its output using the mean and standard deviation of the current batch of inputs.
- The next layers are separable convolutional layers. Separable convolutions consist of first performing convolution for each of the channels present on an image and then mixing the resulting output channels. In the case of color images, a separable convolution will make three operations for the R, G and, B channels, respectively.
- Before the final layer, there is a global average pooling layer. This layer reduces the dimensions, therefore making the more easily classification.
- The final layer is fully connected. This layer will force all the data into the number of nodes the layer has. The nodes are defined by the number of classes the problem has; for this case, there are two classes.

Table 2. Best accuracy and loss value obtained for each model

Model	Best accuracy value	Best loss value
Color-100-7030	87.96	0.277
Color-100-8020	91.09	0.209
Color-200-7030	85.36	0.341
Color-200-8020	92.47	0.186
Grayscale-100-7030	76.68	0.527
Grayscale-100-8020	84.68	0.365
Grayscale-200-7030	75.51	0.511
Gratscale-200-8020	84.81	0.342

After the model takes its input, a processing is applied to the image. All the stages are listed below:

1. Resize the image: the image is down-scaled to achieve the desired size.
2. Flip horizontal: after the image is resized, then a random flip is applied.
3. Flip vertical: similarly, the image is subjected to a random vertical flip.
4. Random rotation: image is turned around by a random factor.
5. Random translation: the final processing is to displace the image in the x-axis and y-axis.

The steps described before are known as image augmentation. Because the original image dataset may be considered sparse, it is a good practice to aid the model by applying this technique. The image augmentation was made with Keras preprocessing tools. It is important to note that the augmentation process is made after the image is loaded to the model before entering the convolutional layers. Thus, the original image is not modified. Image augmentation can help the model to "see" different scenarios where the object to identify might be, i.e., the lemon could be rotated, displaced, or too far in the image. Allowing the model to face these strange situations could help to improve its performance.

For all the convolutional layers, a ReLU activation function was used. This function has proved to be useful for different problems. The *MaxPooling* layer helps to reduce the data's dimensions, so the trainable parameters on the network are reduced before the final layers. The *dropout* layer, as its name suggests it, drops values randomly and can avoid overfitting. For this layer, the values dropped were set to 0.5 or 50%. Because our problem is a classification problem, a sigmoid function was used in the output layer. The sigmoid function will map the results between values 0 and 1. The model's loss function was binary cross-entropy, an Adam optimizer was used with a fixed value of 0.001.

3.4   Training the Models

All the datasets generated were used in the training process. For each of the datasets, the same hyperparameters mentioned before were used. Due to the heuristic nature of the machine and deep learning, little variations in the initial conditions can derive significant differences in the results. Because of this, all models will have the same hyperparameters (the little adjustments made in the optimization algorithms), so the models can begin the training phase with the same conditions. The models were trained for 200 epochs using Google Colaboratory services. We used Google Colaboratory services because it is a free yet powerful tool to develop, train, and test machine and deep learning models. Another interesting feature is that it allows training the models using GPUs so that the training stages can be done faster than in a normal computer. Another advantage is that it is cloud-based, which means that there is no need to install additional software and, the progress made can be saved in a cloud drive.

The metrics used to evaluate the model's performance are the loss value and the accuracy. The loss value is the penalty given to the model for making bad predictions. The loss is a number indicating how bad the model's prediction was on a single example. Ideally, a model's loss value will be 0, i.e., the model can predict correctly on every example of the dataset. Similarly, accuracy is the percentage of correct predictions for the data, either in the training or validation set. On the contrary, an ideal classification model will be 100. That is, the model never gets a prediction wrong.

4   Results

In Table 2 the best value for accuracy (the maximum value) and loss (the minimum value) in the training phase are presented. According to this table, the best models are **Color-100-8020** and **Color-200-8020**. The first one with an accuracy value of 91.09%, while the second achieved an accuracy of 92.47%. Being **Color-200-8020** the best of all the models. The mean accuracy value is around 85%, where models for color or grayscale images got their best accuracy. However, the worst model was the **Grayscale-200-7030** with an accuracy value of 75.51%. Further analysis of these results and predictions against new data will be presented in the next sections.

4.1   Metrics for Color Images

In Fig. 3 the accuracy of the models **Color-100-7030** (blue line) and **Color-100-8020** (orange line) is presented, also this graph includes the loss values for each model. The accuracy value starts near 0.6 and slowly increases during the training stage. Its behavior suggests that accuracy improved at a slow rate. However, both models passed the 0.8 thresholds for accuracy, implying a good result in the training stage. The graph shows a quick decrease for the first epochs for the loss value (green and red line respectively) and continues for the epochs left. Especially the value for the model **Color-100-7030** has minor values than the model **Color-100-80**. The first value goes down to 0.3, while the second goes near to 0.4. These values suggest that distribution with 70-30 gives better results for the training stage.

For the image datasets with size 200 × 200, Fig. 4 shows both the accuracy and loss values for models **Color-200-7030** and **Color-200-8020**. The accuracy (blue and orange lines) starts below the previous models but gets a higher

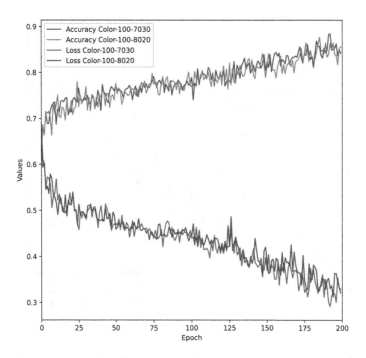

Fig. 3. Accuracy and loss values for the color models with image size 100×100.

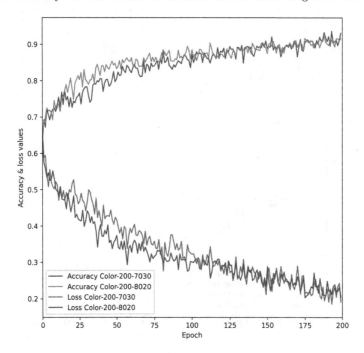

Fig. 4. Accuracy and loss values for the color models with image size 200×200.

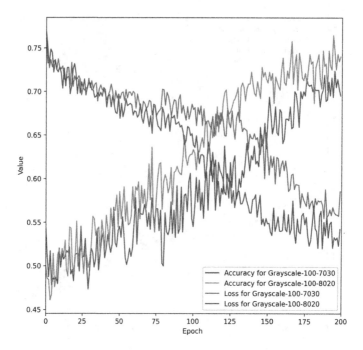

Fig. 5. Accuracy and loss values for grayscale images with image size 100×100

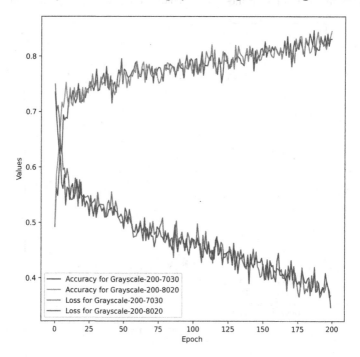

Fig. 6. Accuracy and loss values for grayscale images with image size 200×200.

value at the end of the training stage, achieving values greater than 0.9. The accuracy for the model **Color-200-8020** seems to increase more quickly than its counterpart, where the line is drawn, which suggests the increasing value was slower. The loss values suggest that the training was successful by decreasing an initial value of approximately 0.6 to 0.3. The model **Color-200-8020** seems to decrease more quickly than the model **Color-200-7030**. However, the fact that both loss values do decrease indicates a good performance but there is no overfitting of the data.

4.2   Metrics for Grayscale Images

In Fig. 5 it is shown the accuracy and the loss values for the models trained with datasets **Grayscale-100-7030** and **Grayscale-100-8020**. The accuracy for both models (blue and orange lines) increases from 0.5 to 0.7. This value had a significant increase from epoch 100 but, the accuracy behavior is not continuous, as there are spikes (increments or decrements between epochs) in the values. The loss value (the green and red lines) quickly decreases from above 0.75 to nearly 0.50. However, the values for model **Grayscale-100-8020** decreases more quickly than the **Grayscale-100-7030**, which its values seem to flatten between epoch 75 and epoch 125.

On the other hand, Fig. 6 shows the accuracy and loss behavior for models **Grayscale-200-7030** and **Grayscale-200-8020**. The accuracy for both models (the orange and blue lines) increases quickly in the first epochs, going from 0.50 to 0.70. Then the value increases at a slow rate reaching a value higher than 0.8 in both cases. For the loss value (green and red lines), a similar behavior occurs. The value for both models decreases in the first epochs but, in this case, it continues decreasing for the epochs left. Also, for this case, there are not as many spikes as for the previous models.

4.3   Performance Against New Data

New lemon images are using to evaluate the performance training process. In Fig. 7, the images used for testing are shown. These images were taken after the model's training stage and were segmented with the same process used for the image dataset. In total, there are 18 images available for testing. Also, it is important to mention that these images have not been used before and are not "known"[1] by the models. The images are not labeled but, so a class was given according to its visual appearance. By this criteria, Table 3 was made, where it is shown, the relevant metrics for the model's predictions with the new images. The models with the best results are **Color-200-8020** and **Color-100-8020**, with an accuracy value of 92.47% and 91.09% respectively. The third best model was **Color-100-7030**, with an accuracy value of 87.96%. For the grayscale models, the predictions made were given with a higher confidence value, as the model gives predictions as probabilities. In the case of color models, the predictions are not as confident as their grayscale counterparts.

---

[1] An image not known by the models means that it has been used neither for training nor for validation.

Fig. 7. The 18 images used to test the performance of all the models trained.

Table 3. Predictions for the new lemon images using the color models

Image	True label	Model's predictions							
		Color-100-7030	Color-200-7030	Color-100-8020	Color-200-8020	Grayscale-100-7030	Grayscale-200-7030	Grayscale-100-800	Grayscale-200-8020
Lemon 1	Healthy	Healthy	Faulty	Healthy	Healthy	Faulty	Healthy	Faulty	Healthy
Lemon 2	Healthy	Faulty	Faulty	Healthy	Healthy	Faulty	Faulty	Faulty	Healthy
Lemon 3	Healthy	Healthy	Healthy	Healthy	Healthy	Faulty	Healthy	Faulty	Healthy
Lemon 4	Healthy	Faulty	Faulty	Healthy	Faulty	Faulty	Faulty	Faulty	Healthy
Lemon 5	Healthy	Healthy	Faulty	Healthy	Healthy	Faulty	Healthy	Faulty	Healthy
Lemon 6	Healthy	Healthy	Healthy	Healthy	Healthy	Faulty	Healthy	Faulty	Healthy
Lemon 7	Faulty	Healthy	Faulty	Healthy	Faulty	Faulty	Faulty	Faulty	Healthy
Lemon 8	Faulty	Healthy	Faulty	Healthy	Faulty	Faulty	Faulty	Faulty	Healthy
Lemon 9	Faulty	Healthy	Healthy	Healthy	Faulty	Faulty	Faulty	Faulty	Healthy
Lemon 10	Faulty	Healthy	Faulty	Healthy	Faulty	Faulty	Faulty	Faulty	Healthy
Lemon 11	Healthy	Healthy	Faulty	Healthy	Faulty	Faulty	Faulty	Faulty	Healthy
Lemon 12	Faulty	Faulty	Faulty	Healthy	Faulty	Faulty	Faulty	Faulty	Healthy
Lemon 13	Faulty	Faulty	Faulty	Healthy	Faulty	Faulty	Faulty	Faulty	Healthy
Lemon 14	Faulty	Faulty	Faulty	Healthy	Faulty	Faulty	Healthy	Faulty	Healthy
Lemon 15	Faulty	Faulty	Faulty	Healthy	Faulty	Faulty	Faulty	Faulty	Healthy
Lemon 16	Faulty	Faulty	Faulty	Healthy	Faulty	Faulty	Faulty	Faulty	Healthy
Lemon 17	Faulty	Healthy	Faulty	Healthy	Faulty	Faulty	Faulty	Faulty	Healthy
Lemon 18	Faulty	Faulty	Faulty	Faulty	Faulty	Faulty	Faulty	Faulty	Healthy

5 Conclusions and Future Work

For a larger image size, the accuracy seems to increase, both for color and grayscale images. The best accuracy value was given by model **Color-200-7030** and model **Color-200-8020**, where the value passed beyond 0.9 or 90% for the training stages. The worst accuracy was given by the model **Grayscale-100-7030**, the value was 0.74 or 74%.

However, in the case of grayscale images, a larger size seems to directly impact the model's accuracy. This might show that the grayscale models identify features that, at lower resolutions, are not available or are distorted by the reduction.

When all the models faced new data, color was an essential feature for the classification task. The second lemon (from left to right, top to bottom) does not have visible injuries or defects, but the color is more yellowish than the other fruit. On the other hand, lemon 7 has visible injures on its peel but, some models assigned the class *healthy* even though it is a faulty lemon.

The only "bad model" was **Grayscale-200-8020**, where all the lemons were classified as healthy lemons when, as Fig. 7 shows, there are lemons that do not belong to such class. This behavior can be explained if the model heavily overfitted the data and couldn't adapt to new images.

Color images are more useful than grayscale images. It seems that for deep learning models, the more channels, the better. This happened with models **Color-200-7030** and **Color-200-8020**, where the best accuracies were obtained. Contrary to popular beliefs, working with one channel (when working with grayscale images) may be harmful, as the models might lose important information. A deep analysis of the features considered by the model is required. Knowing these can avoid using information the may no be useful. Also, these features can help to improve the accuracy of the model and generalize the knowledge correctly, which is what is expected of a machine learning model.

Also, as the majority of deep learning models, more data is needed. In order to assure the best performance of the models, more evaluations with new lemon images need to be done. Facing the models against new examples would help identify the opportunity areas, helping to improve the accuracy and the classification results. Another interesting experiment would be to use different color modes like HSV, HSI or, CieLab. Some authors have studied these modes when working with fruit and food. So, it might be possible that better or more useful features would appear when working with the color modes.

References

1. Citrus: World markets and trade. United States department of agriculture. Foreign agricultural service, April 2021
2. The world's top citrus producing countries. World atlas (2021). https://www.worldatlas.com/articles/the-world-s-top-citrus-producing-countries.html
3. Blasco, J., Aleixos, N., Gómez-Sanchís, J., Moltó, E.: Recognition and classification of external skin damage in citrus fruits using multispectral data and morphological features. Biosys. Eng. **103**(2), 137–145 (2009)
4. Blasco, J., Cubero, S., Moltó, E.: Chapter 12 - quality evaluation of citrus fruits. In: Sun, D.-W. (ed.) Computer Vision Technology for Food Quality Evaluation (Second Edition), pp. 305–325. Academic Press, San Diego (2016)
5. Hameed, K., Chai, D., Rassau, A.: A comprehensive review of fruit and vegetable classification techniques. Image Vis. Comput. **80**, 24–44 (2018)
6. Kamilaris, A., Prenafeta-Boldú, F.X.: Deep learning in agriculture: a survey. Comput. Electron. Agric. **147**, 70–90 (2018)
7. Kukreja, V., Dhiman, P.: A deep neural network based disease detection scheme for citrus fruits. In: 2020 International Conference on Smart Electronics and Communication (ICOSEC), pp. 97–101 (2020)
8. Moallem, P., Serajoddin, A., Pourghassem, H.: Computer vision-based apple grading for golden delicious apples based on surface features. Inf. Process. Agric. **4**(1), 33–40 (2017)
9. Moshia, M., Mzini, L.L.: Identification of citrus canker on citrus leaves and fruit surfaces in the grove using deep learning neural networks. J. Agric. Sci. Technol. B, **1**(2) (2020)
10. Saha, R., Neware, S.: Orange fruit disease classification using deep learning approach. Int. J. Adv. Trends Comput. Sci. Eng. **9**(2) (2020)
11. Sujatha, R., Chatterjee, J.M., Jhanjhi, N.Z., Brohi, S.N.: Performance of deep learning vs machine learning in plant leaf disease detection. Microproces. Microsyst. **80**, 103615 (2021)
12. Valdez, P.: Apple defect detection using deep learning based object detection for better post harvest handling. Computing Research Repository (CoRR), abs/2005.06089 (2020)
13. Zhu, L., Spachos, P., Pensini, E., Plataniotis, K.N.: Deep learning and machine vision for food processing: a survey. Curr. Res. Food Sci. **4**, 233–249 (2021)

Detection of Covid-19 by Applying a Convolutional Artificial Neural Network in X-ray Images of Lungs

Gerardo Emanuel Loza Galindo$^{(\boxtimes)}$ ⓘ, Erick Romo Rivera ⓘ,
and Álvaro Anzueto Ríos ⓘ

Bionics Engineering Academy, National Polytechnic Institute, 07340 Mexico City, Mexico

Abstract. COVID-19 is a global disease that first appeared at the end of 2019 in Wuhan, China. The limited information related to this disease and its high level of contagion, which has managed to infect many countries in the world, brings tremendous pressure on the scientific community. It is necessary to focus efforts on finding tools to aid diagnosis and treatment.

In this work, a proposal is presented to help in the diagnosis of COVID-19 by classifying and identifying the disease in images. The dataset (free-access dataset in the Kaggle library) used are X-rays images of lungs previously diagnosed with the pathologies of COVID-19 and Pneumonia, and in addition, reference images of healthy lungs. Because the database used contains images from different sources, the dimensions are varied. It was important to standardize the dimensions, so a statistical analysis of the variations is presented and the size of all the images will be determined. The proposed solution for the classification of images is based on a Convolutional Neural Network architecture. Three different structures were explored in this article in order to compare the performances and determine the best proposal. The analysis of the graphs in the accuracy and loss function values determine the structure with the best performance, which achieves 95% accuracy predicting a diagnostic for the images.

The results show a high efficiency in the diagnosis with the architectures presented, therefore, the development presented can support medical personnel in making decisions when generating a diagnosis.

Keywords: COVID-19 · X-rays images · Pneumonia · Convolutional neural network · Artificial intelligence

1 Introduction

The virus SARS-CoV-2 is a new coronavirus capable of infecting humans and causing the disease known as COVID-19. The first infection detected was at Wuhan, China, in the end of 2019 and it has caused outbreaks in many countries around the world. This virus causes different symptoms to those who get it; from mild respiratory tract infections to pneumonia with multi organ failure and in some cases, death. Infected

M. F. Mata-Rivera and R. Zagal-Flores (Eds.): WITCOM 2021, CCIS 1430, pp. 74–89, 2021.
https://doi.org/10.1007/978-3-030-89586-0_6

patients, symptomatic or asymptomatic, can transmit the virus through saliva's drops [1].

Due to the lack of vaccines or specific drugs to fight the virus, alternative methods, such as real-time polymerase chain reaction (RT-PCR), need to be implemented in order to detect the disease in an early stage, avoiding this way the spread of the virus from the healthy population [2]. However, Cozzi et al. [3] emphasize many limitations that the RT-PCR test has, including delayed diagnostics and a large number on false-negatives tests.

One of the alternative methods could be radiological examination, as the application of X-rays through the human upper body (specifically the chest area) allows to know the health status of infected patients [4]. According to Fleischner Society in [5], chest X-rays show changes in the lungs for patients with advanced symptoms. Therefore, chest X-rays can be used to detect the new coronavirus disease.

Nevertheless, the chest X-rays interpretation requires a certain level of expertise by those who make the coronavirus diagnosis. In [6] a neural architecture of the VGG16 type is presented, which is too complex, so it has a high consumption of computational resources and the performance values achieved are lower than that reported in this work (see architecture 3). Given this, detecting or validating the new coronavirus disease represent a new challenge that needs to be addressed.

Deep learning models such as convolutional neural networks (CNN), could be used as a support tool in order to fight against the coronavirus pandemic. In [7], it is mentioned that CNN have been implemented before on X-rays for to make an analysis of radiological disease characteristics. Hence, this model can be used to aid in the diagnosis of the novel coronavirus.

The presented work uses three different CNN models in order to classify chest X-rays into three different type of patients: healthy, with pneumonia and with COVID-19. This classification is made with the purpose of differencing the different patients' health conditions and in this way, help to diagnose COVID-19. This paper is classified as follows: the related work is presented in Sect. 2. In Sect. 3, the dataset used for developing the work is showed. Then, the methodology of the CNN is described in Sect. 4 and in Sect. 5 the results are presented. Finally, the conclusions of the work are showed in Sect. 6.

2   Related Work

Several researchers have used deep learning models to try to detect the novel coronavirus trough X-ray images, just like in this work.

In [8], Rahimzahed and Attar present various deep convolutional networks models and its training techniques utilized for classifying three kind of patients: health patients, patients with pneumonia and patients infected with COVID-19, by using their chest X-rays. In this mentioned work, a number of training techniques are introduced to help the model learn better with an unequal dataset. In addition, the authors proposed a concatenated neural network of Xception and ResNet50V2. For the work's evaluation, they test the network on 11302 X-ray images, obtaining an average accuracy of 99.5% for COVID-19 cases and an overall average accuracy of 91.4% for the three classes.

The work described in [9] presents a model that could support radiologists to validate the initial COVID-19 diagnosis they determine. This model is an automated COVID-19 detector implemented with 17 convolutional layers, introducing diverse types of filters for each layer; and it is developed to provide diagnostics from chest X-rays for two kind of classifications: binary classification which includes COVID-19 and No-Findings, and multi-class classification including COVID-19, No-Findings and pneumonia. According to Ozturk et al. their presented model reaches an accuracy of 98.08% for binary classes and 87.02% for multi-classes cases.

Further, in [10], Toraman et al. proposed a Convolutional CapsNet neural network in order to detect COVID-19 by classifying X-rays with capsule network with the purpose of offering faster and more accurate diagnostics of the disease. Just like in [9], the authors in [10] work with a binary classification (COVID-19 vs. No-Findings) and a multi-class classification (COVID-19 vs. No-Findings vs. Pneumonia). Toraman et al. firmly believe that their neural network could be an alternative to diagnose COVID-19 as the model's accuracy achieved is 97.24% for binary classification and 84.22% for multi-classification.

In [11], the authors suggested a platform based on the CNN known as VGG16 in order to detect COVID-19 by the use of chest X-rays. The platform consists of a user inserting the desired patient personal information; after that, the patient's chest X-ray will be downloaded, and the image's test will start. After 5 s, the results will be displayed over a PDF containing all the information about the test and the image. All this with the purpose of giving a first diagnosis for COVID-19 in order to aid radiologists. According to the authors, this platform has not been validated by official medical authorities.

Based on the papers review, the conclusion we can reach is that Convolutional Neural Networks are strongly used for analyzing chest X-rays in order to classify different diseases. These classifications will make the medical personal, such as radiologists, to have a more accurate diagnostic.

Just as the papers presented in this section, in this work we propose a solution for the diagnosis of COVID-19 based on Convolutional Neural Networks. The more accurate model out of the three architectures presented in this work has 7 layers; on average, our model manages to correctly classify more than 98% of the presented cases of COVID-19. However, and unlike the works show above, it has an overall precision of more than 95% to classify cases of the three classes presented in the research work (COVID-19, Pneumonia, and Normal). The results suggest great abstraction of characteristic patterns of each class, and a great speed of execution of the algorithm is estimated as it only has 27,163 trainable parameters.

3   Dataset

The data set used in this work has been extracted from Kaggle repository [12], it contains 6432 Chest X-Ray (anteroposterior) films of COVID-19 patients, pneumonia patients, and healthy patients. This dataset was not mean to be tested in deep learning algorithms, thereby it poses bias and great variety of shapes in the images. In order to use this dataset for the purpose of this research, images were discarded and modified based on the analysis applied and presented in this section.

The images were labelled as follows "COVID", "NORMAL", "PNEUMONIA" originally there were 576, 1583 and 4273 samples, respectively. 576 images were taken randomly from each class to form the training and validation set. Two modifications were made to the images; Firstly, the information presented in the images was clear enough represented with one matrix of greyscale, all the images that were in RGB format were transformed in greyscale format. Secondly, the images were reshaped by looking for a size representative of the whole dataset. The Fig. 1 shows the histogram of values found

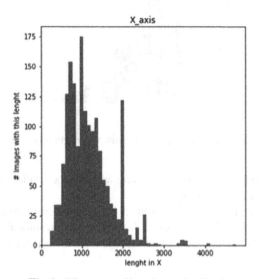

Fig. 1. Histogram of lengths on the X axis.

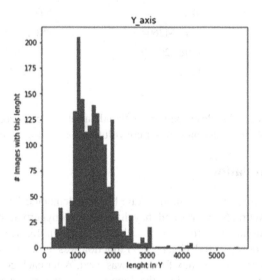

Fig. 2. Histogram of lengths on the Y axis.

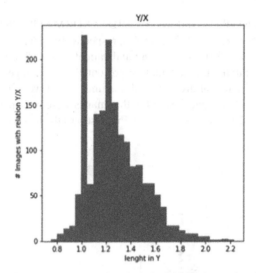

Fig. 3. Histogram of the relation (length Y)/(length X) of each image

for the X axe and the Fig. 2 for the axe Y, along with this the relation between axe X and Y for each image is displayed in Fig. 3.

The tails on the distributions shown in each histogram were cut and the mean was selected as the representative value of each variable. The results displayed in Table 1 were used to select the final reshape values. Images were reshaped to 1150 x 1400 pixels.

Table 1. Mean and STD calculated from the analysis made on the images' shape.

	Mean	STD
X axis	1147.642604	481.158750
Y axis	1408.620710	491.716814
Relation Y/X	1.275045	0.226604

With the pre-processing described above, the data set was prepared to be used in the training and processing of samples in our convolutional neural network models.

4   Model Formulation

For a good analysis, three different models have been implemented. The models are based on Convolutional Neural Networks and they differ on their hyperparameters values. The description of the architecture for each model is presented in this section.

In the given models, the ReLU activation function was implemented on every layer but the last one, where the Softmax function was used. After each convolution, a Max-polling layer is implemented to reduce the dimensions of the matrixes where the information is abstracted. The Figs. 4, 6 and 8 present the information flow in the models,

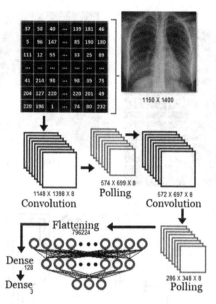

Fig. 4. First model proposed, a convolutional neural network with 8 layers

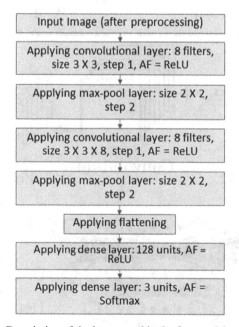

Fig. 5. Description of the layers used in the first model proposed

along with them the Figs. 5, 7 and 8 show the features of each layer for each architecture (Fig. 9).

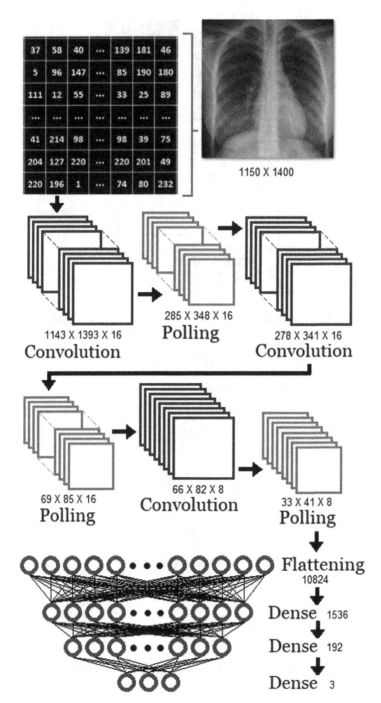

Fig. 6. Second model proposed, a convolutional neural network with 11 layers

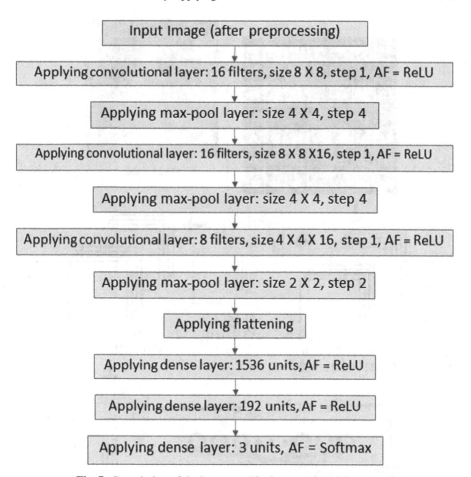

Fig. 7. Description of the layers used in the second model proposed

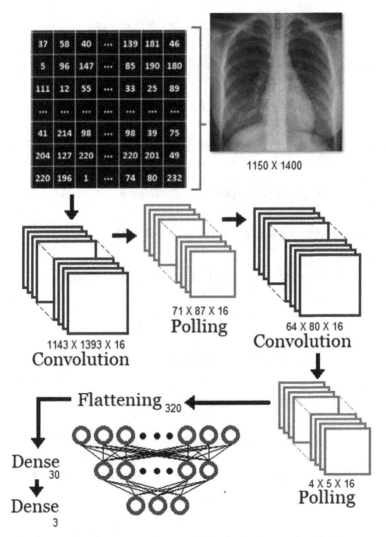

Fig. 8. Third model proposed, a convolutional neural network with 8 layers.

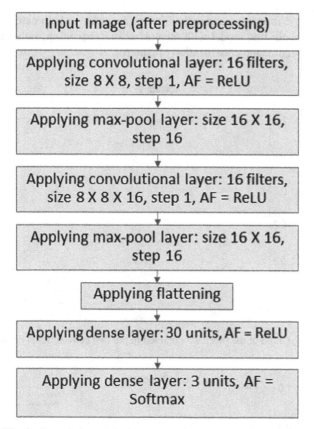

Fig. 9. Description of the layers used in the third model proposed

These CNNs were selected from a broader set of models where different combinations of hyperparameters were tested, trying to reduce the number of trainable parameters and obtain a good performance in the classification of patients. A complete analysis of the results obtained is presented in the following section.

5 Results Evaluation

In order to evaluate the performance of the proposed models the results obtained during the training process and the final validation is presented. All the models were trained using the Adam optimizer, categorical cross-entropy as the loss function and a learning rate of 0.001. The variables selected to evaluate were accuracy of the model and the loss-function value.

CNN1. The Figs. 10 and 11 show the results of the first model presented. In one hand, we can observe that the value of the loss function decreases significantly fast for the training set, within the first epochs the output of the function reaches values close to zero and the accuracy is about 100%. On the other hand, the values of the validation set have not significant changes along the whole training process. Even when the model presents a good performance, above the 90% of accuracy in both cases, this behavior leads to associate our first model with memorization (overfitting) rather than learning through the abstraction and classification of patterns.

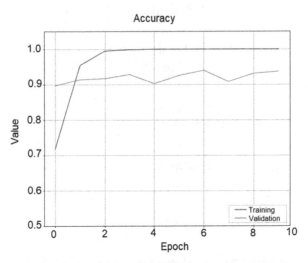

Fig. 10. Graph of the precision obtained in the first convolutional network

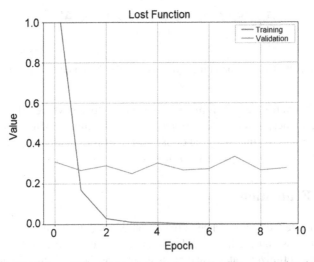

Fig. 11. Graph of the value of the cost function obtained in the first convolutional network during training

CNN2. The accuracy and the value of the lost function during the training for the second model proposed are presented in Figs. 12 and 13, they show a model that ends up with a good performance having more than 90% accuracy in both sets. Also, the changes in the values of accuracy and lost function for the training set along the training process seems to be smoother. This behaviour can be characteristic of the abstraction process; however, the variables reach critical values associated with memorization. On top of that, the values of variables for the validation set differ significantly from the training set, it may be related to a lack of representative patterns of the classes.

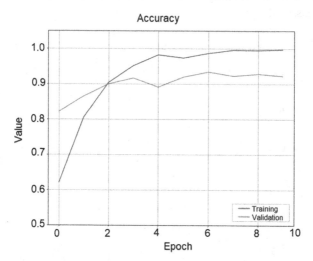

Fig. 12. Graph of the precision obtained in the second convolutional network during training

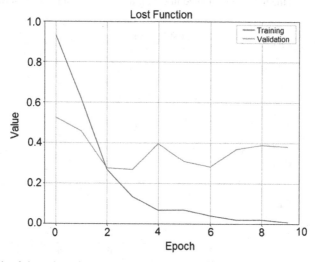

Fig. 13. Graph of the value of the cost function obtained in the second convolutional network during training

CNN3. The last graphs of accuracy and lost function value are presented in Figs. 14 and 15 and they show the performance of the third model. The curves on the training set show smooth changes along the training process that the validation curve follows closely. The values in precision graphs tend to converge to 1 without reaching this value, which is good for the learning process. Additionally, the values of the loss function have values close to zero. This model presents even better accuracy than the previous and shows an abstraction of patterns reflected in the fact that in validation and training set there are similar values of accuracy and lost function between them; also, 95% of images are correctly classified.

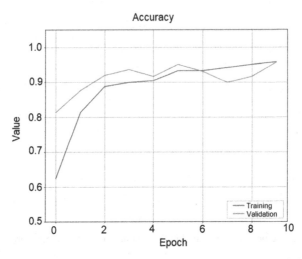

Fig. 14. Graph of the precision obtained in the third convolutional network during training

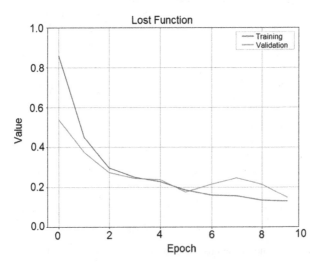

Fig. 15. Graph of the value of the cost function obtained in the third convolutional network during training

The Tables 2, 3 and 4 shows the confusion matrix for each model. The predictions were made on the validation set. The three models have an accuracy above the 90%.

However, only the third model present consistent values of recall and precision for the three classes, this model identifies correctly COVID-19 cases more than 98% of the times.

Table 2. Confusion matrix for first proposed model

CNN1 Class		Predicted		
		COVID	NORMAL	PNEUMONIA
Actual	COVID	115	1	0
	NORMAL	3	106	7
	PNEUMONIA	2	9	105
Precision		0.9583	0.91379	0.9375
Recall		0.9913	0.91379	0.9051
Accuracy		0.9368		

Table 3. Confusion matrix for second proposed model

CNN1 Class		Predicted		
		COVID	NORMAL	PNEUMONIA
Actual	COVID	113	3	0
	NORMAL	1	105	10
	PNEUMONIA	4	9	103
Precision		0.9576	0.8974	0.9115
Recall		0.9741	0.9051	0.8879
Accuracy		0.9224		

The results presented are intended to justify the application of Neural Networks in the medical diagnosis of patients with COVID-19. In the next chapter, a broader discussion about its application is taken.

6 Conclusions

In this work, three Convolutional-type Neural Network architectures are presented for the classification of lung radiographs, which show patients diagnosed as healthy, with pneumonia and with COVID19.

The three of them show a good performance but the best results were found in the third architecture proposed, for this reason, we are currently using this model for further research work. The analysis made on the training process suggests that this architecture does not memorize but instead sets a good abstraction of significant patterns related to

Table 4. Confusion matrix for third proposed model

CNN1 Class		Predicted		
		COVID	NORMAL	PNEUMONIA
Actual	COVID	114	2	0
	NORMAL	0	109	7
	PNEUMONIA	2	4	110
Precision		0.9827	0.9478	0.9401
Recall		0.9827	0.9396	0.9482
Accuracy		0.956896552		

each class. On top of that, it shows a performance above the 95% to correctly classify the images.

The performance of the model presented strongly suggest that convolutional neural networks are a feasible option to aid in the diagnosis of the discussed diseases Currently, the database with images of Mexican patients is being updated, having as a background that knowing the source and the parameters used in the generation of radiological images will allow us to better know the performance of the synthesis of the proposed neural networks.

References

1. Salzberger, B., Glück, T., Ehrenstein, B.: Successful containment of COVID-19: the WHO-Report on the COVID-19 outbreak in China. Infection **48**(2), 151–153 (2020). https://doi.org/10.1007/s15010-020-01409-4
2. Kolta, M.F., Ghonimy, M.B.I.: COVID-19 variant radiological findings with high lightening other coronavirus family (SARS and MERS) findings: radiological impact and findings spectrum of corona virus (COVID-19) with comparison to SARS and MERS. Egypt. J. Radiol. Nucl. Med. **51**(1), 1–8 (2020). https://doi.org/10.1186/s43055-020-00262-7
3. Cozzi, D., et al.: Chest X-ray in new Coronavirus Disease 2019 (COVID-19) infection: findings and correlation with clinical outcome. Radiol. Med. (Torino) **125**(8), 730–737 (2020). https://doi.org/10.1007/s11547-020-01232-9
4. Karar, M.E., Hemdan, E.-D., Shouman, M.A.: Cascaded deep learning classifiers for computer-aided diagnosis of COVID-19 and pneumonia diseases in X-ray scans. Complex Intell. Syst. **7**(1), 235–247 (2020). https://doi.org/10.1007/s40747-020-00199-4
5. Rubin, G.D.: The role of chest imaging in patient management during the COVID-19 pandemic: a multinational consensus statement from the Fleischner Society. Radiology **296**(1), 172–180 (2020)
6. Chandra, T.B.: Coronavirus disease (COVID-19) detection in chest X-yay images using majority voting-based classifier ensemble. Expert Syst. Appl. **165**(2), 113909 (2021)
7. Chouhan, V.: A novel transfer learning-based approach for pneumonia detection in chest X-ray images. Appl. Sci. (Switzerland) **10**(2), 559 (2020)
8. Rahimzadeh, M.: A modified deep convolutional neural network for detecting COVID-19 and pneumonia from chest X-ray images based on the concatenation of Xception and ResNet50V2. Inform. Med. Unlocked **19**, 100360 (2020)

9. Ozturk, T.: Automated detection of COVID-19 cases using deep neural networks with X-ray images. Comput. Biol. Med. **121**, 103792 (2020)
10. Toraman, S.: Convolutional capsnet: a novel artificial neural network approach to detect COVID-19 disease from X-ray images using capsule networks. Chaos Solitons Fractals **140**, 110122 (2020)
11. Tabaa, M.: Covid-19's rapid diagnosis open platform based on X-ray imaging and deep learning. Procedia Comput. Sci. **177**, 618–623 (2020)
12. Kaggle. https://www.kaggle.com/prashant268/chest-xray-covid19-pneumonia. Accessed 03 Jan 2020

Scientific Literature Review for the Search of Vulnerabilities and Pentesting Tools for SCADA System

Eduardo Vásquez[1](✉) (iD) and Helder Castrillón[1,2] (iD)

[1] Universidad Mayor, Av. Manuel Montt 367, Providencia, Chile
eduardo.vasquezp@mayor.cl, hcastrillon@unicomfacauca.edu.co,
helder.castrillon@umayor.cl
[2] Corporación Universitaria Comfacauca, Cl 4 N° 8-30, Popayán, Colombia

Abstract. Information and communication technologies (ICT) have contributed to change the way of doing things in practically all industries and markets worldwide. They make it possible to optimize processes, automate them and have a precise level of control in real time. One of the areas that has evolved and made use of these technologies is industrial control systems (ICS), specifically Supervisory Control And Data Acquisition (SCADA) systems. Using modern ICTs in turn entails embracing both their benefits and associated risks. It is important to know the vulnerabilities that affect these technologies and to analyze in detail those that could directly or indirectly affect and compromise the systems that depend on them. The objective of this systematic review is to identify, analyze and evaluate the published research on ICT vulnerabilities associated with SCADA systems, as well as the methods, methodologies, tools, among others, that can be used for their exploitation and thus to know the current scenario, allowing corrective measures to be taken.

Keywords: Vulnerability · Framework · SCADA · ICS · Tools · Pentesting

1 Introduction

It is important to study the vulnerabilities present in SCADA systems, as these systems are often related to critical processes of a country's infrastructure, such as electricity, drinking water, fuel, among many others. Deploying and maintaining these systems is one of the most important challenges faced by professionals in the sector, who are often unaware of the risks to which they are exposed.

This document aims to make a systematic review of the different vulnerabilities found in SCADA systems, as well as documentation on studies, guides, frameworks, methods, methodologies, among others, that can be found in the current literature related to this topic. At the same time, to find the tools that can be used to perform pentesting on SCADA systems.

It begins with the definition of keywords, with the objective of searching in the bibliographic databases on the topics described above. Once the scientific studies have

© Springer Nature Switzerland AG 2021
M. F. Mata-Rivera and R. Zagal-Flores (Eds.): WITCOM 2021, CCIS 1430, pp. 90–103, 2021.
https://doi.org/10.1007/978-3-030-89586-0_7

been found and obtained, a filter is made with well-defined search criteria, with the purpose of studying only the relevant documentation to answer the three search questions proposed in this document.

2   Systematic Review Process

The systematic review in this research was based on the proposal developed by Barbara Kitchenham [1]. The Systematic Review (SR) responds to a method, which serves to identify, analyze, evaluate, and compare relevant research papers to answer a search question on a specific topic, being able to find new research papers. The main objective of this SR is to identify, analyze and show the vulnerabilities present in SCADA systems, giving way to a future development of a pentesting framework based on these systems of the Efacec brand.

The SR was developed in three stages as shown in Fig. 1. In the first stage, the search protocol was defined, which takes into consideration the search questions, keywords and inclusion/exclusion criteria. In the second stage, the search for research articles corresponding to each question was carried out and those that met the previous criteria were chosen. In the third stage, the quality of the articles was categorized and evaluated for the SR.

Search protocol definition			Conduct research		Data collection process	
Definition of research questions	Keyword definition	Definition of inclusion/exclusion criteria	Search for articles	Reading articles found	Categorization of articles	Evaluate the quality of the articles
▼	▼	▼	▼	▼	▼	▼
Research scope	Search guide	Narrow down article selection	Found articles	Selection of relevant articles	Classified articles	Systematic review results

Fig. 1.   Process of systematic review

2.1   Definition of the Search Protocol

This protocol is used to establish the elements required to carry out the SR, establishing the criteria for searching, selecting and analyzing the information. Each of the elements of the SR process is presented below:

- **Search questions**

  The defined search questions (SQ) that are intended to be answered in the SR are the following:

  - **Search question 1.** What are the main vulnerabilities existing in SCADA systems such as those used in electrical substations?
  - **Search question 2.** What guidelines, methods, methodologies, frameworks have been used to improve the security of SCADA systems?
  - **Search question 3.** What tools have been used in pentesting on SCADA systems?

- **Keyword definition**

  Once the SQs were defined, the keywords associated with each of them were established in English and Spanish, as shown in Table 1. At the same time, the bibliographic databases in which the exploration of the research articles and their respective search strings to use the keywords were identified.

Table 1. Keywords

SQ	English	Spanish
SQ 1	vulnerabilities, vulnerability, risk, informatic security, SCADA, electrical substation	vulnerabilidades, vulnerabilidad, riesgo, seguridad informática, SCADA, subestación eléctrica
SQ 2	framework, guideline, method, methodology, vulnerability, risk, informatic security, SCADA, electrical substations	marco de referencia, guía, método, metodología, vulnerabilidad, riesgo, seguridad informática, SCADA, subestación eléctrica
SQ 3	tools, pentesting, penetration test, kali, framework, method, methodology, vulnerabilities, vulnerability, risk, informatic security, SCADA, electrical substations	herramientas, pentesting, prueba de penetración, marco de referencia, método, metodología, vulnerabilidades, vulnerabilidad, riesgo, seguridad informática, SCADA, subestación eléctrica

- **Definition of inclusion and exclusion criteria**

  To select only those research articles that are related to the objective of the SR and allow the three SQs to be answered, a series of inclusion and exclusion criteria were established, which are presented below:

  - Research articles that did not show a direct relationship with the research objective were excluded: despite containing keywords in the title and/or abstract, the article did not present information relevant to the search question analyzed.
  - Research articles showing similar topics and results were excluded: only articles with more detailed and better-quality results and explanations were taken into consideration.

- Research articles with insufficient information were excluded: articles that did not provide detailed information, were incomplete or were not in line with the stated objective.
- Research articles older than 5 years since their publication were excluded: since it is a research related to ICT, it is necessary to consider updated information and results.
- Research articles published in languages other than English and Spanish were excluded.
- Research articles not related to ICS or SCADA systems were excluded.
- Research articles to which the full document was not accessible were excluded.

2.2 Conducting the Information Search

Once the search protocol was defined, the search for scientific research in various bibliographic sources began.

- **Search for articles**

   For the search of articles, the bibliographic sources IEEE Xplore, ACM and Crossref were used, both directly and using the Google Scholar engine. In each of them, the concatenation of keywords with the site's own format was performed to optimize the exploration of documents. The articles found were catalogued by year of publication and according to the associated SQ.

   A total of 371 articles were found using the databases, of which 195 matched the search criteria of SQ1, 109 with SQ2 and 67 with SQ3. These preliminary results, take with consideration the exclusion of articles that were published before 2016. Then, the articles with relevance to the research were selected, giving a result of 27 for SQ1, 8 for SQ2 and 5 for SQ3. The results are shown in Table 2:

Table 2. List of articles published between 2016 and 2020

SQ	2016	2017	2018	2019	2020	Total
SQ 1	6	5	7	7	2	27
SQ 2	2	3	2	1	0	8
SQ 3	0	2	1	2	0	5
Total studies						40

- **Reading the articles found**

   The selection of the articles to be considered in the research was carried out by applying a three-step criterion, as shown in Fig. 2. In the first step, 331 studies were discarded because they were not considered relevant to the search questions, in the second step the number of studies according to the criterion was maintained, and finally 27 studies were discarded in the third step, resulting in the complete reading of 13 articles as the primary source of information. These articles were catalogued according to the associated SQ.

Step	Preliminary studies	Activity	Selected studies
1 ▶	Q1:195 Q2: 109 Q3: 67 Total: 371	▶ Identify relevant studies by applying the exclusion criteria. ▶	Q1:31 Q2: 14 Q3: 12 Total: 57
2 ▶	Q1:31 Q2: 14 Q3: 12 Total: 57	▶ Identify studies for a comprehensive review ▶	Q1:27 Q2: 4 Q3: 5 Total: 40
3 ▶	Q1:27 Q2: 4 Q3: 5 Total: 40	▶ Obtain main studies for a complete assessment ▶	Q1:8 Q2: 3 Q3: 2 Total: 13

Fig. 2. Steps in the process of reading and selecting articles

3 Results

Thirteen research studies were classified as primary source of information to respond to the SQs. Once the documents had been completely read, an analysis of the vulnerabilities present in the studies and whether they refer to electrical substations was carried out first. This first analysis is related to SQ1. The results are shown in Table 3.

Table 3. Analysis of vulnerabilities found

Vulnerability	Title	Reference	Related to electrical substations?
Denial-of-Service	Simulation and Impact Analysis of Denial-of-Service Attacks on Power SCADA	[2]	No
Default Credentials, Unsupported Unix operating system, SQL Injections, OpenSSH vulnerabilities, Buffer Overflows, DoS, XSS, Browsable Web Directories, Modbus coil access, Cleartext submission of credentials, authentication without HTTPS, Generic paramater injections, web mirroring	Identifying SCADA Vulnerabilities Using Passive and Active Vulnerability Assessment Techniques	[3]	No

(continued)

Table 3. (*continued*)

Vulnerability	Title	Reference	Related to electrical substations?
Replay Attack, Man-in-the-Middle Attack, Brute Force Attack, Dictionary Attack, Eavesdropping, Denial-of-Service Attacks, War Dialing, Default Passwords, Data Modification	Securing Communications for SCADA and Critical Industrial Systems	[4]	No
Architectural Vulnerabilities, Security Policy Vulnerabilities, Software and Hardware Vulnerabilities, Communication Protocol Vulnerabilities	Security of SCADA Systems Against Cyber–Physical Attacks	[5]	Yes (mentioned)
Man-In-The-Middle (MITM) Attack, DoS (Denial of Service) Attack, Replay Attack, Injection Attack, Spoofing Attack, Eavesdropping, Modification, Reconnaissance Attack	Review on Cyber Vulnerabilities of Communication Protocols in Industrial Control Systems	[6]	Yes
Source code design and implementation, Buffer Overflow, SQL Injection, Cross Site Scripting (XSS), Effective patch management application	An Overview of Cyber-Attack Vectors on SCADA Systems	[7]	No
APT (Advanced persistent Attack)	APT Attack Analysis in SCADA Systems	[8]	No
Improper input validation, Buffer overflow, Command injection and Cross-site scripting, Poor code quality, Improper control of a resource, Feeble access control mechanism, Poor authentication, Cryptographic Issues, Poor credential management and maintenance practices, Inadequate policies & procedures, Network Design Fragility, Feeble Firewall, Audit and accountabilities Rules	SCADA (Supervisory Control and Data Acquisition) Systems: Vulnerability Assessment and Security Recommendations	[9]	No

The results of the search for vulnerabilities in SCADA systems give as results, in the first place, the analysis of the nature of the vulnerabilities found and how many times they were found in the different scientific documents analyzed. This is an important data, because it is possible to make a statistic of the probability of their existence when evaluating a SCADA system.

In reviewing the studies found, a total of 27 types of vulnerabilities were detected in SCADA systems, which vary in nature and difficulty of mitigation. It is important to understand that SCADA systems are deployed on common computer systems on common operating systems, so many vulnerabilities can be found in other systems of other natures, for example, data servers. Table 4 shows the different types of vulnerabilities and how many times they were found in the studies:

From the above information, Fig. 3 shows graphically the types of vulnerabilities encountered at times mentioned in analyzed scientific publications.

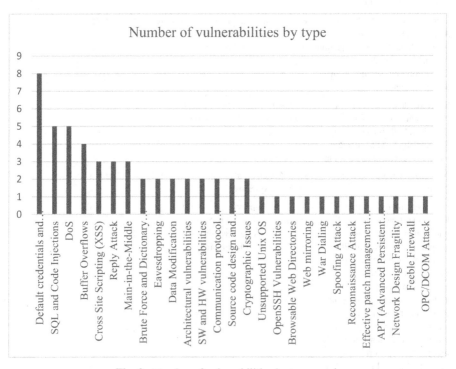

Fig. 3. Number of vulnerabilities by type graph

Table 4. Number of vulnerabilities by type

Vulnerability	Cases	Vulnerability	Cases
Default credentials and authentication	8	Cryptographic Issues	2
SQL and Code Injections	5	Unsupported Unix OS	1
DoS	5	OpenSSH Vulnerabilities	1
Buffer Overflows	4	Browsable Web Directories	1
Cross Site Scripting (XSS)	3	Web mirroring	1
Reply Attack	3	War Dialing	1
Main-in-the-Middle	3	Spoofing Attack	1
Brute Force and Dictionary Attack	2	Reconnaissance Attack	1
Eavesdropping	2	Effective patch management application	1
Data Modification	2	APT (Advanced Persistent Attack)	1
Architectural vulnerabilities	2	Network Design Fragility	1
SW and HW vulnerabilities	2	Feeble Firewall	1
Communication protocol vulnerabilities	2	OPC/DCOM Attack	1
Source code design and implementation	2		

It is possible to see that the greatest vulnerability of SCADA systems is in default credentials and authentication. This means that the username and password remain unchanged from the factory, which allows the attacker to look at the manufacturer's documentation to take control of the system. In turn, this section encompasses credential entry technologies. By not using, for example, HTTPS, it is possible by means of a sniffer to obtain the credentials in plain text once they are entered into the system.

Subsequently, an analysis of the types of documents found and how they contribute to the security of SCADA systems was carried out to respond to SQ2. The results are shown in Table 5 below:

Of the documents analyzed following the search criteria, 54% correspond to studies, 15% to methods, 8% to methodology, 8% to ontology, 8% to report and 7% to guide. No frameworks were found during the filtering of articles. The results are shown graphically in Fig. 4:

Finally, an analysis of the pentesting and vulnerability discovery tools used in the SCADA systems present in the research papers was performed, giving room for SQ3. The results are shown below in Table 6.

Table 5. Types of research and contribution to the study

Type	Title of research	Reference	Contribution and review
Study	Simulation and impact analysis of denial-of-service attacks on power SCADA	[2]	Performs a study of the impact of a denial of service (DoS) attack on a SCADA system. The results show an increase in the response time of the system, but not significant enough to cause it to effectively lose service
Study	Identifying SCADA vulnerabilities using passive and active vulnerability assessment techniques	[3]	It performs a study of the vulnerabilities present in a SCADA system of various brands, using active and passive search techniques, using Nessus and Shodan software. The results are tabulated according to their criticality index and the analyzed brands affected
Guide	Securing communications for SCADA and critical industrial systems	[4]	It reviews the attack vectors affecting SCADA systems and provides recommendations to reduce them. Comprehensive and detailed mitigation methods and controls are present to protect the communication of SCADA systems and industrial control systems (ICS)
Report	Security of SCADA systems against cyber–physical attacks	[5]	It performs an analysis of the layers that make up a SCADA system and in the various markets where they are found (electricity, water, gas, among others). It shows the threat vectors, both internal and external, and the common vulnerabilities found in these systems. At the same time, relevant attacks that have occurred in SCADA systems and their classification are analyzed. Finally, methods of detection and isolation of attacks are shown

(*continued*)

Table 5. (*continued*)

Type	Title of research	Reference	Contribution and review
Study	Review on cyber vulnerabilities of communication protocols in industrial control systems	[6]	It lists the most common communication protocols used in SCADA systems and the cybersecurity problems associated with them, analyzing the taxonomy of possible attacks. The results are tabulated for each communication protocol, finally presenting possible countermeasures
Study	An overview of cyber-attack vectors on SCADA systems	[7]	It studies both hardware and software cyber-attacks on SCADA systems. In the latter category, several vulnerabilities present in these systems are shown. Subsequently, the vulnerabilities present at the communication network level are also shown, ending with graphs detailing the percentage of use of various communication protocols of SCADA systems. For this study, as its title indicates, it responds to a not so deep look of the analyzed topics
Method	Vulnerability Analysis of Network Scanning on SCADA Systems	[10]	It provides a description of vulnerability analysis methods, as well as examples of some of the available active and passive discovery software tools. It also details the technologies present in SCADA and ICS systems in general
Study	APT Attack Analysis in SCADA Systems	[8]	Performs an Advanced Persistent Threat (APT) analysis on a SCADA system. Examples of attacks of this nature in the real world are shown, such as Stuxnet, Havex and Flame, analyzing their characteristics. It is evident from this study that this type of attack is particularly difficult to deal with, due to its complex nature
Ontology	Ontology-based detection of cyber-attacks to SCADA-systems in critical infrastructures	[11]	It proposes a prototype of an open-source IDS, based on an ontology and focusing on an evaluation under realistic conditions

(continued)

Table 5. (*continued*)

Type	Title of research	Reference	Contribution and review
Method	Cyber Security Risk Assessment Method for SCADA of Industrial Control Systems	[12]	It proposes a cybersecurity risk analysis method for a SCADA system. It establishes criteria, identification and risk analysis using a mathematical model
Study	Convergence of IT and SCADA: Associated Security Threats and Vulnerabilities	[13]	It reviews the inherent weaknesses of SCADA systems, breaking them down into three generations: 1°: 1960s, 2°: 1980s and 3°: 2000 to the present. Subsequently, an analysis of threats and vulnerabilities faced by these systems is detailed. The analysis in this document does not go into much depth on the technical part but focuses on making the reading more enjoyable
Methodology	Network security analysis SCADA system automation on industrial process	[14]	Performs a general review of the different elements and equipment that make up a SCADA network and the associated terminology. Subsequently, it performs an analysis of the different sources of threats to these systems and the types of attacks that can be carried out. Next, a methodology for vulnerability analysis of a SCADA system is presented. Kali Linux and Wireshark are used to obtain as a result a pentesting, effects on the human-machine interface and traffic analysis. This study is very complete, taking into consideration the results obtained
Study	Analysis of SCADA Security Using Penetration Testing: A Case Study on Modbus TCP Protocol	[15]	It performs a pentesting study exploiting the Modbus TCP protocol flaws and showing the respective countermeasures. The results obtained using different attack vectors are shown and the detection and prevention methods of these procedures are disclosed. This study shows in detail the results of an exploitation of vulnerabilities of the Modbus TCP protocol, widely used in SCADA systems

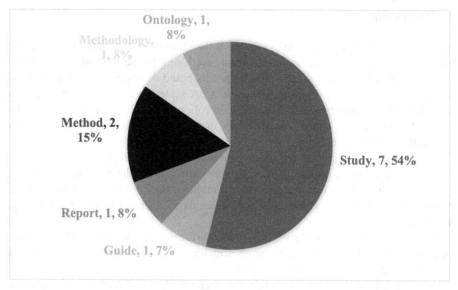

Fig. 4. Graph of percentages of types of research

Table 6. Software tools for pentesting and vulnerability analysis

Tool	Reference	Title
Shodan, Nessus	[3]	Identifying SCADA Vulnerabilities Using Passive and Active Vulnerability Assessment Techniques
Nmap, ZMap, Nessus, Passive Vulnerability Scanner, Shodan, Tshark, Ettercap, Phyton UDP_DoS.py	[10]	Vulnerability Analysis of Network Scanning on SCADA Systems
Kali Linux, Wireshark	[14]	Network Security Analysis SCADA System Automation on Industrial Process
Smod pentesting tool	[15]	Analysis of SCADA Security using Penetration Testing: A case study on Modbus TCP Protocol

4 Discussion

An international supplier of SCADA systems is the Portuguese company Efacec, largely focused on electrical substation implementations. Using the search criteria presented in this document, no publications referring to this brand of systems were found in the databases reviewed. However, the Efacec SCADA system uses elements in common with suppliers of other firms, such as communication protocols and ICT, so it is to be assumed that several or all the vulnerabilities, methods and tools found in this research also apply to these systems.

Through the systematic review carried out in this study, it was possible to recognize the main vulnerabilities present in SCADA systems at a global level. At the same time, the types of documents that are available to improve the computer security of these systems, such as studies, guides, reports and methods, methodologies and ontology, were found.

Finally, examples of software tools used to perform pentesting on SCADA systems were also found, which allow to perform security tests and to take the necessary measures to improve the robustness of these systems.

It is then intended to perform a study of vulnerabilities and pentesting techniques on the Efacec SCADA system, with the purpose of contributing from the approach of this brand, checking in an effective and rigorous way if they are consistent with the results obtained from the research presented in this document.

5 Conclusions

In a detailed analysis of the research work carried out in the last 5 years, it can be concluded that SCADA systems show numerous vulnerabilities often associated with the operating systems in which they are deployed, these systems inevitably share many of the same vulnerabilities. These works answer research question 1 by demonstrating the types of risks to which these systems are exposed and which, without the proper precautions, can put the infrastructure of an industrial control system at risk. It is necessary to understand that these systems are often related to critical processes of the infrastructure of a country, such as electricity supply, drinking water, fuels, among many others.

Regarding search question 2, the types of documentation found, mostly studies, make a description of the different parts that make up the SCADA systems and the cybersecurity risks to which they are exposed. They are complemented by studies of methods, methodologies, ontologies, among others, but none of them proposes a guide that encompasses the critical aspects that can be these vulnerabilities in SCADA systems.

Finally, for search question 3, there are several pentesting tools that can be used in SCADA systems, but not many studies have been found that emphasize this topic. Therefore, as a future work related to this systematic review, is to propose a framework to perform pentesting in SCADA systems of the Efacec brand, with the aim of contributing to the future in analysis and exploitation of vulnerabilities of these systems.

References

1. Kitchenham, B.: Procedures for Performing Systematic Reviews. Keele Univ 33, Keele (2014)

2. Kalluri, R., Mahendra, L., Kumar, R.K.S., Prasad, G.L.G.: Simulation and impact analysis of denial-of-service attacks on power SCADA. In: 2016 National Power Systems Conference, NPSC 2016 (2017). https://doi.org/10.1109/NPSC.2016.7858908

3. Samtani, S., Yu, S., Zhu, H., et al.: Identifying SCADA vulnerabilities using passive and active vulnerability assessment techniques. In: IEEE Conference on Intelligence and Security Informatics Cybersecurity Big Data, ISI 2016, pp. 25–30 (2016). https://doi.org/10.1109/ISI.2016.7745438

4. Bartman, T., Carson, K.: Securing communications for SCADA and critical industrial systems. 69th Annual Conference for Protective Relay Engineers, CPRE 2016 (2017). https://doi.org/10.1109/CPRE.2016.7914914

5. Do, V.L., Fillatre, L., Côte, U., et al.: Security of SCADA systems against cyber – physical attacks (2017)

6. Dorqj, S., Vhyhudo, Z., Dwwdfnv, W.S., Frxqwhuphdvxuhv, D.Q.G.: Review on cyber vulnerabilities of communication protocols in industrial control systems, vol. 4, pp. 1–6 (2015)

7. Irmak, E., Erkek, I.: An overview of cyber-attack vectors on SCADA systems. In: 6th International Symposium on Digital Forensic and Security, ISDFS 2018 – Proceeding, vol. 2018-January, pp. 1–5 (2018). https://doi.org/10.1109/ISDFS.2018.8355379

8. Zhou, X., Xu, Z., Wang, L., et al.: APT attack analysis in SCADA systems. In: MATEC Web Conference, vol. 173, pp. 2–6 (2018). https://doi.org/10.1051/matecconf/201817301010

9. Upadhyay, D., Sampalli, S.: SCADA (supervisory control and data acquisition) systems: Vulnerability assessment and security recommendations. Comput. Secur. **89**, 101666 (2020). https://doi.org/10.1016/j.cose.2019.101666

10. Coffey, K., Smith, R., Maglaras, L., Janicke, H.: Vulnerability analysis of network scanning on SCADA systems. Secur. Commun. Netw. (2018). https://doi.org/10.1155/2018/3794603

11. Krauß, D., Thomalla, C.: Ontology-based detection of cyber-attacks to SCADA-systems in critical infrastructures. In: 2016 6th International Conference on Digital Information and Communication Technology and its Applications, DICTAP 2016, pp. 70–73 (2016). https://doi.org/10.1109/DICTAP.2016.7544003

12. Poletykin, A.: Cyber security risk assessment method for SCADA of industrial control systems. In: International Russian Automation Conference RusAutoCon 2018, pp. 1–5 (2018). https://doi.org/10.1109/RUSAUTOCON.2018.8501811

13. Smurthwaite, M., Bhattacharya, M.: Convergence of IT and SCADA: associated security threats and vulnerabilities. In: IOP Conference Series: Materials Science and Engineering, vol. 790 (2020). https://doi.org/10.1088/1757-899X/790/1/012041

14. Hilal, H., Nangim, A.: Network security analysis SCADA system automation on industrial process. In: 2017 International Conference on Broadband Communication, Wireless Sensors and Powering, BCWSP 2017, vol. 2018-Janua, pp. 1–6 (2018). https://doi.org/10.1109/BCWSP.2017.8272569

15. Luswata, J., Zavarsky, P., Swar, B., Zvabva, D.: Analysis of SCADA security using penetration testing: a case study on modbus TCP protocol. In: 29th Biennial Symposium on Communications, BSC 2018, pp. 1–5 (2018). https://doi.org/10.1109/BSC.2018.8494686

Automatic Diagnosis of Cardiovascular Diseases Using Electrocardiogram Data and Artificial Intelligence Algorithms: A Systematic Review

Roberto Mario Cadena Vega[✉], Efrén Gorrostieta Hurtado,
Marco Antonio Aceves Fernández, and Juan Manuel Ramos Arreguin

Universidad Autónoma de Querétaro, Santiago de Querétaro, Querétaro, Mexico
rcadena16@alumnos.uaq.mx

Abstract. Cardiovascular diseases are now among the top ten causes of death in the world [1] and the electrocardiogram (ECG/EKG) is a very important tool for its diagnosis, as it is non-invasive, inexpensive and easy to access. It has become one of the most used studies by health experts, in addition to offering a useful tool for artificial intelligence algorithms focused on the prediction of anomalies and automatic diagnosis, achieving promising results in this area of health.

This article presents a systematic review of artificial intelligence methods focused on the diagnosis of cardiovascular diseases using ECG data.

Articles were extracted where some type of artificial intelligence algorithm was applied to ECG data in order to classify and give a diagnosis of cardiovascular diseases that were published between 2018 and 2020, the results, conclusions and areas were discussed. Opportunities opened from them.

Current technology, driven by Artificial Intelligence, allows us to carry out medical studies in an easier, faster and more reliable way with new electronic devices, in addition to having access to larger databases for the training of automatic models. Through this work we were able to find that deep learning architectures are increasingly used for their versatility and effectiveness in diagnoses based on medical signals.

There are still challenges to overcome to make this type of instrument efficient, reliable, portable and easily accessible to the general public. It is undoubtedly a research topic of great importance for the health sciences and for the field of artificial intelligence.

Keywords: Electrocardiogram · Artificial intelligence · Automatic diagnosis · Systematic review

1 Introduction

Due to its high availability, low cost and great diagnostic capacity, the electrocardiogram (ECG/EKG) has become one of the most relevant non-invasive medical studies used for the diagnosis of various anomalies and cardiovascular diseases [2], such as premature contractions of the atria (PAC) or ventricles (PVC), atrial fibrillation (AF), myocardial

© Springer Nature Switzerland AG 2021
M. F. Mata-Rivera and R. Zagal-Flores (Eds.): WITCOM 2021, CCIS 1430, pp. 104–116, 2021.
https://doi.org/10.1007/978-3-030-89586-0_8

infarction (MI) and congestive heart failure (CHF). Although the invention of the ECG dates back to 1872 [3], this study has evolved over time and its application method has been developed to make it more accessible and easy to perform, such as the Holter monitor and various portable electronic devices such as the Apple Watch [4] and until a few years ago, data analysis and diagnosis was the exclusive task of trained and qualified physicians, so making the diagnosis automatically has become a subject of research with great scientific importance.

Recently, artificial intelligence algorithms focused on data classification and grouping, as well as deep learning methods have made many advances in the analysis of ECG data for classification and diagnosis [5] and [6]. Therefore, we consider it essential to perform a systematic analysis of the methods used for the diagnosis of cardiac abnormalities and cardiovascular diseases with ECG data from the perspectives of algorithm architectures and application tasks. Furthermore, future research projections are discussed and analyzed, which may serve as the basis for future work [7].

2   Method

2.1   Search Strategy

To carry out the Review as complete as possible, articles published from 2018 to the current year, see the Fig. 2, that implemented some type of artificial intelligence algorithm to perform an automatic diagnosis were searched using ECG data in IEEE Xplore, IOP Science, Science Direct, AHA journals, SciElo and PubMed.

Keywords were used for the search such as: artificial intelligence, electrocardiogram, ECG, EKG, automatic diagnosis, cardiovascular disease, heart disease. All keywords are not case sensitive.

It is worth mentioning that a large number of articles found with any of the keywords aren't directly related to our review topic, which resulted in a large initial set of articles.

2.2   Selection Criteria

The number of articles selected after the search was 72. After deleting the duplicate articles, 68 were obtained. Next, a rapid analysis of the articles was performed to assess their eligibility, reviewing titles and abstracts, excluding some articles. using the following criteria:

1. Do not use ECG data as primary data.
2. Do not use artificial intelligence algorithms.
3. No quantitative evaluations.
4. General classifications (no search for pathologies).
5. Diagnosis of diseases not directly related to the myocardium (sleep apnea, acute cognitive stress, etc.)

As a result, 25 total articles were obtained for the review. See the Fig. 1 shows a schematic diagram of the article selection process.

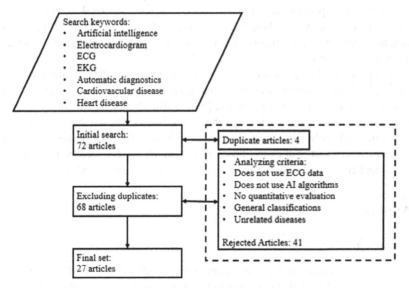

Fig. 1. Item selection process diagram

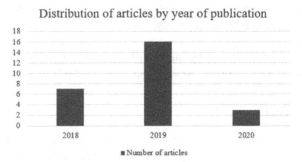

Fig. 2. Distribution of articles by year of publication

3   Data Extraction

Each article was analyzed according to the following aspects of their research: Task, Method and Data.

4 Results

An analysis of the articles was carried out in the aspects of task, method and data.

4.1 Task

Detection of Specific Diseases

The goal of creating an automatic diagnostic system for this purpose is to analyze the input ECG data and map it to the targets of a specific disease output using one or more artificial intelligence algorithms. One of the most common tasks in articles of this type is the detection and classification of cardiac arrhythmias, for example, in [8] a deep neural network and simple ECG were used to classify 12 types of cardiac arrhythmias. Being atrial fibrillation (AF) a particular case of these as shown in [9].

Detection of Abnormalities in the ECG Trace

Given that heart diseases are evident in an ECG causing abnormalities directly in the electrocardiographic trace [10] as in the case of MI causing abnormalities in the ST segment as in [11], in which cases algorithms have been designed to analyze the damage of ECG, specialized in looking for these kind of anomalies in specific segments, in [12] the RR segment of the ECG is analyzed since it is closely linked to different pathologies such as heart failure congestive [13].

4.2 Method

Table 3 shows the distribution of the articles according to the method used and the type of task performed by it.

CNNs: They are a type of deep neural network, which can extract hierarchical patterns through several convolutional, batch normalization, activation, grouped and classification layers [14].

Such is the case of [15] where they use a CNN to analyze fetal ECGs for the detection of congenital heart disease (CHD). They use a private database with 386 fetal ECG records (266 healthy and 120 with CHD) lasting 30 min. They further used a CNN consisting of 6 convolutional layers with residual connections and leaky rectified linear units as activation functions. Training was carried out by increasing the number of recordings by random rotation of the data and 10% was used for validation, then the precision of the model obtained was measured by the formula:

$$Accuracy = \frac{TP + TN}{TP + FP + TN + FN} \tag{1}$$

Where:

TP: *True Positive* | TN: *True Negative*

FP: False Positive | FN: False Negative

Thus, obtaining an accuracy of 76% in the detection of CHD, surpassing the global results of the ultrasonic examination found in the literature, thus de-showing its progress in the field of diagnosis in the prenatal stage.

RNN: This type of network is characterized by the fact that the output of the previous step is used as input for the current step [16], due to this property, an RNN is able to remember information in sequential order.

As in [17] they feed an RNN with ECG data obtained from the MIT-BIH database divided into intervals of 100 beats with long and short term memory (LSTM) to create a model that could automatically detect permanent or intermittent AF.

The LSTM mechanism of the neural network used consists of three primordial layers:

1. Entrance
2. Forget
3. Departure

The algorithm determines which information persists and which is forgotten. The number of LSTM cells in each of the layers were set to twice the length of the input sequence and the global maximum clustering in one dimension between the bidirectional layers or the fully connected layers was used.

The algorithm results were cross-validated ten times. The average training time of an epoch was applied in approximately 215 s and initial experiments showed that the model converged in between 60 and 80 epochs.

The proposed bi-directional LSTM classifier achieves an overall classification accuracy of 98.51% with a stratified 10-fold cross-validation, correctly classifying 98.67% of normal HR sequences and 98.32% of normal HR sequences. HR sequences that correctly show the signs of atrial fibrillation.

CRNN: This type of network is a combination of convolutional neural networks and recurrent networks, this type of architecture is very convenient for the management of ECG signals with varied sequence lengths and multiple input channels. Within the investigations focused on ECG classification, we have found that this type of architecture is the most widely used.

In [18] a residual convolutional model and bidirectional long and short-term memory (LSTM) are used to extract characteristics from raw ECG signals to classify cardiac arrhythmias.

They used as a basis a private database with 10,000 12-lead ECG samples with a duration of 6 to 60 s with a sampling rate of 500 Hz.

Subsequently, they proceeded to unify the samples for a duration of 30 s, obtaining a total database of 6,877 samples labeled in the following proportion (Table 1).

Table 1. Label proportion

Type	Recording	Mean	SD	Min	Median	Max
Normal	918	15.43	7.61	10.00	13.00	60.00
Atrial fibrillation (AF)	1098	15.01	8.39	9.00	11.00	60.00
First-degree atrioventricular block (I-AVB)	704	14.32	7.21	10.00	11.27	60.00
Left bundle branch block (LBBB)	207	14.92	8.09	9.00	12.00	60.00
Right bundle branch block (RBBB)	1695	14.42	7.60	10.00	11.19	60.00
Premature atrial contraction (PAC)	556	19.46	12.36	9.00	14.00	60.00
Premature ventricular contraction (PVC)	672	20.21	12.85	6.00	15.00	60.00
ST-segment depression (STD)	825	15.13	6.82	8.00	12.78	60.00
ST-segment elevated (STE)	202	17.15	10.72	10.00	11.89	60.00
Total	6877	15.79	9.04	6.00	12.00	60.00

The model they used for learning consists of 1-dimensional convolutional layers, batch normalization layers, activation layer linear rectification units (ReLU's), abandonment layers, and max-pooling layers.

The results of the arrhythmia classification were compared with other studies as follows (Table 2):

Table 2. Ranking results against other jobs

Rank	Team	Normal	AF	I-AVB	LBBB	RBBB	PAC	PVC	STD	STE
1	He et al.	0.748	0.920	0.882	0.889	0.883	0.787	0.851	0.780	0.780
2	Cai et al.	0.765	0.927	0.887	0.886	0.880	0.812	0.800	0.784	0.753
3	Chen et al.	0.752	0.930	0.871	0.915	0.839	0.832	0.833	0.800	0.667
4	Mao et al.	0.692	0.940	0.852	1.000	0.899	0.706	0.875	0.762	0.622
5	Yu et al.	0.709	0.907	0.863	0.918	0.838	0.736	0.783	0.714	0.723
6	Zhang et al.	0.757	0.904	0.839	0.887	0.787	0.735	0.755	0.742	0.638

GAN: This model is a type of neural network that consists of two competing submodels, a generative model and a discriminative model that are trained to perform a min-max game.

This type of model is used to a great extent for the generation of images and natural language, however it has also been recently dealt with in the works related to the analysis of ECG, for example, in [19] they perform an anomaly detector in ECG to classify various cardiac pathologies and used a GAN algorithm to perform a data augmentation.

In this case, the GAN model was not used directly for ECG classification, however, it was used to synthesize new samples according to the PhysioNet database increasing them from 47 to 816.

The proposed method solves the challenge well, especially if the audio recordings are transformed into spectrogram form. The solution outperformed the recent wave scattering approach (80%), (84%) in CNN and even the ECG method (80.9%). The system also consisted of 99.66% accuracy in the PhysioNet challenge, the best score after this is 86.02%.

AE: An AE is a type of neural network made up of an encoder module and a decoder module for the purpose of learning a reduced dimensional representation using the encoder module while the decoder tries to reconstruct an original input from this reduced representation. In [20] they use a DAE structure, which are structures that take partially damaged inputs and are capable of recovering the original undistorted input, for a pre-processing stage of their data to eliminate noise from contaminated ECG signals.

FIS: A fuzzy inference system uses representations of inaccurate data in a similar way as human thought does, defining a non-linear correspondence between one or more input variables and an output variable. In [21] they use FIS for the detection of myocardial infarction in the analysis of the peaks of the ST segment in ECG signals due to its flexibility in the linguistic variables.

Others: Some works also worked with fully connected networks (FC), for example in [22] they used them to perform classification on ECG data and detect heart rhythms in extremely short data (10 RR intervals).

U-net networks were also used, such is the case of [23] where they proposed a modified U-net to handle different lengths of ECG sequences for the classification of cardiac arrhythmias.

Table 3. List of methods and tasks of articles

	Arrhythmia	Heart conditions	Atrial fibrillation	Myocardial infarction	ECG abnormalities	Others
CNN	[24]	[15, 19, 25]	[9, 24]	[26, 27]	[11]	[28, 29]
RNN	[22]		[17]			[30]
CRNN	[8, 18, 20, 31]	[32]	[33]			[34, 35]
AE	[20, 36]					
GAN		[19]				
FIS				[21]		
Others	[20, 22, 23]	[12, 37, 38]				

5   Data Description

Many of the articles cited in this document used public databases, thus facilitating the reproduction of the results obtained in these studies.

The data used in all the articles analyzed in this work are ECG data, however, it should be mentioned that they are different from each other due to different aspects.

5.1   Source

Most of the data sets used in the aforementioned works are obtained using medical instrumentation, however, some others were obtained from electronic devices such as smart watches or mobile ECG monitors.

5.2   Number of Leads

Due to the difference in data acquisition devices and the type of ECG requested by a physician, there are simple ECGs (single lead) or 12-lead ECG as in the works of [31] and [36] respectively. An example of a 12-lead ECG sampling with a duration of 10 s is shown in Fig. 3 [39].

5.3   Sample Duration

Again, the type of acquisition device and the type of study play an important role in determining this characteristic, however, it also depends to a great extent on the dimensioning and format of the database used, since there are signal samples. that can last a

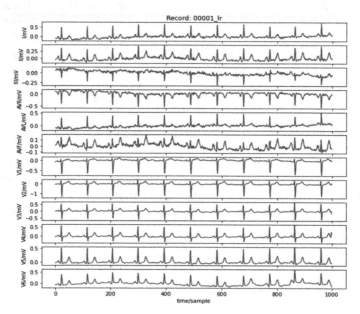

Fig. 3.   12-lead ECG data of 10 s duration.

few seconds or a set number of heartbeats, up to samples lasting minutes [40] or full-day monitoring.

5.4 Annotations and Metadata

Some of the databases used, in addition to the ECG signals, contain annotations made by the capturists, doctors or previous analysts, mainly referring to characteristics and data of the signal (noise explanation, acquisition equipment, markers wave start, peak and end, time annotations, etc.) or previous classifications made by experts or previous algorithms. In addition, still others have additional data (metadata), which present more information about the patients (identifiers, sample collection, date, place, etc.). An example of both data inclusion and annotations can be found in [39].

5.5 Main Databases

Table 4 shows the most used databases in the analyzed articles and their main characteristics.

Table 4. Databases used in the analyzed articles

Name	Samples	Leads	Time	Anotations	Source
MIT-BIH Arrhytmia DB	47	2	30 min	Diagnosis of rhythm and beat level	Hospital Boston's Beth Israel
MIT-BIH AF DB	25	2	10 h	Rhythm: AF, AFL, AV, others	Hospital Boston's Beth Israel
MIT-BIH MVE DB	22	2	30 min	Ventricular tachycardia, ventricular flutter, ventricular fibrillation	Hospital Boston's Beth Israel
MIT-BIH Normal Sinus Rhythm DB	18	2	24 h	Heartbeat: Normal	Hospital Boston's Beth Israel
Physionet CCC-2017	8528/3658	1	30 s	Rhythm: normal, AF, others, noise	AliveCor healthcare device

(continued)

Table 4. (*continued*)

Name	Samples	Leads	Time	Anotations	Source
INCART 12-lead Arrhythmia DB	75	12	30 min	Rhythm: MI, ischemic attack, coronary artery disease, sinus node dysfunction, supraventricular ectopy, atrial fibrillation (SVTA), WPW, AV block	St. Petersburg Institute of Cardiological Technics
PTB Diagnostic ECG DB	549	15	30 s	Rhythm: MI Cardiomyopathy, Dysrhythmia, Myocardial hypertrophy, valve disease, myocarditis	Ph. Tech. Bundesanstalt
PTB-XL	21837	12	10 s	5 super classes and 24 diagnostic subclasses, patient metadata and medical report	Ph. Tech. Bundesanstalt

6 Discussion of Opportunities and Challenges

This section will discuss the current challenges presented by the analyzed papers, related to the classification of ECG data and the diagnosis of heart disease, as well as the potential opportunities that may arise from them.

6.1 Databases

The main variable in the papers presented is the database used to carry out the study, although all are of ECG signals, these present many variations in terms of duration, number of referrals and labels of diseases and metadata, in addition to present a limited number of samples, the latter being one of the greatest impediments to performing a diagnostic system or validating a classification more effectively and accurately, however, in recent years we have been able to observe how to the general public, new databases with a considerable number of samples and labels at different levels, in addition to the fact that the possibility of performing a simple ECG has been increased thanks to the development of smart devices such as Smart Watch or monitoring devices. cardiac monitoring, with what is expected in a few years there will be new, more accessible databases with a greater number of samples.

6.2 Application

Because the algorithms used for ECG diagnosis and classification are dense and complex architectures, we face the great obstacle that is integrating it to simple and portable devices, therefore, a very large opportunity door in this area is the compression of models without compromising their effectiveness.

6.3 Unequal Classes

It is common to find in databases large amounts of samples cataloged as "normal" or similar, because the diseases sought are suffered by the minority of the population analyzed, this can be an obstacle to generate an effective model at the time of training any artificial intelligence architecture. This type of problem has been reduced in the works in different ways, from the creation of data using generative models or designing new loss functions, for example, in [33] the proposed method uses a technical asymmetry of increasing data dynamic driven to balance the distribution of the data.

6.4 Complementary Data

In the studies analyzed, the vast majority of models consider only the data obtained from ECG signals, however, in studies such as [30] the proposed method predicts the morale of the patient in the intensive care unit based on data from ECG, laboratory tests, interventions and vital signs. This type of use of complementary data apart from the ECG signal can also be a very important opportunity to favor the performance of models that predict and diagnose heart diseases and conditions in the investigations of the following years.

7 Conclusion

In this article, we conducted a systematic review of papers that analyzed ECG data and generated a model or diagnostic system to predict or detect heart disease using artificial intelligence methods. We found that automatic diagnosis is taking an important direction with the use of artificial intelligence algorithms, mainly those for deep learning, and that the ECG is one of the most versatile and accessible diagnostic tools in medicine whose sample collection it becomes easier with the advancement of current technology, thanks to which it is possible to have more quantity and better quality in the data to use.

Remembering the importance of the applications of these models, we can estimate a great impact on health and on the reduction of deaths due to heart diseases in the world.

The main contribution of this work is to provide a general description of artificial intelligence applications in the field of cardiology using ECG data in addition to pointing out the current obstacles and some possible solutions to them with which to approach new works.

References

1. World Health Organization. https://www.who.int/news-room/fact-sheets/detail/the-top-10-causes-of-death. Accessed 04 Aug 2021
2. Dimmeler, S.: Cardiovascular disease review series. EMBO Mol. Med. **3**(12), 697 (2011)
3. Rivera, M.: Einthoven's string galvanometer. Tex. Heart Inst. J. **35**(2), 174–178 (2008)
4. Burch, G.: A History of Electrocardiography. 1st edn. Norman Publishing (1990)
5. Mincholé, A.: Artificial intelligence for the electrocardiogram. Nat. Med. **25**(1), 20–23 (2019)
6. Lyon, A.: Computational techniques for ECG analysis and interpretation in light of their contribution to medical advances. J. R. Soc. Interface **15**(138), 15 (2018)
7. Kelley, A.: Artificial intelligence-augmented ECG assessment: The promise and the challenge. J. Cardiovasc. Electrophysiol. 675–678 (2019)
8. Hannun, A.: Cardiologist-level arrhythmia detection and classification in ambulatory electrocardiograms using a deep neural network. Nat. Med. **25**(1), 65–69 (2019)
9. Dang, H.: A novel deep arrhythmia-diagnosis network for atrial fibrillation classification using electrocardiogram signals. IEEE Access **7**, 75577–75590 (2019)
10. Kasper, D., Hauser, S., Jameson, L., Fauci, A., Longo D., Loscalzo, J.: Harrison's Principles of Internal Medicine. 19th edn. McGraw-Hill (2016)
11. Xiao, R.: A Deep learning approach to examine ischemic ST changes in ambulatory ECG recordings. AMIA Jt Summits Transl. Sci. Proc. **2017**, 256–262 (2018)
12. Wang, L.: Deep ensemble detection of congestive heart failure using short-term RR intervals. IEEE Access **7**, 69559–69574 (2019)
13. Libby, P.: Pathophysiology of coronary artery disease. Circulation **111**(25), 3481–3488 (2005)
14. Goodfellow, I.: Deep Learning. MIT Press, Cambridge (2016)
15. Vullings, R.: Fetal electrocardiography and deep learning for prenatal detection of congenital heart disease. In: 2019 Computing in Cardiology (CinC), pp. 1–4 (2019)
16. Bagnato I.: Aprende Machine Learning. Leanpub, La coruña (2020)
17. Faust, O.: Automated detection of atrial fibrillation using long short-term memory network with RR interval signals. Comput. Biol. Med. **102**, 327–335 (2018)
18. He, R.: Automatic cardiac arrhythmia classification using combination of deep residual network and bidirectional LSTM. IEEE Access **7**, 102119–102135 (2019)
19. Wolk, K.: Early and remote detection of possible heartbeat problems with convolutional neural networks and multipart interactive training. IEEE Access **7**, 145921–145927 (2019)
20. Xia, Y.: An automatic cardiac arrhythmia classification system with wearable electrocardiogram. IEEE Access **6**, 16529–16538 (2018)
21. Aghamohammadi, M.: Predicting heart attack through explainable artificial intelligence. In: Rodrigues, J., et al. (eds.) ICCS 2019. LNCS, vol. 11537, pp. 633–645. Springer, Cham (2019). https://doi.org/10.1007/978-3-030-22741-8_45
22. Kimura, T.: A 10-RR-interval-based rhythm classifier using a deep neural network. Circulation **138**, A12693–A12693 (2018)
23. Oh, S.: Automated beat-wise arrhythmia diagnosis using modified U-net on extended electrocardiographic recordings with heterogeneous arrhythmia types. Comput. Biol. Med. **105**, 92–101 (2019)
24. Nurmaini, S.: Robust detection of atrial fibrillation from short-term electrocardiogram using convolutional neural networks. Futur. Gener. Comput. Syst. **113**, 304–317 (2020)
25. Tison, G.: Automated and interpretable patient ECG profiles for disease detection, tracking, and discovery. Cardiovasc. Qual. Outcomes **12**(9), e005289 (2019)
26. Baloglu, U.: Classification of myocardial infarction with multi-lead ECG signals and deep CNN. Pattern Recogn. Lett. **122**, 23–30 (2019)

27. Han, C.: ML–ResNet: a novel network to detect and locate myocardial infarction using 12 leads ECG. Comput. Methods Program. Biomed. **185**, 05138–0518 (2020)
28. Attia, Z.: Screening for cardiac contractile dysfunction using an artificial intelligence–enabled electrocardiogram. Nat. Med. **25**(1), 70–74 (2019)
29. Attia, Z.: Prospective validation of a deep learning electrocardiogram algorithm for the detection of left ventricular systolic dysfunction. J. Cardiovasc. Electrophysiol. **30**(5), 668–674 (2019)
30. Xu, Y.: RAIM: recurrent attentive and intensive model of multimodal patient monitoring data. In Proceedings of the 24th International Conference on Knowledge Discovery & Data Mining, pp. 2565–2573 (2018)
31. Hong, S.: Combining deep neural networks and engineered features for cardiac arrhythmia detection from ECG recordings. Physiol. Meas. **40**(5), 054009 (2019)

Optic Disc and Optic Cup Segmentation Using Polar Coordinate and Encoder-Decoder Architecture

H. J. Sandoval-Cuellar[1]([✉]), M. A. Vázquez Membrillo[2], G. Alfonso-Francia[1],
J. C. Ortega Pedraza[1], and S. Tovar-Arriaga[1]

[1] Facultad de Ingeniería, Universidad Autónoma de Querétaro, Santiago de Querétaro, Mexico
[2] Instituto Mexicano de Oftalmología, IAP, Santiago de Querétaro, Mexico

Abstract. Glaucoma is a disease that affects the vision of those who suffer from it, leading to irreversible vision loss. The cup-to-disc relationship is an indispensable landmark for diagnosing glaucoma; therefore, performing an accurate disc and optic cup segmentation is desirable. In this work, a methodology to separately segment the optic disc and the optic cup from color fundus retina images is presented. For this purpose, the cup and disk sections were manually segmented from the public ORIGA database with the help and of specialists in the field of glaucoma. The complete retina images are cropped, identifying the region of interest (ROI), then converted to polar coordinates to minimize imbalance between classes. Then, an encoder-decoder architecture is applied with residual blocks for segmentation, obtaining an accuracy of 96.94% for the optic disc and 93.2% for the optic cup, as well as an overlap error of 0.088 and 0.0706, respectively.

Keywords: Glaucoma classification · Optic disc segmentation · Optic cup segmentation · Residual block · U-Net

1 Introduction

Glaucoma is the second leading cause of blindness diseases in the world [1], with cataracts number one. Because the disease cannot be cured and is irreversible, the condition is considered more severe than cataracts [2].

Glaucoma refers to a group of clinical diseases with common characteristics, including the deepening or excavation of the optic nerve [3]. This excavation is caused by the loss of axons in the retinal ganglion cells that form the optic nerve fibers. When the loss of optic nerve tissue is important, if the fiber continues to be lost, the visual field will gradually decrease, resulting in complete blindness [4]. The biological basis of the disease is not fully understood, and the factors that enhance its progression have not been fully characterized. Without proper treatment, glaucoma can develop into a visual impairment and eventually lead to blindness [5].

© Springer Nature Switzerland AG 2021
M. F. Mata-Rivera and R. Zagal-Flores (Eds.): WITCOM 2021, CCIS 1430, pp. 117–126, 2021.
https://doi.org/10.1007/978-3-030-89586-0_9

Ophthalmologists use fundus images of the retina to diagnose eye-related diseases. After image capture, the stage of retinal image analysis is considered the cornerstone of the entire diagnostic process. Retinal image analysis includes locating and extracting many retinal structures in a separate view, facilitating diagnosis, providing more information, and improving diagnosis accuracy [6].

Because the initial symptoms of glaucoma are not obvious, patients usually do not feel pain or vision loss. Glaucoma can only be noticed when the disease progresses to a large extent, some symptoms are peripheral vision loss or total blindness [7]. Early detection and timely treatment are the keys to preventing vision loss in patients, so effective diagnostic methods must be developed [8].

As one of the important structures of fundus images, the size and shape of the optic disc are the main auxiliary parameters for judging various eye diseases [9]. The optic disc is also a key part of detecting other retinal structures [10]. Therefore, the analysis of the retinal optic disc in fundus images is a very important research topic.

The cup-to-disk ratio (CDR) is manually estimated by a professional ophthalmologist. This is labor-intensive and time-consuming. In order to automate accurate CDR quantification and help glaucoma diagnosis, optic disc (OD) and optic cup (OC) segmentation is attracting a lot of attention [11]. In general, a larger CDR suggests a higher risk of glaucoma [12].

The segmentation of the optic disc in the retinal fundus image plays a primary role in diagnosing various pathologies and abnormalities related to the retina of the eye. Most of the abnormalities related to the optical disc will cause structural changes in the internal and external areas of the optical disc. The segmentation of the optic disc at the image level of the entire retina increases the detection sensitivity of these regions [13].

In recent years, deep learning has been widely used in computer vision, thanks to the rapid development of convolutional neural networks [14]. Several successful medical image processing has been applied using deep learning.

All methods designed for retinal image analysis or other objects include three main stages: preprocessing, processing, and post-processing. The preprocessing stage is considered the preliminary stage because it will affect the quality of the subsequent stages and affect the overall segmentation effect [15].

U-Net is a Convolutional Network architecture for image segmentation, this network consists of a contracting path and an expansive path, giving it the U-shaped architecture [16]. The contracting path is a typical convolutional network consisting of the repeated application of convolutions, each followed by a Rectified Linear Unit and a max-pooling operation [17].

Ronneberger et al. [18] proposed an architecture that consists of a contraction path and an expansion path. At each down-sampling step, the number of functional channels will be doubled. Each step in the expansion path includes upsampling the feature map. In the last layer, 1×1 convolution is used to map each 64-component feature vector to the required number of classes. They modify and extend an U-Net architecture such that it works with very few training images and yields more precise segmentations.

Cheng et al. [19] proposed an experiment using 2326 images of 2326 different eyes, including 650 from the Singapore Malay Eye Study (SiMES) and 1676 from the Singapore Chinese Eye Study (SCES). In the image, the intervertebral disc and cup boundaries from the 650 SiMES dataset of size 3072 × 2048 have been manually marked by trained professionals in a previous study for the segmentation of intervertebral discs and cups. They evaluated the proposed disc and cup segmentation methods using manual boundaries as ground truth.

Fu et al. [20] proposed for the global image stream and segmented guidance network, data enhancement is completed on the training set through random rotation (0/90/180/270°) and random flip. During training, they used stochastic gradient descent to optimize the depth model. The learning rate we use gradually decreases from 0.0001, while the momentum starts from 0.9.

The method used by Afolabi et al. [22] is based on 2 phases. In the first phase, the segmentation process is carried out, and in the second, the detection. For segmentation, a U-Net lite model is used while detection is performed with an extreme gradient boost (XGB. The decoding layer concatenates the sampled feature maps with the output from the encoding layer. Up-sampling was performed using 2 × 2 convolutional layers. They segment the optic disc and cup.

The network architecture proposed by Yin et al. [23] consists of a U-shaped network, multiscale guided filter modules, and lateral exit layers. The network has RGB images as input. The architecture is similar to U-Net, that is, it has an encoding path and a decoding path. ReLU is used as activation. The decoding path generates a feature map using convolutions.

The contribution of this paper is to have achieved one of the best metrics using an image management technique where the images are converted to polar coordinates before being fed into the neural network. We use an architecture U-Net, which is a U-shaped encoder-decoder network architecture consisting of encoder blocks and decoder blocks that are connected through a bridge, with residual blocks.

2 Methods

2.1 Preprocessing

Images of 3072 × 2048 pixels were used, and their size was reduced four times to execute the algorithm faster. The reduction was selected taking into account that at that size the image still has a good resolution to locate the optical disc and the computing power does not allow the use of large images. The 650 images from the ORIGA database were used.

To locate the region of interest and to be able to crop the image to reduce processing time, the images were converted to grayscale with a specific color ratio. The channels to be used were determined by obtaining the histograms of channels of the image, in this way it was determined that the channels that influenced the most were the red and green channels, since a greater contrast is noted in the image. This proportion is shown in Eq. 1.

$$Img_{gray} = R * 0.9 + G * 0.5 \qquad (1)$$

Where Img_{gray} is the grayscale image, and R and G are the corresponding red and green channels.

Once the grayscale image was obtained, techniques were used where a kernel moves along the image while obtaining the average brightness in each pixel and thus indicates where the optical disk is located. Therefore, where the region of interest is located, and it gives us a cropped image.

Using this method to obtain the region of interest, it is possible to cut the image correctly in 99.69% of the images. To obtain this percentage of correctly cropped images, specialists in the field of glaucoma were asked to indicate which images were suitable for making a diagnosis, and with them, the percentage was obtained, that is, of the 650 images used, only 2 were not cropped correctly.

2.2 Architecture

In order to feed the architecture, shown in Fig. 3, the image is converted to polar coordinates, to increase the proportion that the cup and the disk occupy since, before the transformation, they only occupied 5% and 13%, respectively. After transformation, they occupied, on average, 21% and 66% respectively. Achieving class balance is important as algorithms tend to favor the class with the highest proportion of observations, which can lead to biased accuracy metrics. This can be particularly problematic when we are interested in the correct classification of a minority class. The equations used to convert the images to polar coordinates are shown in Eqs. 2 and 3 [18].

$$u = u_0 + r * \cos(\theta + \varphi) \tag{2}$$

$$v = v_0 + r * \sin(\theta + \varphi) \tag{3}$$

Once the image is obtained at the output of our architecture, it is necessary to convert the output image back from polar to cartesian coordinates. For this, the equations were used 4 and 5.

$$r = \sqrt{(u - u_0)^2 + (v - v_0)^2} \tag{4}$$

$$\theta = tan^{-1}\left(\frac{v - v_0}{u - u_0}\right) - \varphi \tag{5}$$

Where $p(u, v)$ is the point in the cartesian plane, r and θ are the radius and directional angle, u_0 and v_0 are the disc center points, and φ is the polar angle.

The conversion of the images from Cartesian to polar coordinates can be seen in Figs. 1 and 2.

Fig. 1. Fundus image and ground truth on Cartesian Coordinate.

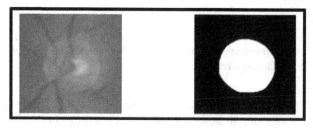

Fig. 2. Fundus image and ground truth on Polar Coordinate.

The architecture uses an encoder-decoder configuration. It starts with a residual modulus, then a 3×3 convolution is performed, followed by a rectified unit (ReLU) and a 2×2 grouping operation. Each of the steps in the expansion process samples the above feature map. In the last layer [21], a 1×1 convolution is used so that it is possible to obtain a 2-channel output because, due to the nature of our problem, the classification will be binary, that is, each of the pixels in the image will have values of 0 or 1. In Fig. 3, it is possible to see how the architecture is composed. The architecture is used for both the optic disc and the optic cup.

2.3 Training and Testing

For the training phase, 100 images of the disc and 50 images of the optic cup were used. The original images were obtained from the ORIGA public database, which contains 650 retinal images annotated by trained professionals from Singapore. These images were segmented with the help of Instituto Mexicano de Oftalmología supervised by glaucoma specialists.

The algorithm was developed in Python and ran on a computer with an Intel Core i7-3160QM 2.3 GHz CPU and 8 GB of RAM.

The learning rate used was 0.001 as a training parameter, and the Adaptive Moment Estimation (ADAM) optimization was used. Because the segmentation it will has values that only represent 2 classes, the loss function that best matched it and the one used in this work was Binary Cross-Entropy, since this function compares each of the predicted

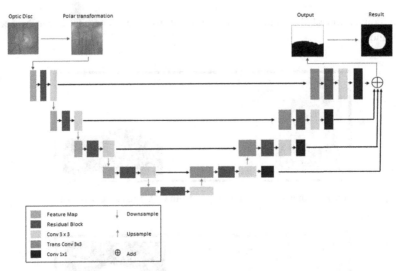

Fig. 3. The proposed architecture is composed of a U-Net with residual blocks [21], converting the input image into polar coordinates.

probabilities with the real output of the class, which can be 0 or 1. In total, 300 epochs were performed with a stop if the loss function was not different in 25 iterations. 80% of the test images were used for training, and 20% were left for validation. A cross-validation with a 5-fold was used. To validate the results, it was repeated 5 times with the same architecture, in this way it was possible to average the results to obtain the estimate. It was determined to repeat the experiment 5 times seeking to have a balance between the execution time and having enough tests to obtain the average in the results.

To evaluate the algorithm, the overlapping error and the accuracy were used, and the results were compared with other architectures shown in Table 3. The equations used for these metrics are shown in 6 and 7.

$$Error = 1 - \frac{Area(S \cap G)}{Area(S \cup G)} \tag{6}$$

$$Accuracy = \frac{TP + TN}{TP + FP + TN + FN} \tag{7}$$

Where G is the ground truth that was manually segmented and S the output image, TP is the predicted value was positive and agrees with the true value, TN is the predicted value was negative and agreed with the true value, FP represents when the model is classified as a positive class, and the true value is negative. FN is when the model is classified as a negative class, and the actual value is positive.

To reinforce the work carried out, sensitivity and specificity metrics were also used. What sensitivity will tell us is what proportion of the positive class was correctly classified, while specificity will tell us what proportion of the negative class was correctly classified. The equations are shown in 8 and 9.

$$Sen = \frac{TP}{TP + FN} \tag{8}$$

$$Spe = \frac{TN}{TN + FP} \tag{9}$$

Where TP, TN, FP and FN have the same meaning as Eqs. 6 and 7.

3   Results and Discussion

In the present work, the algorithm was executed by individually segmenting the optic disc and the cup. In this way, better results were obtained segmenting the cup than doing it jointly as do some of the works with which it is compared.

Table 1 shows the sensitivity and specificity results for the disc and the optic cup.

Table 1. Sensitivity and specificity results.

Method	Sensitivity $_{Disc}$	Specificity $_{Disc}$	Sensitivity $_{Cup}$	Specificity $_{Cup}$
U-Net + residual block	0.82	0.97	0.74	0.96
U-Net + residual block with polar transformation	0.85	0.99	0.83	0.97

Table 2 shows the results applying the polar transformation and those obtained without applying the said transformation.

Table 2. Comparison of the method using polar coordinates and without using them.

Method	Accuracy $_{Disc}$	Overlapping error Disc	Accuracy $_{Cup}$	Overlapping error Cup
U-Net + residual block	93.21	0.171	90.4	0.0758
U-Net + residual block with polar transformation	96.94	0.088	93.2	0.0706

Table 3 makes a comparison with other works against the proposed method.

Table 3. Comparison of the proposed method with those seen in the literature.

Method	Accuracy $_{Disc}$	Overlapping error $_{Disc}$	Accuracy $_{Cup}$	Overlapping error $_{Cup}$
U-Net [18]	95.9	0.115	90.1	0.287
Superpixel [19]	96.4	0.102	91.8	0.264
M-Net with polar transformation [20]	98.3	0.071	93.0	0.071
U-Net Lite and Extreme Gradient [22]	–	0.1	–	0.21
Deep Guidance Network [23]	–	0.071	–	0.220
Proposed	96.94	0.088	93.2	0.0706

In Fig. 4 are showed some results. The results obtained for the optic disc and those obtained for the cup are shown separately.

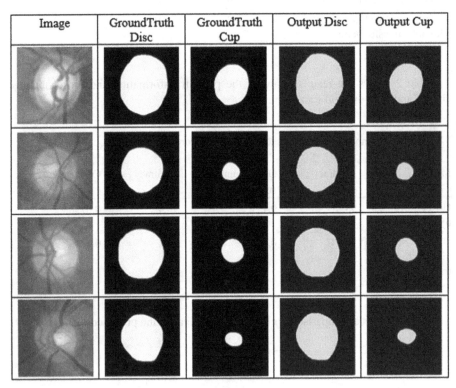

Fig. 4. Some results comparing the ground truth with the output.

4 Conclusions

Achieving a correct segmentation of the disc and the optic cup is an important job to help make a correct diagnosis of glaucoma. In the present work, it can be observed how better results were obtained for retrieving the cup by separating the segmentation of the disc and the cup, than doing it jointly as do some of the works with which it is compared. It must be taken into account that achieving good segmentation is a task that requires high computational power. By separating the segmentation into two parts, it can make the task less demanding and the processing faster.

The results obtained with the data set used show satisfactory results. Being able to get the area of interest in almost every image helps to focus only on the desired region. An important step was to convert the images to polar coordinates, which help reduce the class imbalance. To better visualize the images, they are converted back from polar coordinates to Cartesian at the departure from our architecture.

As future work, it is planned to continue working with this type of architecture to improve the metrics obtained. The implementation of an algorithm that can obtain the relationship between the cup and the disc is also pending so that in this way it can better observe possible cases of glaucoma.

Acknowledgment. We want to give thanks to Dr. Miguel Ángel Vázquez Membrillo, Dr. Edgar Daniel Fuentes Pérez and the entire team of the Mexican Institute of Ophthalmology for allowing us to make short research stay to clear up doubts about the disease and for their support with the segmentation of the images used in this work. We also want to thank Conacyt for the support received for the development of this work.

References

1. Pascolini, D., et al.: Global update of available data on visual impairment: a compilation of population-based prevalence studies. Ophthalmic Epidemiol. **11**(2), 67–115 (2004)
2. Kazi, A., Ajmera, M., Sukhija, P., Devadkar, K.: Processing retinal images to discover diseases. In: International Conference on Current Trends towards Converging Technologies, pp. 1–5. IEEE (2018)
3. Pinto, A.: Machine learning for glaucoma assessment using fundus images. Universitat Politècnica de València (2019)
4. Piñero, R.T., Lora, M., Andrés, M.I.: Glaucoma: patogenia, diagnóstico y tratamiento. Offarm: Farmacia Soc. **24**(2), 88–96 (2005)
5. Weinreb, R., Khaw, P.: Primary open-angle glaucoma. Lancet **363**(9422), 1711–1720 (2004)
6. Gopalakrishnan, A., Almazroa, A., Raahemifar, K., Lakshminarayanan, V.: Optic disc segmentation using circular Hough transform and curve fitting. In: 2nd International Conference on Opto-Electronics and Applied Optics, pp. 1–4. IEEE (2015)
7. Huang, G., Hsiang, T.: A simplified deep network architecture on optic cup and disc segmentation. In: International Joint Conference on Neural Networks, pp. 1–7. IEEE (2020)
8. Yin, F., et al.: Automated segmentation of optic disc and optic cup in fundus images for glaucoma diagnosis. In: 25th IEEE International Symposium on Computer-Based Medical Systems, pp. 1–6. IEEE (2012)

9. Maninis, K.-K., Pont-Tuset, J., Arbeláez, P., Van Gool, L.: Deep retinal image understanding. In: Ourselin, S., Joskowicz, L., Sabuncu, M.R., Unal, G., Wells, W. (eds.) MICCAI 2016. LNCS, vol. 9901, pp. 140–148. Springer, Cham (2016). https://doi.org/10.1007/978-3-319-46723-8_17

10. Mittapalli, P., Kande, G.B.: Segmentation of optic disk and optic cup from digital fundus images for the assessment of glaucoma. Biomed. Signal Process. Control **24**, 34–46 (2016)

11. Jonas, J.B., Bergua, A., Schmitz-Valckenberg, P., Papastathopoulos, K.I., Budde, W.M.: Ranking of optic disc variables for detection of glaucomatous optic nerve damage. Invest. Ophthalmol. Vis. Sci. **41**(7), 1764–1773 (2000)

12. Joshi, G.D., Sivaswamy, J., Krishnadas, S.R.: Optic disk and cup segmentation from monocular color retinal images for glaucoma assessment. IEEE Trans. Med. Imaging **30**(6), 1192–1205 (2011)

13. Almotiri, J., Elleithy, K., Elleithy, A.: An automated region-of-interest segmentation for optic disc extraction. In: 2018 IEEE Long Island Systems, Applications and Technology Conference, pp. 1–6. IEEE (2018)

14. Pan, F., Lu, Z., Chen, D., Xue, D.: An optic disk semantic segmentation method based on weakly supervised learning. In: 2020 Chinese Control and Decision Conference, pp. 4791–4794. IEEE (2020)

15. Daneshzand, M., Zoroofi, R.A., Faezipour, M.: MR image assisted drug delivery in respiratory tract and trachea tissues based on an enhanced level set method. In: Proceedings of the 2014 Zone 1 Conference of the American Society for Engineering Education, pp. 1–7. IEEE (2014)

16. Zhang, Z., Liu, Q., Wang, Y.: Road extraction by deep residual u-net. IEEE Geosci. Remote Sens. Lett. **15**(5), 749–753 (2018)

17. Sevastopolsky, A.: Optic disc and cup segmentation methods for glaucoma detection with modification of U-Net convolutional neural network. Pattern Recognit. Image Anal. **27**(3), 618–624 (2017). https://doi.org/10.1134/S1054661817030269

18. Ronneberger, O., Fischer, P., Brox, T.: U-net: convolutional networks for biomedical image segmentation. In: Navab, N., Hornegger, J., Wells, W., Frangi, A. (eds.) MICCAI 2015. LNCS, vol. 9351, pp. 234–241. Springer, Cham (2015). https://doi.org/10.1007/978-3-319-24574-4_28

19. Cheng, J., et al.: Superpixel classification based optic disc and optic cup segmentation for glaucoma screening. IEEE Trans. Med. Imaging **32**(6), 1019–1032 (2013)

20. Fu, H., Cheng, J., Xu, Y., Liu, J.: Glaucoma detection based on deep learning network in fundus image. In: Lu, L., Wang, X., Carneiro, G., Yang, L. (eds.) Deep Learning and Convolutional Neural Networks for Medical Imaging and Clinical Informatics. ACVPR, pp. 119–137. Springer, Cham (2019). https://doi.org/10.1007/978-3-030-13969-8_6

21. He, K., Zhang, X., Ren, S., Sun, J.: Deep residual learning for image recognition. In: Proceedings of the IEEE Conference on Computer Vision and Pattern Recognition, pp. 770–778 (2016)

22. Afolabi, O.J., Mabuza-Hocquet, G.P., Nelwamondo, F.V., Paul, B.S.: The use of U-net lite and extreme gradient boost (XGB) for glaucoma detection. IEEE Access **9**, 47411–47424 (2021)

23. Yin, P., Yuan, R., Cheng, Y., Wu, Q.: Deep guidance network for biomedical image segmentation. IEEE Access **8**, 116106–116116 (2020)

Forecasting the Behavior of Electric Power Supply at Yucatan, Mexico, Using a Recurrent Neural Network

R. A. Ancona-Osalde[1]⬤, M. G. Orozco-del-Castillo[1,2]⬤,
J. J. Hernández-Gómez[2,3(✉)]⬤, M. R. Moreno-Sabido[1]⬤,
and K. López-Puerto[1]⬤

[1] Departamento de Sistemas y Computación, Tecnológico Nacional de México/IT
de Mérida, Mérida, Yucatán, Mexico
[2] AAAI Student Chapter at Yucatán, México (AAAIMX), Association
for the Advancement of Artificial Intelligence, Mérida, Mexico
[3] Instituto Politécnico Nacional, Centro de Desarrollo Aeroespacial,
Mexico City, Mexico
jjhernandezgo@ipn.mx

Abstract. The forecast of electric power generation and supply with respect to an expected demand is a matter of national strategy for countries around the world as well as of vital importance for the assurance and viability of current societies. In the state of Yucatan, Mexico, power generation authorities often experience overproduction due to estimations that are done based on historical data in an statistical manner. In this work, we propose the implementation of a long short-term memory recurrent neural network to predict the consumption of electrical power in the aforementioned state. The main outcome shows that this approach implies a reduction in the error of the estimations of 39.53% provided by the neural network forecast with respect to previous estimations by local power generation experts.

Keywords: Recurrent neural networks · RNN · ANN · Artificial
neural networks · Electric power supply forecasting · Mexico ·
Yucatan · México, Yucatán

1 Introduction

The electric power industry produces and delivers electricity to over 5 billion people worldwide [1]. Normally, industries can use some form of inventory to store their products, however, electricity cannot be massively stored and therefore must be generated and delivered as it is consumed so to have a balance between supply and demand. This fundamental inability makes it necessary to carry out energy forecasts to operate the grid, i.e., forecasts of supply, demand, and price. Nowadays, these variables have become volatile and unpredictable [2], thus requiring increasingly complex approaches to energy forecasting. While oil and

M. F. Mata-Rivera and R. Zagal-Flores (Eds.): WITCOM 2021, CCIS 1430, pp. 127–137, 2021.
https://doi.org/10.1007/978-3-030-89586-0_10

gas forecasting has become a subdomain of energy forecasting [3], in this paper we consider the term "energy forecasting" related exclusively with power systems, particularly electricity demands. When talking about energy forecasting, there are differences among its different subdomains, but there are some common challenges, which include data cleansing, probabilistic forecasting methodologies, forecast combination, and integration [2].

Efforts for forecasting long-term load for planning have been carried out for over a hundred years [1], and short-term load forecasting has gradually attracted more attention from researchers [3]. The process of forecasting electricity consumption has evolved from counting light bulbs, to engineering approaches to manually forecast using charts and tables, to statistical approaches and simulation methods, to approaches related to artificial intelligence (AI) [1], leading to a significant restructuring of the electric power industry in the last two decades [4]. AI-related applications usually employ machine learning approaches, which often focus on artificial neural networks (ANN), a computational model which emulates the operation of a biological model, the human brain. One particular architecture of ANNs which has shown remarkable capabilities of learning features and long-term dependencies from sequential data, normally represented as time series, are recurrent neural networks (RNN). RNNs are ANNs with recurrent connections made of high dimensional hidden states with non-linear dynamics, which enable them to store, remember, and process past complex signals for long time periods [5].

RNNs have been successfully employed in several fields, for instance, in medicine-related applications. In [6], two long short-term memory (LSTM) models are mentioned to make predictions in the transmission of the SARS-CoV-2 through two distinct models. The first one was trained and evaluated with a collection of data from Canada and scored a Root-Mean-Squared Error (RMSE) of 34.83 daily confirmed cases. On the other hand, the second model was trained and evaluated with a collection of data from Italy to predict short-term infections, reaching an RMSE of 51.46 daily confirmed cases in short-term infections. In [7] the prediction of hospital readmission for patients with lupus is explored, using an LSTM RNN, which was key to ensure the optimal use of health care resources. The data collection used in such project was extracted from the Cerner HealthFacts databases between the years 2000 and 2015. The Cerner database consists of data collected from approximately five hundred health care service facilities in the United States and approximately sixty-three million anonymous patients from which information was extracted only from patients with lupus; the results had an accuracy rate of 70.54%.

In applications related to energy forecasting, RNNs have been extensively used. In [8], a hybrid AI system based on an LSTM RNN is presented to find patterns in energy consumption in the residential sector of France, a sector that represents 27% of global energy consumption [9]. In [10], a project focused on the recognition of patterns for the prediction of energy consumption in the non-residential sector of China is presented. Specifically, the k-means algorithm is used to classify non-residential consumers and subsequently an LSTM RNN is applied to predict energy consumption, showing an RMSE of 36.07 kW. In [11], an LSTM RNN is implemented to predict the workload of cloud servers in three data collections, the first data collection D_1 contains two months of all HTTP requests (communication protocol in the web) to the space center server Kennedy of NASA in Florida. The second data collection D_2 is made up of all HTTP requests of approximately one year to the server of the department of computer science located in Calgary, Alberta, Canada. Finally, the third data collection D_3 consists of seven months of requests to a university server in Saskatchewan, Canada. The best predictions scored an RMSE of 2.18, 2.02, and 1.7 (requests) for D_1, D_2, and D_3, respectively.

In countries where their energy demands have rapidly grown, forecasting studies constitute a vital part of their energy policies. Such is the case of Mexico, whose developing economic structure and growth in recent years have provoked a quickly increasing energy demand [12]: the consumption has increased from 150 TWh in 2000, to around 181.5 TWh in 2009, and has been projected to reach around 370 TWh by 2025 [12]. In this work, still in progress, the implementation of an LSTM RNN to predict the consumption of electrical power in the state of Yucatan, Mexico, is described. The objective is to provide an accurate forecast of the consumption of electrical power, considering current demand tendencies of the market. We used public information provided by the Mexican government agency Federal Commission of Electricity (CFE, Spanish for *Comisión Federal de Electricidad*) in the period from January 1st, 2006 to December 31st, 2015, in order to train the model.

This work is organized as follows: Sect. 2 is devoted to present the theoretical background about LSTM RNNs, as well as data gathering and pre-processing. Section 3 presents both the implementation of the RNN and its main results, while finally, Sect. 4 poses some final remarks, including possible future work.

2 Materials and Methods

2.1 Artificial Neural Networks

An ANN is a structure consisting of a number of nodes connected through directional connections. Each node represents a processing unit and the connections between the nodes specify the causal relationship between the connected nodes. The main objective of an ANN is to imitate the synapse generated in neurons, which are the fundamental unit of the nervous system and are made up of a nucleus and a system of inputs and outputs called dendrites and axons, respectively [13]. An ANN can be thought of as a massively parallel distributed processor that has a natural propensity to store experimental knowledge and make it available for its use [14]. Its main similarity with the human brain is that through a learning process, the network is capable of acquiring knowledge that it stores in the so-called synaptic weights. Some of the advantages of ANNs that distinguish them from conventional computational methods are (1) the direct way in which they acquire information about the problem through the training stage, (2) their ability to work with both analog and discrete data, (3) their robustness, and (4) their tendency to describe non-linear behaviors, among others [15].

Recurrent Neural Networks. RNNs are a type of ANN which provide a way to deal with time-sequential data [16]. Some of the applications of RNNs include natural language processing, language generation, video processing, time series prediction, among others [17]. A simple RNN is composed of a function F_t that is applied iteratively to an input sequence $X = (X_1, \cdots, X_t)$, the function generates a hidden state h_t of the current input and of the previous output, $h_t = F_h(X, h_{t1})$ [18]. In other words, each neuron in the RNN is able to memorize and perform computations based on both the current and the previous input values. There are many types of RNNs: simple RNNs (previously described), LSTM RNNs, long-term memory RNNs of Coordinated Gate-Long-Short Term Memory (CG-LSTM), among others [19]. The present work considers a LSTM RNN.

LSTM RNNs are recognized as one of the main ANNs for modeling sequential data structures, since they were developed to solve deficiencies that exist in simple RNNs [19], such as the gradient fading problem, which is the main cause that simple RNNs are not able to handle long-term dependencies [20]. The basic unit in the hidden layer of an LSTM is the memory block (see Fig. 1), which contains one or more memory cells and a pair of multiplicative and adaptive activation functions (sigmoid and hyperbolic tangent) to control the inputs and outputs to all the cells of the block. Each memory cell contains within its core a recurrent auto-connected, the so called Constant Error Carousel (CEC) [21], which is the accepted solution for the gradient fading problem. Additionally, the memory block has a *forget gate*, responsible for remembering a certain amount of information from previous steps [19].

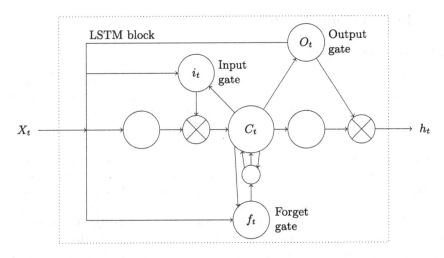

Fig. 1. LSTM RNN block memory [22].

There is a wide variety of ANN optimizers [23], such as the Gradient Descent whose purpose is to reduce the objective function by replacing parameters in contrary directions of the objective function's gradient, the Stochastic Gradient Descent, which is a variation of the Gradient Descent, but randomly picks samples, and Adaptive Moment Estimation (ADAM), which has demonstrated to achieve satisfactory results in stochastic-gradient optimization with lower memory requirements.

2.2   Electric Power Time Series from Yucatan, Mexico

Official data from CFE were obtained through two time series with a resolution of 1 day: the first one was the expected by CFE experts generation for the next day based on historical data, and the second one corresponds to the generated/demanded electrical power in such a day. The time series, which can be observed in Fig. 2, represent the power from the electric power plants at Yucatan State within the time span from January 1st, 2006, and December 31st, 2015, according to public availability of the data [24].

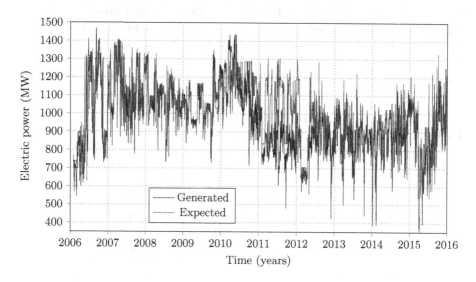

Fig. 2. The time series corresponding to the expected by CFE (red) and generated/demanded (blue) electric power in Yucatan State, Mexico, from January 2006 to December 2015. Data provided by CFE [24]. (Color figure online)

The statistical analysis of both time series can be observed in Table 1. It should be noted that on average, CFE daily power generation is 48.2487 MW (Mega Watts) above the real power consumption at Yucatan State, which yields an overproduction of 17,610.7682 MW per year on average, that represents an excess in production costs. Moreover, the RMSE of the expected by CFE power generation is of 120.6463 MW, which is not negligible as it is discussed later in the manuscript.

Table 1. Statistical data from time series shown in Fig. 2.

	Expected power (MW)	Generated power (MW)
Number of instances	3652	3652
Mean	962.218	1010.871
Standard deviation	181.172	177.901
Minimum value	355.600	388.300
First quartile	835.066	889.450
Second quartile	954.867	1015.937
Third quartile	1083.742	1143.312
Maximum value	1468.942	1412.250

3   Development and Results

In order for the time series to be an adequate input for the RNN, it was pre-processed by normalizing values to 1 (as the activation function that provided best results is sigmoid). From several lengths of input that were tested, we determined that the best configuration is to take 30 consecutive instances $X = X_0, \cdots, X_{29}$ (one month of data) to yield one output (the next day forecast), Y. Thus, the input is a vector of 30 elements consisting of normalized values, as it can be observed in Table 2.

Table 2. Sample of the input vector (X) and the output (Y) for the RNN, after the normalization of the time series shown in Fig. 2.

X_0	X_1	$\cdots$	X_{29}	Y
0.388539	0.358971	$\cdots$	0.355992	0.342675
0.358971	0.402424	$\cdots$	0.342675	0.366896
0.402424	0.402927	$\cdots$	0.366896	0.332892
0.402927	0.386116	$\cdots$	0.332892	0.343644

The input layer consists of 30 input neurons, corresponding to the length of the input vector X. Two hidden layers of 20 neurons each, were considered empirically for yielding better results. For the training stage, the data were split as follows: 75% of data were used for training and 25% of data for validation. Data were taken randomly, through a cross-validation technique to reduce training errors and biases. A batch size of 32 was used to avoid both a poor training as well as over-fitting. The output layer is made up of a neuron Y, which represents the obtained prediction. Adam optimizer was implemented as it has proven to be effective in problems related to prediction in time series [25]. The architecture of the RNN is summarized in Table 3.

Table 3. Parameters of the RNN.

Feature	Value
Number of input layers	1
Number of output layers	1
Number of hidden layers	2
Number of neurons per hidden layer	20
Number of inputs	30
Number of outputs	1
Activation function	Sigmoid
Number of epochs	100
Optimizer	Adam
Error	RMSE

The RMSE for 100 epochs of training was computed and can be observed in Fig. 3. It can be observed that after 40 epochs, RMSE does not vary significantly between training and validation data, indicating that the RNN does not tend to over-fit, nor it trained poorly.

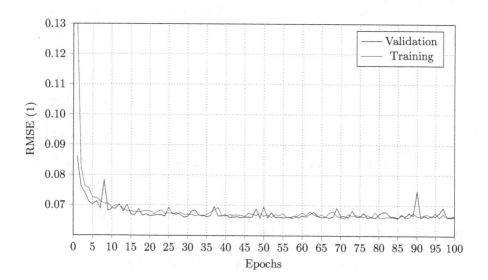

Fig. 3. RMSE for training and validation datasets.

In Fig. 4, both the original time series of generated electric power and the forecast done by the RNN can be observed. A simple visual inspection between the RNN forecast and the previously expected by CFE experts time series in

Fig. 2 shows that the forecast is clearly more accurate to the real generated power in the time span under study.

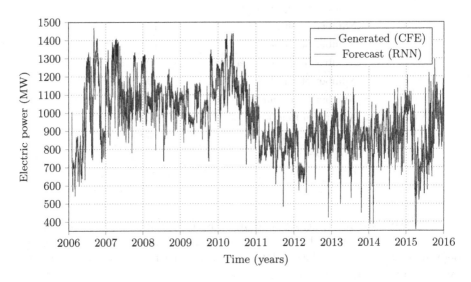

Fig. 4. The time series corresponding to the forecast from the RNN (red) and the real generated/demanded (blue) electric power in Yucatan State, Mexico, from January 2006 to December 2015. Generated/demanded data provided by CFE [24]. (Color figure online)

In order to make a more quantitative assessment of the behavior of the RNN with respect to previous estimations of power generation in the region, both the RMSE as well as the correlation index between the real generated/demanded and both the expected and the forecasted time series were computed, and can be observed in Table 4. It is clear that in both metrics the forecast by the RNN performs better than the previous estimations by CFE experts based on historical data.

Table 4. RMSE and correlation index of both the expected (CFE) and the forecasted (RNN) time series with the generated/demanded power one.

Time series	RMSE (MW)	Correlation index (1)
Expected by CFE	120.6463	0.8044
Forecast by RNN	72.9562	0.9135

Considering the RMSE of the generated/demanded power with the expected average capacity, an RMSE of 120.751 MW is obtained. On the other hand, after training the algorithm and restoring it to its original scale, an RMSE of 78.03

MW was obtained for data from training and of 77.98 MW for validation data (see Fig. 3). In this way, the model shows the ability to reduce the human error by approximately 39.53%. Based on these results and the average daily cost of MW [24], by implementing the RNN, CFE would have been able to save about $4,051,847.52 MXN each year.

With respect to the correlation index [26, 27], the higher value of the forecast time series represents that the degree of correlation between it and the generated/demanded electric power is very high, representing the similarity of their behavior.

4   Conclusions

In this work, still in progress, a LSTM RNN was presented in order to better forecast the electric power consumption in Yucatan, Mexico, through the analysis of official time series from CFE. The study is aimed primarily at improving the estimations previously made by CFE experts based on historical consumption data, but lastly to reduce power production costs as well as its environmental impact.

Based on the results obtained in this study, it is possible to predict electrical energy consumption in Yucatan State in a more satisfactory way, since the proposed RNN model does not show neither undertraining, nor, overtraining. It is worth mentioning that the error of the forecast obtained by the model is just under half the human error, so the proposed goal was achieved. Finally, it should be mentioned that this model is currently under consideration for its implementation in Yucatan's electric power plants to improve their generation efficiency.

5   Future Work

Despite this being a work in progress, the results are clearly encouraging. This work can be expanded in the following directions:

- To carry out a study that allows predicting power consumption at a federal level in Mexico.
- To study if there is any relationship between the power consumption and the increase of temperatures in Yucatan State, or of any other meteorological variable of potential influence.
- To extend this model to be able to provide accurate long-term forecasts.

Acknowledgements. This work was supported by projects 8285.20-P and 10428.21-P from Tecnológico Nacional de México/IT de Mérida, as well as by projects SIP 20210925, 20211789 and EDI grant, by Instituto Politécnico Nacional/Secretaría de Investigación y Posgrado.

References

1. Hong, T.: Energy forecasting: past, present, and future. Foresight Int. J. Appl. Forecast. **32**, 43–48 (2014)
2. Hong, T., Pinson, P., Fan, S., Zareipour, H., Troccoli, A., Hyndman, R.J.: Probabilistic energy forecasting: global energy forecasting competition 2014 and beyond. Int. J. Forecast. **32**(3), 896–913 (2016)
3. Hong, T., Pinson, P., Wang, Y., Weron, R., Yang, D., Zareipour, H.: Energy forecasting: a review and outlook. IEEE Open Access J. Power Energy **7**(August), 376–388 (2020)
4. Conejo, A.J., Contreras, J., Espínola, R., Plazas, M.A.: Forecasting electricity prices for a day-ahead pool-based electric energy market. Int. J. Forecast. **21**(3), 435–462 (2005)
5. Caterini, A.L., Chang, D.E.: Recurrent neural networks. In-Teh (2008)
6. Chimmula, V.K.R., Zhang, L.: Time series forecasting of COVID-19 transmission in Canada using LSTM networks. Chaos Solitons Fractals **135**, 109864 (2020)
7. Reddy, B.K., Delen, D.: Predicting hospital readmission for lupus patients: an RNN-LSTM-based deep-learning methodology. Comput. Biol. Med. **101**, 199–209 (2018)
8. Kim, T.Y., Cho, S.B.: Predicting residential energy consumption using CNN-LSTM neural networks. Energy **182**, 72–81 (2019)
9. Nejat, P., Jomehzadeh, F., Taheri, M.M., Gohari, M., Majid, M.Z.A.: A global review of energy consumption, CO2 emissions and policy in the residential sector (with an overview of the top ten CO2 emitting countries). Renew. Sustain. Energy Rev. **43**, 843–862 (2015)
10. Jiao, R., Zhang, T., Jiang, Y., He, H.: Short-term non-residential load forecasting based on multiple sequences LSTM recurrent neural network. IEEE Access **6**, 59438–59448 (2018)
11. Kumar, J., Goomer, R., Singh, A.K.: Long short term memory recurrent neural network (LSTM-RNN) based workload forecasting model for cloud datacenters. Procedia Comput. Sci. **125**, 676–682 (2018)
12. Morales-Acevedo, A.: Forecasting future energy demand: electrical energy in Mexico as an example case. Energy Procedia **57**, 782–790 (2014)
13. Basogain Olabe, X.: Redes neuronales artificiales y sus aplicaciones. Med. Intensiva **29**, 13–20 (2005)
14. Hayati, M., Mohebi, Z.: Application of artificial neural networks for temperature forecasting. World Acad. Sci. Eng. Technol. **28**(2), 275–279 (2007)
15. Nannariello, J., Fricke, F.: Introduction to neural network analysis and its application to building services engineering. Build. Serv. Eng. Res. Technol. **22**(1), 58–68 (2001)
16. Schuster, M., Paliwal, K.K.: Bidirectional recurrent neural networks. IEEE Trans. Signal Process. **45**(11), 2673–2681 (1997)
17. Pan, P., Xu, Z., Yang, Y., Wu, F., Zhuang, Y.: Hierarchical recurrent neural encoder for video representation with application to captioning. In: Proceedings of the IEEE Conference on Computer Vision and Pattern Recognition, pp. 1029–1038 (2016)
18. Dixon, M.: Sequence classification of the limit order book using recurrent neural networks. J. Comput. Sci. **24**, 277–286 (2018)
19. Gelly, G., Gauvain, J.L.: Optimization of RNN-based speech activity detection. IEEE/ACM Trans. Audio Speech Lang. Process. **26**(3), 646–656 (2017)

Forecasting the Behavior of Electric Power Supply at Yucatan, Mexico   137

20. Shewalkar, A.: Performance evaluation of deep neural networks applied to speech recognition: RNN, LSTM and GRU. J. Artif. Intell. Soft Comput. Res. **9**(4), 235–245 (2019)
21. Gers, F.A., Schmidhuber, J., Cummins, F.: Learning to forget: continual prediction with LSTM. Neural Comput. **12**(10), 2451–2471 (2000)
22. Abdel-Nasser, M., Mahmoud, K.: Accurate photovoltaic power forecasting models using deep LSTM-RNN. Neural Comput. Appl. **31**(7), 2727–2740 (2019)
23. Okewu, E., Adewole, P., Sennaike, O., et al.: Experimental comparison of stochastic optimizers in deep learning. In: Misra, S. (ed.) ICCSA 2019. LNCS, vol. 11623, pp. 704–715. Springer, Cham (2019). https://doi.org/10.1007/978-3-030-24308-1_55
24. Comisión Federal de Electricidad: Consulta de archivos de costo unitario y capacidad promedio prevista y realizada diaria (2020). https://app.cfe.mx/Aplicaciones/OTROS/costostotales/ConsultaArchivoCostosyCapacidades.aspx. Accessed 11 Oct 2020
25. Do, D.T., Lee, J., Nguyen-Xuan, H.: Fast evaluation of crack growth path using time series forecasting. Eng. Fract. Mech. **218**, 106567 (2019)
26. Kvasov, B.I.: Cubic Spline Interpolation, pp. 37–59. World Scientific (2000)
27. Sharma, A.K.: Text Book of Correlations and Regression. Discovery Publishing House, New Delhi (2005)

Methodological Proposal for Privilege Escalation in Windows Systems

Diego Muñoz Espinosa$^{(\boxtimes)}$ ⓘ, David Cordero Vidal$^{(\boxtimes)}$ ⓘ,
and Cristian Barría Huidobro$^{(\boxtimes)}$ ⓘ

Centro de Investigación en Ciberseguridad, Universidad Mayor, Vicerrectoria de Investigación,
Santiago, Chile
{diego.munoze,david.cordero}@mayor.cl, cristian.barria@umayor.cl

Abstract. One of the operating systems most used today is Windows, created by the Microsoft company since its launch on November 20, 1985. As a result of the popularity that the use of the Windows operating system generated in companies and individuals, also called the attention of Cybercriminals who began to exploit different security breaches in these systems, and in a few years an exponential exploitation of equipment, theft of confidential information, impersonation, among many other attacks began. With the evolution of offensive security, there are different tasks that must be executed to evaluate the level of security of the systems. For this, researchers use methodologies that contribute to the development of their activities. The purpose of this work is to propose a procedural alternative to execute actions to raise privileges in Windows 7, 8, 8.1 and 10 systems to support post-exploitation work by professionals in the offensive security area.

From the work methodology exposed in this research, which allows to be able to evaluate in an orderly way different activity associated with the enumeration, which becomes a background for the selection of techniques for raising or escalating privileges, within of a post-exploitation process.

Keywords: Pentesting · Elevation · Privilege · Cybersecurity · Privsec

1 Introduction

With the arrival of technology, the world has developed different capacities to automate and improve people's lives, many of these technological advances are supported thanks to what we know today as "operating systems". The operating system is the software that allows controlling the hardware (physical component), the central processing unit CPU, memory and the multiple activities or tasks that can be carried out when interacting with a computer, such as reading documents, browsing the Internet, connecting to the network of networks, etc., [1], to meet the demands of users in the execution of specific tasks [2].

One of the most widely used operating systems today is Windows, created by the Microsoft company since its launch on November 20, 1985, it has been marketed in such a way that it became an indispensable element for both public and/or business

M. F. Mata-Rivera and R. Zagal-Flores (Eds.): WITCOM 2021, CCIS 1430, pp. 138–150, 2021.
https://doi.org/10.1007/978-3-030-89586-0_11

organizations. As for personal use, therefore, it is not strange nowadays that when buying computer equipment, I already integrated this operating system by default [3].

Its popularity continues to grow, considering that it began life as a desktop operating system, using its graphical user interface (GUI) as its main feature, as Matthew Hickey points out [4].

As a result of the popularity that the use of the Windows operating system generated in companies and individuals, it also attracted the attention of Cybercriminals who began to exploit different security gaps in these systems, and in a few years an exponential exploitation of equipment began, theft of confidential information, spoofing, among many other attacks [5]. In addition, researchers, analysts or specialists in cybersecurity and ethical hacking also began to exploit flaws in the different S.O. to detect these gaps ahead of time and to be able to prevent these attacks [6].

As a result of the above, there is a great variety of techniques and procedures to be able to access a system by taking advantage of different vulnerabilities. One of the stages of a system auditing or hacking process is post-exploitation, which has as a key task to be able to raise or increase privileges once a target has been entered with a user, usually from fewer privileges, for example, if we access a system as the "guest" user, we must find the path that allows us to become an administrator and take full control of the system. Identifying in this way the problem that exists when carrying out a privilege escalation procedure on Windows systems as there are different alternatives to achieve this and with the purpose of being a contribution for the different cybersecurity professionals, this research seeks to delimit and establish different activities associated with the enumeration and elevation to face post-exploitation challenges in a objective system, establishing a procedure that allows to function in these environments in an orderly and standardized way, contributing to the time factor, to the detection of critical gaps and to the search for and obtaining the maximum possible privileges, which through an analysis and categorization could allow organizations to analyze their risks with significant impact.

2 Methodology of Search, Diagnosis, Validation and Analysis of the Data

For the development of activities related to research, an experimental design was carried out that encompasses three development areas, the first; that allows to know referentially the current situation of the computers with Windows operating system in a certain sample, the second; that allows to identify techniques for elevation of privileges and the third; that I evaluated the results to discern in the final stage of procedural proposal.

Using shodan, according to Yongle Chen, is a great threat to the security of systems, especially industrial systems due to its ability to analyze and extract information [7] for this reason and based on the impact it could have on cybersecurity, is that this study will consider the shodan results for the definition of variables and objectives.

By dividing the process into three stages based on the proposed experimental design, the first task is to identify popular assets by acquiring antecedents such as types of operating system, versions, quantity, name, among other data that the platform provides. The second, to identify privilege elevation techniques considering the current resources or system utilities that the operating systems themselves have, such as internal commands or characteristics within control configurations, to finally support this work with third-party tools. Such as those developed by Microsoft or independent researchers. Finally, based on the data collected, carry out the procedural proposal by comparing the results executed in the controlled environments of the research through a validation of the previous phase and a subsequent data extraction.

The process includes a phase of diagnosis, analysis, validation and extraction of the data obtained in the different stages of the experimental design; the process can be summarized in Fig. 1.

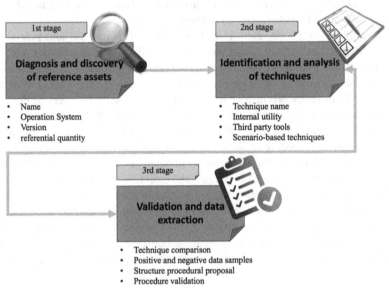

Fig. 1. Design processes privesec analysis

To meet the specific objectives presented in this research, the aforementioned processes of the experimental design must be executed, where the entire study referring to assets present on the internet through the shodan engine and the identification of variables such as: name, operating system, version and reference quantity are part of the first specific objective, the process of identification of technique, laboratory configuration to execute techniques based on scenarios, the use of utilities or internal commands of the operating system cover the second specific objective, and the validation and extraction of data, a process where a comparison and evaluation of the applied techniques is carried out to materialize and validate a procedural proposal, are part of the third and fourth specific objectives of this research.

2.1 Environment Configuration Based on Experimental Design

To define an acceptable path on elevation of privilege, different techniques will be executed in laboratories with similar characteristics, but with a different operating system.

With the data collected, its effectiveness will be studied, considering what type of enumeration and technique gave a favorable result when facing a scenario of elevation of privileges, in this way, an impact can be generated both in time and in results using the following model (Fig. 2).

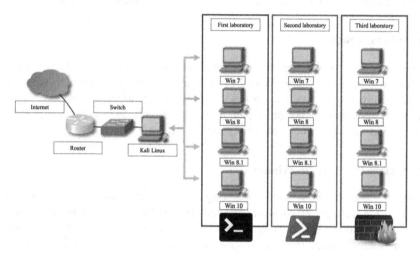

Fig. 2. Outline of the testing laboratory

To validate different tests, three types of labs were configured with the aforementioned operating systems in three possible scenarios, one with standard privileges for a normal user, which can execute typical Windows system commands such as: network, for queries of registers, processes, applications, etc., another with higher privileges, being able, for example, to use "powershell", modify processes and services belonging to a group with similar privileges but not total of an "NT Authority System", and finally, a last modification enabling security measures such as the Windows firewall and, in the latest versions, Windows defender.

2.2 Universe and Sample

In order to have a complete vision, an initial data in support of the research is the number of computers with Windows operating system connected to the internet, as conducting a worldwide study of this magnitude is difficult from the point of view of establishing an exact and precise number, there is the alternative of using "shodan" [8]. Shodan is an online platform also known as the Internet of Things search engine, with this service we can view different connected computers through simple searches or advanced filters. As shodan results may vary, we use the data with the longest antecedents, these were taken the week between March 22–28, 2021, between 09:00 a.m. and 11:00 p.m.

To know exposed equipment and whose main characteristic is the operating systems to be evaluated, it is possible to use a filter or advanced operator by putting the word "os:" in front of the shodan search engine, which will serve as a basis to identify assets exposed on the internet on the operating systems of this study, for example: "os: Windows 7".

As a result of the above, it is possible to define objectives to be evaluated based on pre-configured laboratories in three environments with different levels of security, the samples used for the identification of techniques that allow the elevation of privileges, are directly related to the effectiveness of this in controlled environments.

2.3 Windows Services

In Windows, a series of system services are executed, these work in the background, for this reason to be able to study or visualize them, a command or system tools are required for their study, if a user with less privilege has the ability to view or alter services that run as a system, this can become a path for exploitation through existing gaps in those services, in some cases due to misconfigurations or assignments.

2.4 System Privileges in Windows

Microsoft, developer of Windows operating systems, within its official literature, disseminates the different privileges associated with its OS, especially the most modern versions of Windows 10 and its derivatives [9], When studying these privileges, we can see that when exploited they have an "impact" that allows administrator-type access through different means.

To identify which variables achieve a critical impact within an objective, it is important to highlight the importance of administration privileges, the final objective for the total control of a team, although there are other types of privileges within the system, These require more than one action to take full control, that is why they can be classified as risks or threats that could produce some interference in the business without the need to become an authenticated user of the "NT Authority System" type through these privileges. Computers with Windows operating system.

2.5 Techniques and Instruments for Data Collection

From the scope of the investigation, the data to obtain an exact amount is limited, due to constant technological changes and the low accuracy regarding Windows computers that are currently used. Due to this, through an analysis of the effectiveness of techniques, the following table of evaluation criteria was designed (Table 1):

Table 1. Effectiveness evaluation criteria

Evaluation	Characteristic		
1st configuration	To carry out a statistic of the results of each elevation technique, different types of tests will be carried out which must be executed satisfactorily in the different configured laboratories, which have privileges from less to more robust to evaluate security and possible gaps, including modern versions of Windows		
2nd configuration			
3rd configuration			
Evaluation criteria	Less than 25% **Unfavorable**	Between 26% and 55% **Favorable**	Between 57% and 100% **Outstanding**

2.6 Windows Asset Identification

The result delivers a quantity of 43,650 devices detected by the shodan engine, the most popular being Windows 10 Home 19041. In summary, there is a wide range of users who use these devices with any of the operating systems, it is evident There are many more, however, to have a reference to the amount of existing equipment, this study was carried out using shodan and its ability to extract information from a query. The most popular is the latest version of Windows in its "home" version, used mainly for tasks around the home.

2.7 Analysis of Techniques on Elevation of Privilege

The process of elevation of privilege requires a series of stages or enumeration methods to be able to identify security gaps, which will allow access as an administrator user, for this, it is necessary to identify which are these techniques, both for the phase of enumeration as well as for the execution of activities that allow the elevation, in this chapter the study of these steps is evidenced considering the topology or configuration of the laboratory of the experimental design.

2.8 Search for Techniques and Variables to Consider

Identifying techniques for the elevation of privileges can be a complex task, however, with the evolution or new developments of researchers, it is possible to know about different styles or ways to achieve this task, for this, there are some variables to consider achieving an analysis and subsequent execution in the configured laboratory. These variables correspond to the identification of the name of the technique, how an action is executed, and the programming language associated with the technique, this last point is important because depending on the access that is had on a victim computer can be possible to install or use a specific programming language for the execution of lifting actions.

Obviously, the use of these techniques can be executed satisfactorily depending on the state and configuration of the victim objective, for this reason it is essential to study new methodologies and tools that may arise over time, it should be noted that the work of pentesting. They are associated with constant feedback on offensive cybersecurity matters. In addition, part of what can be obtained today, such as automated scripts for the elevation of privileges, can be adapted, as Haubris explains in his research where he explains that it is possible to adapt different existing tools for processes. Or specific methodologies, optimizing results [10].

2.9 Comparison of Techniques Based on Scenarios

To make a comparison of the attacks that are effective and those that are not, it is necessary to execute these in the different configured laboratories and compare their effectiveness in both the old and new versions. For the purposes of the present study, some of the randomly configured scenarios will be used as an example in this research, using different techniques.

2.10 Variables to Consider in the Execution of Techniques

For the present tests, a number of attacks were used through the execution of techniques for the elevation of privilege, the number of actions is related to the difficulty of each technique, for example, those that are possible to execute in more than one service or the process will be carried out three times on the same objective, repeating the process in the three laboratory settings.

An attack with meterpreter was developed by executing the "eternal blue" exploit, in the different laboratories, giving a total of 12 tests related to this technique, in the same way that Boyanov carried out tests of this type in the Faculty of Technical Sciences by Konstantin Preslavsky [11].

The development of a reverse shell was also contemplated using "msfvenom" with a malicious executable in ".exe" format, which was executed directly, without intervention by other system processes or secondary actions, in addition, this executable also supports the results of the other techniques of elevation of privileges for the activities of the laboratory, which was named "shell_reverse.exe".

Finally, the execution of scripts for the elevation of privileges was carried out automatically, these can be executed to support the procedure in the phases of the procedure related to its function. The variables measured in this stage are the techniques used in Table 2.

Table 2. Variables associated with the evaluation

Variable/techniques	Number of attacks	Description
Meterpreter	12	Attack with meterpreter by executing the "eternal blue" exploit
Unsafe services permit	36	Evaluación de 03 servicios inseguros en los diferentes laboratorios
Reverse shell with msfvenom	12	Elaboration of a reverse shell for execution in a direct and complementary way for the other techniques
Unquoted Service Path	36	Evaluation of 03 vulnerabilities in services with "Unquoted Service Path" in the different laboratories
Weak Registry Permissions	36	Evaluation of 03 vulnerabilities of "Weak Registry Permissions" in the different laboratories
Insecure Service Executables	36	Evaluation of 03 vulnerabilities of "Insecure executable services" in the different laboratories
Automatic executions	12	Evaluation of an automatic execution present in the different laboratories
Passwords on record	12	Evaluation of passwords obtained in the registry present in the different laboratories
Stored passwords	12	Evaluation of passwords obtained in the equipment present in the different laboratories
Security Manager (SAM) Account	12	Evaluation of the extraction or visualization of SAMe present in the different laboratories
Passing the Hash	12	Evaluation and use of "Hashs" obtained in the techniques related to credentials obtained in the different laboratories
Scheduled Tasks	12	Evaluation of a programmed task present in the different laboratories
Insecure GUI Apps	12	Evaluation of an insecure application GUI present in the different labs

(continued)

Table 2. (*continued*)

Variable/techniques	Number of attacks	Description
Startup Apps	12	Configuration of applications by a user for their execution fulfilling a certain condition
Impersonation - Rogue Potato	12	It allows to impersonate the identity of a user plus the retransmission of information to obtain system privileges
Impersonation PrintSpoofer	12	Lets you take advantage of the ability to grant elevated privileges to service accounts
Privilege Scripts Escalation	60	Execution of scripts that contribute to the elevation of privileges in each laboratory
Kernel	12	Running kernel exploits with versions defined from this study
Total	**360**	

3   Procedural Proposal

The procedure to be carried out consists of three phases, it is important to remember that to reach this stage there must already be exploitation of the system and have at least one user authenticated in it, after this mandatory requirement, the following is proposed task execution to consolidate a successful elevation of privilege.

First, carry out a complete enumeration of the system, based on the different queries that can be made both by internal system utilities and automated external tools.

Second, execute privilege elevation techniques as we have reviewed in the execution of the different scenarios, this stage is carried out following a Third, check the results and the level of privileges obtained, this mainly because it is sometimes possible to access an administrator-type user in a system, but not with full privileges, rather a user named "Admin" but with permissions to execute limited actions anyway, it is evident that this type of user, created to fulfill special functions, may not be useful if the objective is a total control to generate persistence in a team, however, if the test of Penetration considers this last point as final, the post-exploitation of the target victim can be considered successful in the same way (Fig. 3).

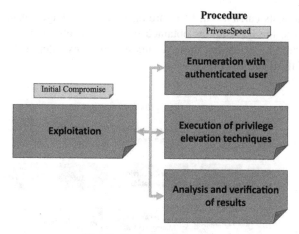

Fig. 3. Procedural proposal

To carry out a complete enumeration process, the following procedure is established in Fig. 4.

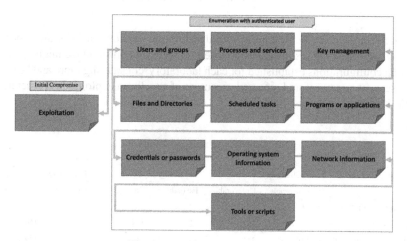

Fig. 4. Enumeration techniques

Through the tests carried out, there are different percentages of success based on lifting techniques, the laboratories obtained favorable results with access to the "NT Authority System" by executing these techniques, both by internal Windows utilities and by tools of third parties (Fig. 5).

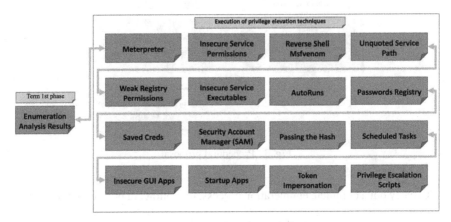

Fig. 5. Privilege elevation techniques

Based on different laboratories, with the different versions of Windows operating systems, the following results are established by executing different techniques with the different configurations established for each laboratory, considering more and less privileges, security measures and repeated execution of attacks on exploitable characteristics (Table 3).

Table 3. Laboratory results

Operating system	Version	Lab config 1		Lab config 2		Lab config 3	
		Favorable	Unfavorable	Favorable	Unfavorable	Favorable	Unfavorable
Windows 7	SP 1	53	307	48	312	04	356
Windows 8	N	28	332	22	338	01	359
Windows 8.1	Pro Build 9600	19	341	16	344	01	359
Windows 10	Home	12	348	05	355	00	260

4   Conclusions

Organizations of different nature have a huge challenge ahead considering the rapid evolution of technologies, especially when it comes to cybersecurity, if there are security gaps in any asset, both physical and human, auditors, analysts, chiefs or security officers must be constantly updated regarding the disciplines of cybersecurity.

The objectives imposed must be aimed at reducing risks to provide quality services that reflect a satisfactory security status of organizations for society security of organizations and achieve a state of maturity in cybersecurity issues in these [12]. Data leakage, security breaches, zero-day attacks, among others that continue to occur too frequently and become commonplace reported by the media, for this reason any tool that allows to combat these threats can positively impact an organization [13]. Starting to work in a structured way is something that many entities have chosen to execute, but since everything must evolve and adapt to the current reality, contributing with methodologies to favor the work of multidisciplinary teams is an advantage for the fulfillment of objectives in matters of cybersecurity.

The importance of this research not only contributes to technical auditors, but also contributes to the different lines or hierarchical areas within an organization to select procedural routes with respect to security evaluations, especially those related to pentesting or hacking. Ethics that impact both time and results.

While each methodological model that is freely available on the Internet in this new world or global networked society [14], can have both advantages and disadvantages and part of this an uncertain lifespan, using what really serves organizations due to internal discrimination can make a difference in the execution of offensive activities to detect gaps and solve them, supporting mitigation in a reduced time. In addition, with the arrival of new technologies, it is necessary to continue studying new operating systems that have the difficult mission of improving their security and having the ability to adapt to propose new methodologies on said systems.

References

1. Milenkovic, M.: Sistemas operativos: conceptos y diseños, no. 005.44 M642s2 (1999)
2. Terrasa, S., Balbastre, P., Roselló, M., Ripoll, I.: Time Logger: Una Herramienta Software de Soporte a la Docencia de Sistemas Operativos de Tiempo Real (2021)
3. Lemmons, P.: Microsoft Windows. A mouse with modest requirements. BYTE Magazine (1983)
4. Helmuth, C., Feske, N.: A Nitpickers guide to a minimal-complexity secure GUI. In: Computer Security Applications Conference, 21st Annual (2006). https://doi.org/10.1109/CSAC.2005.7
5. Cortés, C.: Microsoft entre monopolio y ciberseguridad. Chasqui revista latinoamericana de comunicación, p. 85 (2004). https://doi.org/10.16921/chasqui.v0i85.440
6. Astudillo, K.: Hacking Etico 101, Babelcube Inc. (2017)
7. Chen, Y., Lian, X., Yu, D., Lv, S., Hao, S., Ma, Y.: Exploring Shodan from the perspective of industrial control systems. In: IEEE (2020). https://doi.org/10.1109/ACCESS.2020.2988691
8. Search Engine for the Internet of Things. Shodan. https://shodan.io. acceso 01 Junio 2021
9. Microsoft: Privilege Constants (Authorization) (2020). https://docs.microsoft.com/en-us/windows/win32/secauthz/privilege-constants. acceso 22 Mayo 2021
10. Haubris, K.P., Pauli, J.J.: Improving the efficiency and effectiveness of penetration test automation. In: 10th International Conference on Information Technology: New Generations. IEEE (2013)
11. Boyanov, P.: Educational exploiting the information resources and invading the security mechanisms of the operating system windows 7 with the exploit eternalblue and backdoor doublepulsar. Association Scientific and Applied Research (2018)

12. Barria, C., Cordero, D., Galeazzi, L., Acuña, A.: Proposal of a multi-standard model for measuring maturity business levels with reference to information security standards and controls. In: Dzitac, I., Dzitac, S., Filip, F.G., Kacprzyk, J., Manolescu, M.-J., Oros, H. (eds.) ICCCC 2020. AISC, vol. 1243, pp. 121–132. Springer, Cham (2021). https://doi.org/10.1007/978-3-030-53651-0_10
13. Pelleti, S.: Modeling and predicting cyber hacking breaches (2021). https://doi.org/10.22214/ijraset.2021.36168
14. Krieger, D., Belliger, A., Krieger, D.: Hacking Digital Ethics. Introduction: Ethical Hacking and Hacking Ethics (2020)

Satisfaction of Members of a Facebook Group with the Credible Information Provided to Reduce Medical Misinformation in Obstetrics During the COVID-19 Pandemic in Peru

Yuliana Mercedes De La Cruz-Ramirez[1]([⊠]) [iD], Augusto Felix Olaza-Maguiña[1] [iD], and Nadezhda Tarcila De La Cruz-Ramirez[2] [iD]

[1] Universidad Nacional Santiago Antúnez de Mayolo, Centenario 200, Huaraz 02002, Peru
{ydelacruzr,aolazam}@unasam.edu.pe
[2] Hospital Víctor Ramos Guardia, Luzuriaga 1248, Huaraz 02001, Peru

Abstract. The present investigation was carried out to determine the satisfaction of the members of a Facebook group created and directed by obstetricians with respect to the credible information provided to reduce medical misinformation in obstetrics during the COVID-19 pandemic in Peru, identifying said satisfaction according to the age and sex of the participants. A cross-sectional study was conducted with 268 members, who completed an online questionnaire. The information was processed through the SPSS V23.0 program, using the Chi-square statistical test. Regarding the results, all active members were satisfied with the information shared by obstetricians in the Facebook group, with scores higher than 4 in all dimensions, highlighting the confidence in the source of the information and the resolution of doubts by obstetricians as the dimensions with the highest scores (4.71 and 4.68, respectively). Likewise, statistically significant differences were found in the aforementioned satisfaction results with respect to the age and sex of the participants ($p < 0.05$). It was concluded that all members of Facebook group created and directed by obstetricians stated that they were satisfied with the credible information provided to reduce medical misinformation in obstetrics during the COVID-19 pandemic in Peru, being able to improve the respectful treatment.

Keywords: Social networks · Medical misinformation · Obstetrics · COVID-19

1 Introduction

The increasingly frequent use of social media has meant many benefits in communication, such as the speed and ease of exchange of information between users from different parts of the world, speeding up the performance of many activities typical of work, education, health and entertainment [1].

However, the aforementioned benefits have not prevented an increasingly frequent and dangerous reality related to dis/misinformation that mainly occurs on social networks

M. F. Mata-Rivera and R. Zagal-Flores (Eds.): WITCOM 2021, CCIS 1430, pp. 151–162, 2021.
https://doi.org/10.1007/978-3-030-89586-0_12

[2]. This situation is product in some cases of ignorance and in other cases, from the lack of scruples that leads a person to share false information in a totally intentional way [3–5], without taking into account the terrible consequences that this attitude can cause [6] for example in the area obstetric health, where medical misinformation can lead a pregnant woman, her partner or family to make wrong decisions by putting into practice behaviors that can be risky to her own health, her baby, her family and to that of society as a whole [7].

On the other hand, the effects of the COVID-19 pandemic have been related not only to the high mortality caused by the viral infection, but also to the health consequences related to the existing medical misinformation [2], reality of which obstetrics have also been a part. Faced with this situation, a Facebook group directed by obstetricians was created, who are professionals dedicated to pregnancy care and sexual and reproductive health overall attention in Peru, with the purpose of provide credible information to reduce medical misinformation in obstetrics during the COVID-19 pandemic. It is important to mention that although this type of interventions had already been developed before by health professionals [8, 9], none of these cases had occurred during situations as extreme as those of a pandemic, not having determined until now, the degree to which the information needs of people are being met, findings that would allow us to identify improving to the prevention and health promotion work of obstetric professionals.

Another important aspect that justifies this research is the particular reality that Peru is going through, due to the lack of knowledge of digital tools to evaluate the credibility of health information, as well as the high levels of poverty, which have increased medical misinformation and its potential risks in people. This reality is even worse in the most vulnerable population groups such as pregnant women and their families, whose access to reliable information has been restricted not only as a result of the economic and educational deficiencies they suffer, but also because of the mistakes of the Peruvian authorities, who have not promoted personalized counseling strategies based on the needs of the people during the pandemic, allowing the dissemination of erroneous information, without quality control and the supervision of trained professionals such as obstetricians.

In this sense, the problem to be investigated was how satisfied people could be with the credible information released by trained health professionals such as obstetricians and in what aspects could improvements be applied to reduce existing medical misinformation?. Taking into consideration the mentioned problem, the objective of this research was to determine the satisfaction of the members of a Facebook group created and directed by obstetricians with respect to the credible information provided to reduce medical misinformation in obstetrics during the COVID-19 pandemic in Peru, identifying said satisfaction according to the age and sex of the participants.

The outcomes obtained in the present research have made it possible to know that in general the members of Facebook group created and directed by obstetricians stated that they were satisfied with the credible information provided during the COVID-19 pandemic, showing statistically significant differences regarding the age and sex of the participants. Likewise, it was identified that it is possible to improve the respectful treatment between members.

2 Methodology

2.1 Research Design and Population Under Study

A cross-sectional design investigation was developed. The population under study consisted of 349 active members of a Facebook group created and directed by obstetricians. The inclusion criteria were belonging to the Facebook group for 3 months, 4 weekly participations with the other people in the group and Peruvian residence. Within the exclusion criteria, it was considered being less than 18 years of age (age of legal recognition as an adult in Peru) and abandonment of the Facebook group.

2.2 Variables

Demographic Variables. Age (18–34 years, ≥ 35 years), sex (male, female) and location in Peru (urban area, rural area).

Research Variables. Satisfaction of the members of a Facebook group created and directed by obstetricians with respect to the credible information provided to reduce medical misinformation in obstetrics during the COVID-19 pandemic, evaluating 6 dimensions (thematic variety, importance of the information, utility perception, confidence in the source of the information, resolution of doubts by obstetricians and respectful treatment). The evaluation was carried out with Likert-type questions, the responses of which received a rating from 1 to 5, from totally dissatisfied (equal to 1) to totally satisfied (equal to 5).

2.3 Data Collection Procedure

The authors of this research, in the absence of a validated instrument to assess people's satisfaction with the information provided on medical issues in obstetrics during a health emergency situation, decided to elaborate a questionnaire consisting of 4 questions referring to demographic characteristics and 6 questions related to the satisfaction of the members of Facebook group with respect to the credible information provided.

In order to ensure the content validity of the questionnaire, the opinion of 7 experts in health promotion through social networks was requested, to whose responses the Kendall concordance test was applied, demonstrating the content validity mentioned above ($p = 0.001$). Likewise, through a pilot test with 35 active members of the Facebook group, the reliability of the instrument was evaluated, applying the test-retest technique after 5 weeks, with a qualitative and quantitative analysis using the kappa index (0.865) and the intraclass correlation coefficient (0.813) respectively, followed by Cronbach's alpha index (0.842).

After making the necessary corrections to the questionnaire, its final application was made during December 2020, for which an online form was prepared, whose link was sent to each member via Messenger, where the participation was voluntary.

2.4 Statistical Analysis

The statistical package SPSS, version 24.0 for Windows, was used, performing a descriptive analysis through absolute frequencies, percentages, the mean as a measure of central tendency and the standard deviation as a measure of dispersion. To determine possible differences in satisfaction according to age and sex of the members of Facebook group, the Chi-square test was used with a significance level of $p < 0.05$, as well as 95% confidence intervals (CI) of the difference in proportions.

2.5 Ethical Considerations

During the development of research, the right to privacy and confidentiality of the data was respected, considering previously the filling of an online form with the voluntary acceptance of their participation as well as the declaration of informed consent, as established by the World Medical Association and the Declaration of Helsinki [10]. It is important to mention that the Ethics Committee of the Santiago Antúnez de Mayolo National University (Huaraz-Peru) approved the execution of the research protocol, through registration N° 010-2020.

3 Results

Regarding participation, 268 active members of the Facebook group responded to the online questionnaire (Table 1), not including in this group the 35 members who collaborated in the pilot test. Likewise, 32 people did not accept to participate and in the case of 14 members, no response was obtained to the invitation sent, making a total of 349 active members of the study population.

Table 1. Demographic characteristics.

Characteristic	n	%
Age		
- 18–34 years	144	53.7
- ≥35 years	124	46.3
Sex		
- Male	115	42.9
- Female	153	57.1
Location in Peru		
- Urban area	164	61.2
- Rural area	104	38.8

The results of the satisfaction of the members of Facebook group created and directed by obstetricians with respect to the credible information provided to reduce medical misinformation in obstetrics during the COVID-19 pandemic in Peru are reported in Table

2, where it stands out that all active members were satisfied with the information shared. It was evidenced scores higher than 4 in all dimensions, highlighting the confidence in the source of the information and the resolution of doubts by obstetricians as the dimensions with the highest scores (4.71 and 4.68, respectively). Likewise, the lowest score corresponded to the respectful treatment with 4.24.

Table 2. Satisfaction responses of Facebook group members.

Dimensions	Mean	Standard deviation
Thematic variety	4.36	0.481
Importance of the information	4.54	0.527
Utility perception	4.51	0.506
Confidence in the source of the information	4.71	0.611
Resolution of doubts by obstetricians	4.68	0.535
Respectful treatment	4.24	0.458

In Table 3 and Table 4 the responses expressed by the active members of Facebook group have been grouped into 2 categories, the first corresponding to the satisfied members, where the highest satisfaction scores are included (4 and 5) and the second one that represents dissatisfied members with low scores (1 and 2), which also includes the neutral position (3). The results of these categories are presented by age (Table 3) and sex (Table 4) of the participants, having shown statistically significant differences in both tables in all the satisfaction dimensions evaluated with respect to the aforementioned demographic characteristics ($p < 0.05$), where the highest percentages of satisfaction corresponded to the participants women (57.1%) between 18 and 34 years old (53.7%).

Table 3. Satisfaction of the members by age.

Dimensions	18–34 years		≥35 years		Total		P-value*	IC 95%
	n	%	n	%	n	%		
Thematic variety								
- Satisfied	132	49.2	99	37.0	231	86.2	0.005	2.7–21.0%

(continued)

156   Y. M. De La Cruz-Ramirez et al.

Table 3. (*continued*)

Dimensions	18–34 years		≥35 years		Total		P-value*	IC 95%
	n	%	n	%	n	%		
- Neutral or dissatisfied	12	4.5	25	9.3	37	13.8		
Importance of the information								
- Satisfied	139	51.9	107	39.9	246	91.8	0.002	2.7–17.7%
- Neutral or dissatisfied	5	1.8	17	6.4	22	8.2		
Utility perception								
- Satisfied	135	50.3	105	39.2	240	89.5	0.016	0.9–17.3%
- Neutral or dissatisfied	9	3.4	19	7.1	28	10.5		
Confidence in the source of the information								
- Satisfied	143	53.3	106	39.6	249	92.9	<0.001	6.7–20.9%
- Neutral or dissatisfied	1	0.4	18	6.7	19	7.1		
Resolution of doubts by obstetricians								
- Satisfied	140	52.2	108	40.3	248	92.5	0.002	2.9–17.4%
- Neutral or dissatisfied	4	1.5	16	6.0	20	7.5		
Respectful treatment								
- Satisfied	127	47.4	95	35.5	222	82.9	0.012	1.7–21.5%
- Neutral or dissatisfied	17	6.3	29	10.8	46	17.1		
Total	144	53.7	124	46.3	268	100		

*Chi square test.
IC: confidence interval of the difference of proportions.

Table 4. Satisfaction of the members by sex.

Dimensions	Male		Female		Total		P-value*	IC 95%
	n	%	n	%	n	%		
Thematic variety								
- Satisfied	90	33.6	141	52.6	231	86.2	0.001	4.5–23.3%
- Neutral or dissatisfied	25	9.3	12	4.5	37	13.8		
Importance of the information								
- Satisfied	100	37.3	147	54.9	247	92.2	0.006	1.5–16.8%
- Neutral or dissatisfied	15	5.6	6	2.2	21	7.8		
Utility perception								
- Satisfied	97	36.2	143	53.4	240	89.6	0.016	0.6–17.6%
- Neutral or dissatisfied	18	6.7	10	3.7	18	10.4		
Confidence in the source of the information								
- Satisfied	98	36.6	151	56.3	249	92.9	<0.001	6.0–21.0%
- Neutral or dissatisfied	17	6.3	2	0.8	19	7.1		
Resolution of doubts by obstetricians								
- Satisfied	99	36.9	148	55.2	247	92.1	0.001	3.0–18.3%
- Neutral or dissatisfied	16	6.0	5	1.9	21	7.9		
Respectful treatment								
- Satisfied	83	31.0	139	51.9	122	82.9	<0.001	8.5–28.8%
- Neutral or dissatisfied	32	11.9	14	5.2	46	17.1		
Total	115	42.9	153	57.1	268	100		

*Chi square test.
IC: confidence interval of the difference of proportions.

4 Discussion

In relation to the main objective of the study, it was determined that all active members of Facebook group created and directed by obstetricians reported their satisfaction with the credible information provided in said group during the COVID-19 pandemic. This finding is similar to what was found in other studies, where the information provided made it possible to reduce the existing medical misinformation in various countries afflicted by the consequences of the health emergency caused by COVID-19, an effect that in turn was directly related to the actions and efforts made by the authorities [11, 12] and health professionals to retrieve reliable information in different health specialties [1, 7].

In this sense, in the current circumstances, many sources of unregulated information on the Internet offer a variety of references related to all kinds of activities, which do not necessarily obey a particular topic. The lack of quality control for communication in public health during the COVID-19 pandemic [13], would explain why when this variety of information responds to an important aspect in a person's life, such as health care in the obstetric area, becomes a highly valued resource that generates satisfaction in human beings, as happened with the active members of Facebook group created and directed by obstetricians, who were able to access information on various topics related to an area of interest with quality control, as part of an intervention focused on their needs [14, 15].

Regarding the importance of the information and the utility perception of what is shared, it is shown that these dimensions received a rating of satisfaction in the present research, probably due to the lack of said characteristics on social media without the accompaniment of a professional properly trained, which exposes the person to receive potentially life-threatening pseudoscientific advice [16–18], especially in situations of uncertainty in the face of unknown circumstances such as COVID-19. This situation, added to the lack of economic resources and low educational preparation becomes a deadly combination for many people, especially in low and middle-income countries such as Peru, where, in addition to the lack of knowledge of the strategies for evaluating the credibility of health information that is applies in other countries [19–22], a series of errors and deficiencies have been evidenced as in the educational campaigns promoted by the authorities, with the consequent increase in medical misinformation among the most vulnerable population groups.

With regard to the confidence in the source of the information provided in the Facebook group, dimension that obtained the highest percentage of satisfaction, said result would be explained because unregulated sources of information have a direct effect on the appearance of erroneous beliefs and wrong health protection behaviors [23], which generate a lot of anxiety in people, so having the means of disseminating credible information is, according to some researchers, one of the main components of assessment of care during the COVID-19 pandemic [14, 24].

The resolution of doubts by obstetricians was the second aspect most valued and recognized by the participants of the present research, a situation that had already been recognized as a need for individualized personal communication during the health emergency that is being experienced worldwide [25]. In this way, it should be promoted in health professionals, the application of a critical and skeptical approach regarding the information that is shared, in order to ensure the quality of the educational work that can be carried out during the health emergency [26].

On the other hand, the respectful treatment among the members of Facebook group was the dimension that resulted with the lowest percentage of satisfaction among the participants who responded to the online questionnaire, which fortunately did not mean the occurrence of frequent events and/or unpleasant confrontations between the people of the group. This fact would be related to the high levels of anxiety that have been evidenced in people worldwide as a result of the measures taken to control the COVID-19 pandemic [27, 28], among them social distancing, which in many cases has increased fear and inaccurate communication between people [29], causing an increase in the risk of accepting for certain information released by unreliable sources [30–32]. The aforementioned emotional effects could be taken into account in other studies, where the relevance of strategies based on multidisciplinary care can be evaluated, in which through the use of digital media, it can contribute to the attention and access of credible information regarding the physical and emotional consequences of COVID-19, even considering the influence of family and cultural factors in the regulation of shared information.

Likewise, in the present research statistically significant differences were evidenced in the satisfaction results of the active members of Facebook group with respect to age and sex, a result similar to that observed in other studies, where the search, access and satisfaction with credible information were associated with the age and sex of the people [1, 27, 33]. The difference with these studies is that in their case, access to information was given with greater emphasis on males from advanced age [14], who had preconceived ideas about the Internet technologies which increased their confidence and satisfaction with the information provided by health professionals [34]; while in the present research, the highest satisfaction percentages corresponded to women between 18 and 34 years old, who in other studies showed higher levels of anxiety related to COVID-19 [27], which in turn would influence their need search for information and the respective satisfaction when they access credible information.

On the other hand, it is necessary to highlight the existing limitations with respect to the present research, referring mainly to the cross-sectional design of the study, which did not allow long-term evaluation of satisfaction. Likewise, it is important to remember that this research has been carried out in the context of the COVID-19 pandemic and its repercussions on the health care of obstetric patients in Peru, situation that would affect the application of the findings in other realities, where the restrictive measures could have been different from those applied by the Peruvian authorities; limitations that do not decrease the importance of the findings found.

5 Conclusions and Future Steps

5.1 Conclusions

All the members of Facebook group created and directed by obstetricians stated that they were satisfied with the credible information provided to reduce medical misinformation in obstetrics during the COVID-19 pandemic in Peru, showing statistically significant differences in the aforementioned satisfaction results regarding the age and sex of the participants. This evidence could provide greater support for the use of social networks such as Facebook, for the dissemination of reliable information, as long as the participation of professionals duly trained for this purpose is counted on, especially in circumstances as difficult as those of a pandemic.

5.2 Future Steps

Based on the aforementioned findings, it is suggested to carry out new studies based on other research designs, including qualitative approaches, as a way of approaching the subject of study from other points of view, as well as identify methods and/or digital resources for the retrieval of credible information that could be used by health professionals in the obstetric area where they have not yet been evaluated, thus avoiding possible deficiencies and negative consequences on the health of the general population.

Acknowledgements. To the active members of Facebook group who participated in this study. To the students of the Professional School of Obstetrics of the Santiago Antúnez de Mayolo National University (Huaraz-Peru), for their constant support in managing the content of Facebook group.

Financing. This research was self-funded.

Conflict of Interest. The authors declare that they have no conflict of interest.

References

1. Wang, P., et al.: COVID-19-related information sources and the relationship with confidence in people coping with COVID-19: Facebook survey study in Taiwan. J. Med. Internet Res. **22**, e20021 (2020). https://doi.org/10.2196/20021
2. Silva, M., Benevenuto, F.: Analyzing the use of COVID-19 ads on Facebook. In: WebMedia 2020: Proceedings of the Brazilian Symposium on Multimedia and the Web, pp. 21–24. ACM Press, New York (2020). https://doi.org/10.1145/3428658.3431088
3. Ghenai, A., Mejova, Y.: Fake cures: user-centric modeling of health misinformation in social media. In: Proceedings of the ACM on Human-Computer Interaction, pp. 1–20. ACM Press, New York (2018). https://doi.org/10.1145/3274327
4. Apuke, O., Omar, B.: User motivation in fake news sharing during the COVID-19 pandemic: an application of the uses and gratification theory. Online Inf. Rev. **45**(1), 220–239 (2021). https://doi.org/10.1108/OIR-03-2020-0116
5. Ardèvol-Abreu, A., Delponti, P., Rodríguez-Wangüemert, C.: Intentional or inadvertent fake news sharing? Fact-checking warnings and users' interaction with social media content. Profesional de la información **29**, e290507 (2020). https://doi.org/10.3145/epi.2020.sep.07
6. Saiful, M., et al.: COVID-19–related infodemic and its impact on public health: a global social media analysis. Am. J. Trop. Med. Hyg. **103**, 1621–1629 (2020). https://doi.org/10.4269/ajtmh.20-0812
7. Datta, R., Yadav, A., Singh, A., Datta, K., Bansal, A.: The infodemics of COVID-19 amongst healthcare professionals in India. Med. J. Armed Forces India **76**, 276–283 (2020). https://doi.org/10.1016/j.mjafi.2020.05.009
8. McCarthy, R., Byrne, G., Brettle, A., Choucri, L., Ormandy, P.: Midwife-moderated social media groups as a validated information source for women during pregnancy. Midwifery **88**, 102710 (2020). https://doi.org/10.1016/j.midw.2020.102710
9. McCarthy, R., Choucri, L., Choucri, L., Brettle, A.: Midwifery continuity: the use of social media. Midwifery **52**, 34–41 (2017). https://doi.org/10.1016/j.midw.2017.05.012
10. World Medical Association: Declaration of Helsinki – Ethical principles for medical research involving human subjects. https://www.wma.net/policies-post/wma-declaration-of-helsinki-ethical-principles-for-medical-research-involving-human-subjects/. Accessed 26 June 2021
11. Lovari, A.: Spreading (dis)trust: Covid-19 misinformation and government intervention in Italy. Media Commun. **8**, 458–461 (2020). https://doi.org/10.17645/mac.v8i2.3219
12. De Blasio, E., Selva, D.: Affective governance during the COVID-19 crisis: building leadership, trust, and good citizens. Tripodos **1**, 67–86 (2020)
13. Mejova, Y., Kalimeri, K.: COVID-19 on Facebook ads: competing agendas around a public health crisis. In: COMPASS 2020: Proceedings of the 3rd ACM SIGCAS Conference on Computing and Sustainable Societies, pp. 22–31. ACM Press, New York (2020). https://doi.org/10.1145/3378393.3402241

14. Sallam, M., et al.: COVID-19 misinformation: mere harmless delusions or much more? A knowledge and attitude cross-sectional study among the general public residing in Jordan. PLoS ONE **15**, e0243264 (2020). https://doi.org/10.1371/journal.pone.0243264

15. Obiała, J., Obiała, K., Manczak, M., Owoc, J., Olszewski, R.: COVID-19 misinformation: accuracy of articles about coronavirus prevention mostly shared on social media. Health Policy Technol. **10**(1), 182–186 (2021). https://doi.org/10.1016/j.hlpt.2020.10.007

16. Teovanović, P., Lukić, P., Zupan, Z., Lazić, A., Ninković, M., Žeželj, I.: Irrational beliefs differentially predict adherence to guidelines and pseudoscientific practices during the COVID-19 pandemic. Appl. Cognit. Psychol. **35**(2), 486–496 (2021). https://doi.org/10.1002/acp.3770

17. Dhoju, S., Uddin, M., Ashad, M., Hassan, N.: Differences in health news from reliable and unreliable media. In: WWW 2019: Companion Proceedings of the 2019 World Wide Web Conference, pp. 981–987. ACM Press, New York (2019). https://doi.org/10.1145/3308560.3316741

18. Ghenai, A.: Health misinformation in search and social media. In: DH 2017: Proceedings of the 2017 International Conference on Digital Health, pp. 235–236. ACM Press, New York (2017). https://doi.org/10.1145/3079452.3079483

19. Song, S., Zhang, Y., Yu, B.: Interventions to support consumer evaluation of online health information credibility: a scoping review. Int. J. Med. Inform. **145**, 104321 (2021). https://doi.org/10.1016/j.ijmedinf.2020.104321

20. Boyer, C., Frossard, C., Gaudinat, A., Hanbury, A., Falquet, G.: How to sort trustworthy health online information? Improvements of the automated detection of HONcode criteria. Procedia Comput. Sci. **121**, 940–949 (2017). https://doi.org/10.1016/j.procs.2017.11.122

21. Wang, Z., Sun, Z.: Can the adoption of health information on social media be predicted by information characteristics? Aslib J. Inf. Manag. **73**(1), 80–100 (2021). https://doi.org/10.1108/AJIM-12-2019-0369

22. Oroszlányová, M., Teixeira, C., Nunes, S., Ribeiro, C.: Predicting the quality of health web documents using their characteristics. Online Inf. Rev. **42**, 1024–1047 (2018). https://doi.org/10.1108/OIR-01-2017-0028

23. Allington, D., Duffy, B., Wessely, S., Dhavan, N., Rubin, J.: Health-protective behaviour, social media usage and conspiracy belief during the COVID-19 public health emergency. Psychol. Med. 1–7 (2020). https://doi.org/10.1017/S003329172000224X

24. Erceg, N., Ružojčić, M., Galić, Z.: Misbehaving in the Corona crisis: the role of anxiety and unfounded beliefs. Curr. Psychol. (2020). https://doi.org/10.1007/s12144-020-01040-4

25. Hornik, R., Kikut, A., Jesch, E., Woko, C., Siegel, L., Kim, K.: Association of COVID-19 misinformation with face mask wearing and social distancing in a nationally representative US sample. Health Commun. **36**, 6–14 (2021). https://doi.org/10.1080/10410236.2020.1847437

26. Armitage, L., Lawson, B., Whelan, M., Newhouse, N.: Paying SPECIAL consideration to the digital sharing of information during the COVID-19 pandemic and beyond. BJGP Open **4**, 34–41 (2020). https://doi.org/10.3399/bjgpopen20X101072

27. Sallam, M., et al.: Conspiracy beliefs are associated with lower knowledge and higher anxiety levels regarding COVID-19 among students at the University of Jordan. Int. J. Environ. Res. Public Health **17**, 4915 (2020). https://doi.org/10.3390/ijerph17144915

28. Sharov, K.: Adaptation to SARS-CoV-2 under stress: role of distorted information. Eur. J. Clin. Invest. **50**, e13294 (2020). https://doi.org/10.1111/eci.13294

29. Malhotra, P.: Relationship-centered and culturally informed approach to studying misinformation on COVID-19. Social Media Soc. **6**, 1–4 (2020). https://doi.org/10.1177/2056305120948224

30. Xiao, H., et al.: Social distancing among medical students during the 2019 coronavirus disease pandemic in China: disease awareness, anxiety disorder, depression, and behavioral activities. Int. J. Environ. Res. Public Health **17**, 5047 (2020). https://doi.org/10.3390/ijerph17145047

162   Y. M. De La Cruz-Ramirez et al.

31. Husky, M., Kovess-Masfety, V., Swendsen, J.: Stress and anxiety among university students in France during Covid-19 mandatory confinement. Compr. Psychiatry **102**, 152191 (2020). https://doi.org/10.1016/j.comppsych.2020.152191
32. Dean, D., et al.: Cross-cultural comparisons of psychosocial distress in the USA, South Korea, France, and Hong Kong during the initial phase of COVID-19. Psychiatry Res. **295**, 113593 (2021). https://doi.org/10.1016/j.psychres.2020.113593
33. Zhao, Y., et al.: Concerns about information regarding COVID-19 on the internet: cross-sectional study. J. Med. Internet Res. **22**, e20487 (2020). https://doi.org/10.2196/20487
34. Zhang, Y., Song, S.: Older adults' evaluation of the credibility of online health information. In: CHIIR 2020: Proceedings of the 2020 Conference on Human Information Interaction and Retrieval, pp. 358–362. ACM Press, New York (2020). https://doi.org/10.1145/3343413.3377997

Content Distribution and Storage Based on Volunteer and Community Computing

Francisco de Asís López-Fuentes[(✉)] [iD]

Department of Information Technology, Universidad Autónoma Metropolitana - Cuajimalpa,
Av. Vasco de Quiroga 4871, Cuajimalpa, 05348 México City, Mexico
`flopez@cua.uam.mx`

Abstract. In recent years, the users need to discover and use a diversity of resources in the Internet to do their tasks. These resources such as massive storage, processing and distribution capacity are generally decentralized and geographically dispersed, however they can be shared to solve large-scale problems in a collaborative way. Peer-to-peer (P2P) networks are an attractive alternative to implement collaborative solutions. This work presents a P2P collaborative for content distribution and store management in small communities based on volunteer and community computing.

Keywords: P2P networks · Collaboration · Distributed systems · Simulation

1 Introduction

Information and communication technologies have significantly altered the ways people communicate, entertain, work, negotiate, govern, or socialize on a global scale. The Internet, better computing and communication capabilities have led to an interest in decentralizing and sharing geographically dispersed resources to solve large-scale problems. Under this approach, various computing resources such as processing capacity, massive storage and high capacity networks are offered as services. Resource management and application programming in large-scale distributed systems is a hard task, since different scenarios such as the variable number of available resources and the different requirements defined by users must be evaluated to improve their performance. However, users do not know how the computational structure of these systems have been constructed because a resource agent hides this complexity to the users during the interaction. Many of these services are based on centralized approaches, which introduce various limitations related to locality, dependency and a single point of failure.

Collaborative computing infrastructures such as peer-to-peer networks have emerged as an important solution for managing distributed resources on the Internet, but they still have open problems [16]. The Internet has triggered a social revolution due to the way in which people interact with each other on a planetary scale. Thus, people with common interests but geographically separated can create small communities around the world for cooperation between them. This approach can be based on community and volunteer computing. Community computing is a model where all computing services

M. F. Mata-Rivera and R. Zagal-Flores (Eds.): WITCOM 2021, CCIS 1430, pp. 163–173, 2021.
https://doi.org/10.1007/978-3-030-89586-0_13

are based on a cooperative resource-sharing approach between users [1]. Community computing is studied by many researchers for several applications mainly related with cloud computing [3, 4]. For example, community cloud can be used by organizations with the same requirements and needs in order to save costs [25]. On the other hand, voluntary computing refers to idle computing resources that are shared by public participants to support computationally expensive projects [2]. Volunteer computing uses the distributed resources as an important strategy to do large-scale tasks [5] such as potential processing and storage [6, 7]. For example, the users of a social network may share their heterogeneous computing resources to form a in a social ad hoc could [24].

Although community and voluntary computing have been studied during the last years, these paradigms still presents different challenges and opportunities. Future directions related to cloud and fog computing, security, privacy, and reliability are open. Also, new applications based on community and voluntary computing for organizations with common interests may be deployed. In the present work, we propose a P2P collaborative infrastructure as a possible solution for supporting the generation and dissemination of contents in small communities. Our main motivation in this work is to create an open collaborative platform where we can evaluate new protocols and algorithms for the distribution and storage of content. Our second motivation is to propose an open architecture to small communities with common interests that want to share their resources without using commercial applications.

Our paper continues with the following organization. Information about community and volunteer computing architectures is presented in Sect. 2. Concepts related to P2P networks are described in Sect. 3. In Sect. 4, we present our proposed P2P collaborative architecture. Because our work is in progress, in Sect. 5 we present a basic evaluation of our proposed architecture to know its impact in terms of collaboration. The article concludes in Sect. 6.

2   Related Work

Peer-to-peer networks are a promising paradigm in the distributed computing [10], and it has been used as a way to spread digital content to a large audience [9]. Interest in this paradigm is growing because they allow geographically distributed computational resources to be coupled to solve large-scale problems. These new approaches help to solve complex problem in several areas related to science and engineering [8] because the data and computational resources can be exchanged, selected aggregated regardless their physical location. P2P systems still present open issues and research opportunities, and P2P networks has been used to deploy IoT (Internet of Things) [17], blockchain [18] or grid solutions [19].

Authors in [1] propose a cooperation scheme using community computing in order to model and describe cooperation effectively. This model gives an introduction about the conflict resolution in the community computing. Authors presents some case studies to evaluate the community computing and its model. Babaoglu et al. [20] introduce a P2P architecture for providing cloud services. This work presents how a fully decentralized P2P cloud has been designed and implemented. A distributed computing infrastructure allows for organizations and individuals to use existing resources for allocating different tasks. Main problem to been solved is the coherency of the structure under unreliable conditions of the computing resources. Overlay network is constructed on top of the physical network using gossip-based communication protocols. Resources are partitioned into multiple slices in order to avoid that individual failures in a node affect the overall network. The resource partitioning process receives special attention in this work, because it must be conducted in an efficient and reliable way in any cloud architecture. A prototype of this architecture was implemented as a way to demonstrate the effectiveness of this proposal.

Marzal-Romeu et al. in [19] review information and communication technologies related to the microgrids. In this work is investigated which is the most suitable network topologies and protocols for smart microgrids. Because microgrids and P2P networks have a dynamic behavior, the authors conclude in their study that P2P technology can play a powerful role for distributed self-management and control schemes in the power grids. In [18] is presented a conceptual model for managing sensitive information such as the personal health information. This proposal uses information from different health-care providers and it is supported by blockchain technology and P2P networks. The authors also do a security analysis for the proposed model. Data integrity is guaranteed, and the blockchain technology is used to offer an immutable of the data record. The authors state that the model presented a good experimental performance in term of data dissemination. On the other hand, several IoT data marketplaces have been deployed on P2P networks. For example, a review system is proposed in [17], which can confirm the reputation of a data owner or the data traded in the P2P data marketplace. This study is based on Etherum model and P2P networks, which is used to face the limitations of the client-server model such as security vulnerability or server administrator's malicious behavior. The integrity and immutability of the registered reviews are assured too.

3   P2P Background

A P2P network is an overlay network which is established through TCP (Transport Control Protocol) or HTTP (Hypertext Transfer Protocol) connections [14]. An example of a P2P network is shown in Fig. 1. Here, the participating nodes form the overlay P2P network on the top of the physical network [12].

P2P networks can be classified as unstructured and structured. Participating nodes in an unstructured P2P network are chosen randomly. This type of network is often used for distributed and heterogeneous systems [15], where it is not possible to maintain strict restrictions on the placement of control data and network topology. Unstructured P2P networks use flooding communication protocols which cause a large amount of network traffic [11]. Unstructured P2P networks can be further divided in centralized P2P, pure P2P and hybrid P2P. On the other hand, structured P2P networks maintain a close coupling between the network topology and the location of data using a hash table (DHT) [13]. This table is used to precisely define the data placement and lookup operations, and the DHT mechanism handles the peers joining/leavings on the overlay. Each peer has a routing table with information of links to a small subset of peers.

A computing system involves different computer resources, policy, management strategies and applications with a variety of computing requirements. The users of a system either as producers or consumers of resources have different objectives, strategies

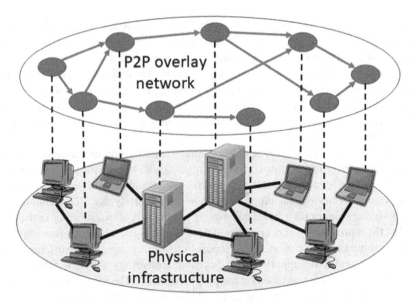

Fig. 1. A P2P network is an overlay network.

and demand patterns which cloud be considered during the design of the system. In most cases, users and resources are dispersed through the world. The management of these distributed resources is often complex because traditional approaches based on centralized schemes to optimize performance measures cannot be used. This work reviews some collaborative computing infrastructures to achieve better connectivity and efficiency in the dissemination of content. In some scenarios, collaboration occurs between nodes that work as peers (or equals) to distribute content, while in other cases sources collaborate with each other to distribute their workload. P2P networks introduces different benefits such as decentralization, cost reduction, resource aggregation, scalability, dynamism, fault resilience, self-organization and anonymity. Since the Napster advent, a significant number of P2P applications have been developed. P2P applications have become a large category, which have been categorized into major areas such as file sharing, distributed computing, collaboration, media streaming. In this work, a P2P collaborative architecture for content distribution and storage is proposed.

4   P2P Collaborative Architecture

Our proposal architecture is shown in Fig. 2. Our architecture is an extension of our works presented in [21] and [22]. This architecture has two levels. In the first level there is the main pool, which contain a defined number of trackers. In the second level there are different pools with peers and different function. For example, pool 1 can be used to storage and distribute video files, while pool 2 can be used to storage and distribute music files. Thus, we can assign different function to each pool. Nodes in each pool work as peers, and they collaborate with each other to store files, in such a way that a virtual storage space is created throughout the system. Trackers in the main pool can be coordinate with each other to distribute the different file types through the system.

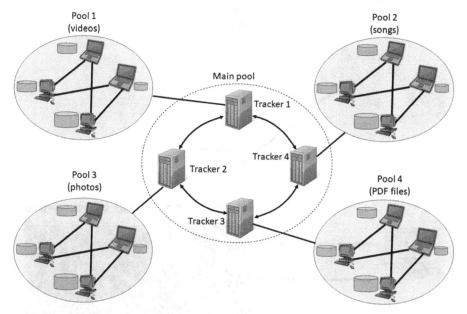

Fig. 2. Proposed collaborative P2P architecture.

Different transparency levels for the users can be considered in this architecture. In this way, operation details of the system are hidden from the user. P2P infrastructure is used by the system to support operations of storage, back up, and file synchronization and sharing. In addition, the trackers control parameters related to availability, reliability and quality of service of the peers in each pool. Therefore, these parameters are also transparent to the users. On the other way, the system can be initialized by any tracker in the main pool. In each pool, the communication between the peers is done via the tracker application, which manages the database where are registered the reports generated by the peers and their content list to be shared.

In our architecture the trackers are not storage servers, therefore they do not store files. Thus, when a file is received by the tracker from a peer, this file is redirects to another peer to be stored. Otherwise, when a peer wishes recover a file, it is requested by the tracker to peer where the file is stored. A tracker contain the database with information of each peer in the pool. This information is related to store capacity, dynamism and availability of each peer, which allow to define the reliability of the peer in the pool. In this scenario, all participating nodes are registered in the main server (tracker), which also monitors the behavior of each node in the system. The interaction between a tracker and a peer is shown in Fig. 3. In this case, each node in the P2P network runs a peer application, such that each node must receive and send files at the same time. To reach time goal, peer application performs both tasks simultaneously. The peer application also supervises each peer and reports its shared resources and behavior to the tracker in each pool. The peer application has a server part and a client part. The server part always is active to listen the request from the other peers, while the client part is responsible to upload files, display files and exit. Also, client part reports to the tracker all information related to the storage and upload capacity of its local computer in the pool.

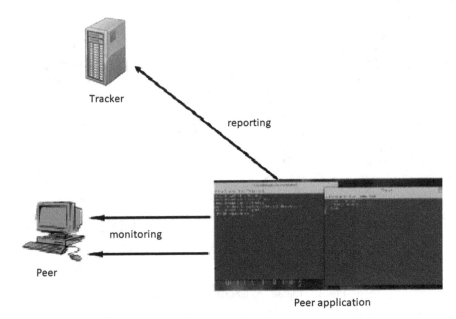

Fig. 3. Interaction between a peer and a tracker.

The tracker in each peer can classify the priority and importance of each file received and decides where (a specific peer) it should be stored. The tracker is responsible for establishing the communication between peers and routing the contents. Flow diagram of tracker operation is shown in Fig. 4. Each tracker has a database which has been designed to register and monitor information related to the peers. For each peer in the pool the following information is recorded in this database: physical address, IP address, date and time of the last connection, available space in disk, availability and dynamicity. To store content received from a sending peer, the tracker looks for host peers with similar level of reliability as the sending peer. The localization transparency is offered by the tracker to all users in the system. Thus, a sending peer does not know where is placed its content in the pool, because this activity is done by the tracker. When a peer wishes to recover a content, it should be requested through the tracker, which addresses the requested content from the host peer to the requesting peer.

Security in distributed and collaborative environments is a very important issue to be considered to reduce the risks to the information that is shared in different devices and physical places [23]. Therefore, there are various preventive, detective and corrective measures that must be considered to protect the information. Among the most important objectives that security services must meet are confidentiality, integrity, authentication, and non-repudiation. Cryptography enables these objectives to be achieved by allowing the meaning of the original messages to be altered through encryption and encoding. Cryptography can be symmetric and asymmetric (or public). The first method uses one key on both sides of the communication while the second method uses two keys, a different one on each side of the communication (private key and public key). The symmetric encryption algorithms perform their encryption by blocks of bits the size of the key, which is chosen randomly. Examples of symmetric encryption algorithms are DES, triple DES, RC2, RC4, AES [23].

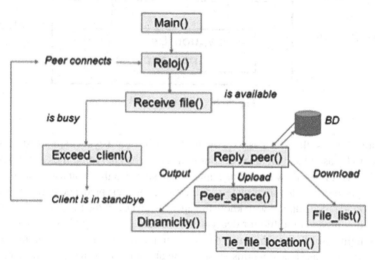

Fig. 4. Flow diagram of tracker operation.

Our proposal architecture considers a privacy and authentication framework to encrypt the files to be distributed and stored by the peers. Figure 5 shows how the security scheme interacts with the peer and tracker applications. There are a database with the passwords which are used to access to the system, and to store a file in a peer or to distribute a file from a peer to one or more peers. This database is managed by the tracker application in each pool. Each tracker also manages the authentication process. When a node arrives to the system it is authenticated by the tracker in each pool. Privacy is reached via encryption techniques. After a file is encrypted it will stored in a database located in a local peer. Our P2P collaborative architecture plans to use the AES encryption algorithm because it does not consume many resources when encrypting video files. This is very important, since this task can be done by each user on their own computers, so the computing capacities are variable. Therefore, if an algorithm is not efficient or consumes a lot of resources, it could cause problems with the equipment, such as making the encryption process take a long time.

The authentication process is done from point to point, that is, every time a user wants to enter the system, a message must be sent with their username and password so that it can be verified by the tracker with the database. If both data match then access is allowed. The password is stored in MD5 format by the tracker. Every time the password is authenticated, it is sent in MD5 format so as not to be visible to intruders. In the

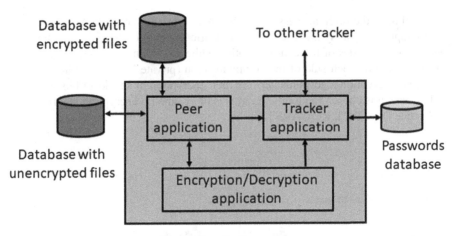

Fig. 5. Security framework.

encryption process, the user has to provide three different keys which are stored in the database, to be used later. In the encryption process, the encrypted files are stored in an attached folder of the software and its name is also stored in the database to be used when decrypting. When the files are transferred, they are sent encrypted, and together with this, a query is made to the database to know the encryption key of the file, which is sent to the user who downloaded the file for decryption. The data is managed through a database, which contains user data such as username, login password, and access permissions. In addition, the database also contains information about the files that users upload, which helps to make the search more efficient. These data are concentrated in the trackers, which helps to avoid losses in searches as normally happens in pure P2P systems where information is sometimes lost.

5   Evaluation

Our work is in progress. However, to evaluate our collaboration concept we have done an initial implementation of our proposed architecture. This prototype uses different entities such as entities are peers, trackers and databases, which are deployed on Linux using language C/C++. We used a reduced number of peers to compare the performance of a P2P network against a client-server network. In this case, 4 files of 28 MB are distributed between the same number of nodes for both networks, and the performance is measured in term of distribution time of the files to all nodes. Results are shown in Fig. 6.

We can see how nodes using the collaborative model can distribute the four files in a less time compared with the client-server model. This is because the client-server architecture needs to broadcast the four files to all nodes, while P2P model uses the collaboration between peers to distribute the four files to the all peers. Collaboration strategy reduce delivery time to all end-users.

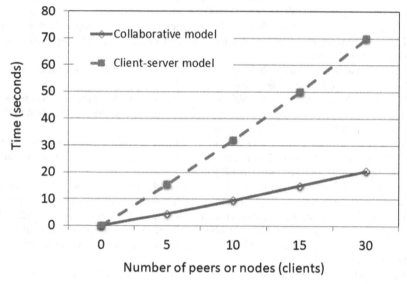

Fig. 6. Comparison of distribution time.

6 Conclusions

Content storage and distribution on Internet is very popular currently. In this paper, we present a P2P collaborative architecture for content distribution and storage management. Our proposed architecture integrate different strategies to face the different challenges for content distribution and storage such as authentication, privacy, quality of service, scalability and heterogeneity. We believe that collaborative P2P based on volunteer computing represent a good opportunity for small communities with common interests, because these paradigms represent a way to share resource and save money.

Our work is in progress, however initial results show benefits of collaboration compared with the traditional client-server model. Our work can be extended to different scenarios. For example, we can integrate in our architecture a coordination mechanism between the trackers, network coding or information dispersion techniques and its respective evaluations. Also, different security schemes can be studied in order to evaluate the encryption times and its impact in the file privacity.

References

1. Jung, Y., Lee, J., Kim, M.: Community computing model supporting community situation based strict cooperation and conflict resolution. In: Obermaisser, R., Nah, Y., Puschner, P., Rammig, F.J. (eds.) SEUS 2007. LNCS, vol. 4761, pp. 47–56. Springer, Heidelberg (2007). https://doi.org/10.1007/978-3-540-75664-4_6
2. Durrani, M.N., Shamsi, J.A.: Volunteer computing: requirements, challenges, and solutions. J. Netw. Comput. Appl. **39**, 369–380 (2014)
3. Bruque-Cámara, S., Moyano-Fuentes, J., Maqueira-Marín, J.M.: Supply chain integration through community cloud: effects on operational performance. J. Purchasing Supply Manag. **22**(2), 141–153 (2016)
4. Goyal, S.: Public vs private vs hybrid vs community-cloud computing: a critical review. Int. J. Comput. Netw. Inf. Secur. **6**(3), 20–29 (2014)
5. Nov, O., Anderson, D., Arazy, O.: Volunteer computing: a model of the factors determining contribution to community-based scientific research. In: Proceedings of the WWW 2010, Raleigh, NC, USA, pp. 741–750. ACM Press (2010)
6. Anderson, D.P., Fedak, G.: The computational and storage potential of volunteer computing. In: Proceedings of the 6th IEEE International Symposium on Cluster Computing and the Grid, Washington, DC, pp. 73–80. IEEE (2006)
7. Cunsolo, V.D., Distefano, S., Puliafito, A., Scarpa, M.: Volunteer computing and desktop cloud: the Cloud@Home paradigm. In: Proceedings of the 8th IEEE International Symposium on Network Computing and Applications, Cambridge, MA, USA, pp. 134–139. IEEE (2009)
8. Buyya, R., Murshed, M.: GridSim: a toolkit for the modeling and simulation of distributed resource management and scheduling for grid computing. Concurr. Comput. Pract. Exp. **14**(13–15), 1175–1220 (2002)
9. Androutsellis-Theotokis, S., Spinellis, D.: A survey of peer-to-peer content distribution technologies. ACM Comput. Surv. **36**(4), 335–371 (2004)
10. Milojicic, D.S., et al.: Peer-to-Peer Computing (Technical report HPL-2002-57R1). HP Labs, Palo Alto (2002)
11. Schollmeier, R.: A definition of peer-to-peer networking for the classification of peer-to-peer architectures and applications. In: Proceedings of the First International Conference on Peer-to-Peer Computing, Linköping, Sweden, pp. 101–102. IEEE (2001)
12. López-Fuentes, F.A.: Video Multicast in Peer-to-Peer Networks, Doctoral dissertation, Technische Universität München, Germany (2009)
13. Zheng, W., Liu, X., Shi, S., Hu, J., Dong, H.: Peer-to-peer: a technique perspective. In: Wu, J. (ed.) Handbook of Theoretical and Algorithmic Aspects of Ad Hoc, Sensor, and Peer-to-Peer Networks, pp. 591–616. Auerbach Publications, Boca Raton (2005)
14. Ripeanu, M., Foster, I., Iamnitchi, A., Rogers, A.: In search for simplicity: a self organizing multi-source multicast overlay. In: Proceedings of the 1st IEEE International Conference (SASO 2007), Boston, MA, USA, pp. 371–374. IEEE (2007)
15. Li, J., Vuong, S.: An efficient clustered architecture for P2P networks. In: 18th International Conference on Advanced Information Networking and Applications, Fukuoka, Japan, pp. 278–283 (2004)
16. Bandara, H.D., Jayasumana, A.P.: Collaborative applications over peer-to-peer systems—challenges and solutions. Peer-to-Peer Netw. Appl. **6**, 257–276 (2013)
17. Park, J.S., Youn, T.Y., Kim, H.B., Rhee, K.H., Shin, S.U.: Smart contract-based review system for an IoT data marketplace. Sensors **18**, 3577 (2018)
18. Rahmadika, S., Rhee, K.: Blockchain technology for providing an architecture model of decentralized personal health information. Int. J. Eng. Bus. Manag. (2018)

19. Marzal-Romeu, S., Salas-Puente, R., González-Medina, R., Figueres, E., Garcerá, G.: Peer-to-peer decentralized control structure for real time monitoring and control of microgrids. In: Proceedings of the 26th International Symposium on Industrial Electronics (ISIE), Edinburgh, UK, pp. 140–145. IEEE (2017)
20. Babaoglu, O., Marzolla, M., Tamburini, M.: Design and implementation of a P2P cloud system. In: Proceedings of the 27th Annual ACM Symposium on Applied Computing (SAC 2012), Trento, Italy, pp. 412–417. ACM Press (2012)
21. López-Fuentes, F.A., García-Rodríguez, G.: Collaborative cloud computing based on P2P networks. In: Proceedings of the 4th International Workshop on Collaborative Enterprise Systems (COLLABES-2016) co-located with the IEEE-AINA, Crans-Montana, Switzerland (2016)
22. López-Fuentes, F.A., Orta-Cruz, C.A.: A secure P2P architecture for video distribution. In: Proceedings of the First International Workshop on Internet-Scale Multimedia Management (WISMM 2014), co-located with the ACM Multimedia Conference, Orlando, FL, USA (2014)
23. Stalling, W.: Network Security Essentials: Applications and Standards, 4th edn. Pearson (2011)
24. Varghese, B., Buyya, R.: Next generation cloud computing: new trends and research directions. Future Gener. Comput. Syst. **79**, 849–861 (2018)
25. Dubey, K., Shams, M.Y., Sharma, S.C., Alarifi, A., Amoon, M., Nasr, A.A.: A management system for servicing multiorganizations on community cloud model in secure cloud environment. IEEE Access **7**, 159535–159546 (2019)

Classification of Cardiac Arrhythmias Using Machine Learning Algorithms

Christian García-Aquino[1]($\boxtimes$) (ID), Dante Mújica-Vargas[1] (ID),
and Manuel Matuz-Cruz[2] (ID)

[1] Tecnológico Nacional de México, CENIDET, Cuernavaca, Mexico
m21ce012@cenidet.tecnm.mx
[2] Tecnológico Nacional de México, Campus Tapachula, Mexico City, Mexico

Abstract. This article proposes a method to classify cardiac arrhythmias using feature extraction and dimensionality reduction techniques. The experiment was carried out with the QRS complexes of the electrocardiographic signals, which are part of the Physionet MIT-BIH arrhythmia database. The machine learning algorithms used to perform the classification were k Nearest Neighbors, Linear SVM, RBF SVM, Decision Tree, Random Forest, Neural Net, AdaBoost, Naive Bayes and QDA. To measure the efficiency and quality of the proposed method, the metrics of Accuracy, Precision, Recall, F1 Score, as well as the Cohen Kappa score and the Mathews correlation coefficient were used. The results obtained show a better classification performance in the neural network with 96.33%, 96.33%, 96.33%, 96.32%, 1.0 and 1.0 of the aforementioned metrics.

Keywords: Arrhythmia · ECG · Feature extraction · Dimensionality reduction · QRS complex

1 Introduction

In recent years, cardiovascular diseases have been the leading cause of deaths around the world. Among them, cardiac arrhythmias are very common conditions that require novel approaches in terms of early detection and effective treatments, and thus prevent heart problems. Cardiac arrhythmia, on the other hand, is a series of disturbances in which the heart rate varies between excessively fast, excessively slow or irregular [1].

Electrocardiography records the electrical activity of the heart, which is the most used technique in the diagnosis of patients during clinical practice [2]. The signals present in the electrocardiogram (ECG) present morphological and temporal characteristics of multiple components, which provide an improvement in the diagnosis and treatment planning processes, as well as in the control and prediction of cardiovascular diseases such as: arrhythmias, acute coronary syndromes, among other congenital or genetically unknown cardiovascular diseases, as studied in [3], [4] and [5].

© Springer Nature Switzerland AG 2021
M. F. Mata-Rivera and R. Zagal-Flores (Eds.): WITCOM 2021, CCIS 1430, pp. 174–185, 2021.
https://doi.org/10.1007/978-3-030-89586-0_14

The diagnosis that is usually used to interpret ECG signals requires a demand in the use of highly precise devices accompanied by experienced doctors [6]. Generally, cardiologists perform ECG waveform inspections digitally. However, it is often necessary to analyze ECG signals lasting hours and even days [7]. According to the aforementioned, it is a procedure which is too time consuming and this leads to a limitation regarding the impartiality of the diagnosis [8]. This limitation can be eliminated by using computational techniques for the classification of arrhythmias.

In the literature, investigations are detailed in the context of deep learning approaches such as recurrent convolutional neural networks (RNN-CNN) [9], convolutional neural networks with bidirectional layers of LSTM cells (CNN-BiLSTM) [10] or a radial base function descriptor data network (RBFDD) [11]. In the context of signal processing there are works that perform basic noise reduction, detection of QRS complexes and their segmentation as studied in [12], [13] and [14].

However, the works focused on proposing deep models for the automatic classification of arrhythmias when carrying out a complex construction, suppose a huge computational expense in training, accompanied by high amounts of data that, in some cases, require data increases in the training sessions unbalanced classes in order to achieve acceptable ranking performance. Likewise, the works that focus on signal processing, since these do not reach high degrees of robustness and quality in processed data since they propose methods that do not achieve a correct elimination of noise and can even lose important data from the signals ECG mistaking them as a noisy signal.

The purpose of this article is to propose a new method to classify cardiac arrhythmias using feature extraction and dimensionality reduction techniques. The main idea of this approach is to perform a robust and efficient treatment of ECG signals by decomposing wavelet packets, which will allow us, as indicated above, to obtain a reduced vector of characters by extracting features and the reduction of dimensionality of these. In addition, the reduced vector of characters by having statistical characteristics, facilitates the classification tasks by obtaining an improvement in the performance of machine learning algorithms. The ECG signals used for this research come from the well-known MIT-BIT arrhythmia database [15].

The rest of this document is organized as follows. In Sect. 2, a brief introduction about packet wavelets decomposition, as well as the classification algorithms used during experimentation. The treatment of ECG signals of the proposed method is indicated in Sect. 3. The results obtained from experimentation and a comparative analysis are presented in Sect. 4. Conclusions are mentioned in the final section and future work is described.

2 Background

2.1 Wavelets

Discrete Wavelet Transform. The discrete wavelet transform (DWT) is a computational algorithm, which is commonly used in recent years for signal processing, that allows dividing a time series into coefficients or components that describe the variation of the series over a wide range of both high and low frequencies [16]. The high and low frequency components of an input signal x are determined as follows [17]:

$$\psi_{high}[k] = \sum_{t=1}^{n} x[t]g[2k - t] \tag{1}$$

$$\psi_{low}[k] = \sum_{t=1}^{n} x[t]g[2k - t] \tag{2}$$

Where ψ_{low} the detailed signal is calculated using a high-pass filter and ψ_{high} is known as an approximation signal. To keep the length constant, downsample with two passes is applied for each filter.

2.2   Classifiers

Classification algorithms were used in this research are briefly described.

K-Nearest Neighbors. In [18], the k-Nearest Neigbors (kNN) algorithm uses the standard Euclidean distance to measure the variability between training instances and test instances. The standard Euclidean distance is defined in the following Eq. (3).

$$d_E\left(P_e, Q_r\right) = \sqrt{\sum_{j=1}^{n} \left(v_j\left(P_{ej} - Q_{rj}\right)\right)^2} \tag{3}$$

kNN calculates the common class of nearest neighbors, therefore it allows estimating the class of the test instance. Finally, the kNN algorithm is defined in the Eq. (4) [19].

$$v_q\left(x\right) = mjr\sum_{l=1}^{k} \xi\left(v, v\left(w_l\right)\right) \tag{4}$$

Where $w_{l...k}$ is the closest neighbors of an instance of the test data set, k is the number of neighbors, and v represents the finite set of class labels.

Linear SVM. The algorithm Linear Support Vector Machine (SVM) builds a hyperplane in a multidimensional space iteratively for class separation which is used to minimize an error, in other words, SVM calculates a marginal hyperplane that best fits the classification of the data set and thus finally identify the points closest to the hyperplane data which are support vectors [20]. SVM linear classification is defined in the expression (5).

$$\phi_n\left(x\right) = \begin{cases} 1, if \sum_{l \in \nu} \xi_i^* y_i x_i^T x - \frac{1}{|\nu_o|}\sum_{l \in \nu}\sum_{k \in \nu_o} \xi_i^* y_i x_i^T x + \frac{1}{|\nu_o|}\sum_{k \in \nu_o} y_i > 0, \\ 0, otherwise \end{cases} \tag{5}$$

RBF SVM. The SVM with radial basis function (RBF), is a kernel which is used when the data set cannot be separated linearly [20]. The Gaussian classification kernel is represented in the following expression:

$$k\left(x, x'\right) = \exp\left(-\psi \left\|x, x'\right\|^2\right), for\ \psi > 0 \tag{6}$$

Decision Tree. The decision tree is a classification tool generally used for multidimensional data. The classifier has a binary tree structure, because the internal nodes divide the x feature space into many regions proportionally to the number of existing leaf nodes. The set of leaf nodes is denoted by ψ [21]. The general prediction function f corresponding to the decision tree is written as:

$$f\left(x\right) = \sum_{j \in \psi} f^j\left(x\right) 1\left\{x \in \phi_j\right\} \tag{7}$$

Random Forest. Random forests generate multiple decision trees using replacement sampling, and decisions are made on a rule-based basis, where a decision tree ensemble voting system is often performed. In other words, the random forest seeks to improve precision with a reduced variance and thus avoid overfitting [21]. The prediction function random forest is described as:

$$fRF\left(x\right) = \frac{1}{B} \sum_{j=1}^{B} f\delta_b^*\left(x\right) \tag{8}$$

Neural Net. A neural network is intuitively based on the functioning of the biological neuron in the brain. An artificial neuron (perceptron) receives a set of inputs $x = (x_1, x_2, ..., x_p) \in \mathbf{R}^\mathbf{P}$, which is weighted by the corresponding scalar part $w = (w_1, w_2, ..., w_p)$, generating a signal if the total weight is greater than some threshold. The mathematical representation of a neuron is observed in the Eq. (9).

$$\sum_{k=1}^{p} w_k x_k - b \tag{9}$$

The ability of abstraction that has an artificial neuron is only at the level of linear classification (binary), therefore, the neural network is composed of several neurons organized in layers, the input layer in which are values input x. Each layer generates output information, these outputs subsequently serve as inputs to the layer that precedes it, whether they are hidden layers or the output layer. Since the network seeks the non-linear classification of a data set, activation functions are added that guarantee non-linearity [22]. The most common are the hyperbolic tangent: $\varrho(y) = \frac{e^y - e^{-y}}{e^y + e^{-y}} \in [-1, 1]$, the sigmoidal: $\varrho(y) = \frac{e^y}{e^y + 1} \in [0, 1]$ and rectified linear unit (ReLu): $\varrho(y) = \max(0, y) \in [0, \infty)$.

AdaBoost. AdaBoost is an algorithm which is a variation of the method called Boosting, whose objective is to make a set of weak learning algorithms to give rise to a strong learning process to solve a classification problem [23]. AdaBoost's strong classifier output can be seen in the Eq. (10).

$$Y_{fnl}(x) = sign\left(\sum_{u=1}^{U} b_u m_u(x)\right) \tag{10}$$

Naive Bayes. The Bayesian classifier is in charge of estimating the probabilities of all alternative models or hypotheses, providing data as evidence, and from this finding the classification with the highest probability that will be assigned to each new entry [24]. The main idea of Bayesian classifiers is the Bayes theorem, which can be observed in the Eq. (11).

$$prob(I|T) = \frac{prob(T|I)\,prob(I)}{prob(T)} \tag{11}$$

Where $prob(I|T)$ estimates the posterior probability for a hypothesis, given the data set T.

Quadratic Discriminant Analysis. The quadratic discriminant analysis is a supervised classification method of qualitative variables in which two or more groups or classes are known a priori and the new ones are classified in one of them based on their characteristics, also considering that each class k has its own covariance matrix (sum_k) and as a consequence, the quadratic discriminant function can be seen in the Eq. (12) [25].

$$\log(P(Y = k|X = x)) = -\frac{1}{2}\log\left|\sum_k\right| - \frac{1}{2}(x - \mu_x)^T \sum_k^{-1}(x - \mu_x) + \log(\pi_k) \tag{12}$$

3   Implementation

In order to classify arrhythmias, a methodology for classifying electrocardiographic signals is analyzed in this section, starting with their acquisition and the segmentation of the QRS complexes present. Likewise, the process of extraction of statistical characteristics is analyzed, which are subjected to a dimensionality reduction. Finally, the classification is performed with machine learning algorithms. A description of the aforementioned can be seen in Fig. 1.

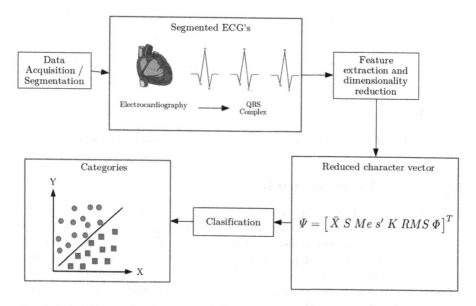

Fig. 1. Proposed classification method

3.1 Data Acquisition/Segmentation

The original MIT-BIH arrhythmia database was used, from which the ECG signals were obtained concentrated in a file called MITBIH_ECG.mat that contains 5 variables identified as ECGN, ECGAPC, ECGPVC, ECGLBBB and ECGRBBB. Each variable contains a matrix where the ECG signals are represented in columns and each signal is identified as the "QRS Complex" containing 320 samples. The variable ECGN encompasses the segments of the signals that were annotated with N (normal beat), ECGAPC contains segments of the signals that were annotated with A (premature atrial beat), ECGPVC contains segments of the signals that were annotated with V (ventricular contraction premature), ECGLBBB contains segments of the signals that were annotated with L (beat of left bundle branch block) and ECGRBBB contains segments of the signals that were annotated with R (beat of right bundle branch block). Having 74512, 2546, 6902, 8072 and 7257 extracted signals labeled as N, A, V, L and R respectively. A graphic representation of the signals present in the ECG's can be seen in Fig. 2.

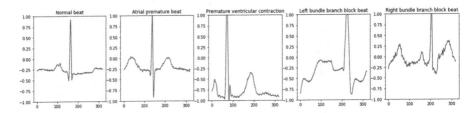

Fig. 2. ECG's with normal heartbeat and common arrhythmias

3.2   Feature Extraction and Dimensionality Reduction

After the segmentation of the signals extracted from the MIT-BIH database, the next step is to decompose the signals by transforming them into wave packets (WPT) in 6 levels of decomposition. Being the WPT it is an extension of the wavelet transform which will provide us with a complete level-by-level decomposition, which will allow us to extract the characteristics of signals that combine stationary and non-stationary characteristics with an arbitrary time-frequency resolution [29]. The two orthogonal bases of wave packets in a parent node (i, p) are given by the following forms [30]:

$$\Psi_{1+1}^{2p}(k) = \sum_{n=-\infty}^{\infty} l[n]\Psi_i^p(k - 2^i n) \tag{13}$$

where l[n] is a low pass filter (scaling),

$$\Psi_{1+1}^{2p}(k) = \sum_{n=-\infty}^{\infty} h[n]\Psi_i^p(k - 2^i n) \tag{14}$$

where h[n] is the high pass (wavelet) filter.

After performing the decomposition of the signals, a dimensionality reduction is performed by means of a reduced vector of statistical characteristics made up of:

- Mean values of each sub-band
- The standard deviation of each sub-band
- Median values of each sub-band
- The skewness of each sub-band
- Kurtosis of each sub-band
- Root mean square of each sub-band
- The ratio of each sub-band

3.3   Classification

Finally, for the classification of the characteristics obtained, in this case, the class with the least number of signals is label A, which has 2546 signals, so all other labels will be normalized with the same quantity. The column "classes" in the DataFrame indicates what is the signal class of that row, as we provided the parameter classes as A, V, N, L, R, the 0 means A, 1 means V, and so then. As we specified 2546 signals per class and A, V, N, L, and R for the classification classes, the rows from 0 to 2545 store extracted features for the A signals, the rows from 2546 to 5091 store extracted features for the V signals, the rows from 5092 to 7637 store extracted features for the N signals, the rows from 7638 to 10183 store extracted features for the L signals and the rows from 10184 to 12729 store extracted features for the R signals. And finally the data was divided into 70% for training and 30% for validation.

4   Experimentation and Results

The performance and time for segment extraction and arrhythmia classification are quantified and compared using the MIT-BIH arrhythmia database obtained from PhysioNet. The experimentation was carried out in a computer that consists of an Intel (R) Core (TM) i5-6300HQ CPU @ 3.20 GHz processor with 4 cores and 16 GB of RAM memory; as well as an NVIDIA GTX 960M GPU, with 640 cores and 4 GB of dedicated VRAM memory. The project was programmed in Python language in addition to the library for the use of Scikit-learn machine learning algorithms. Regarding the machine learning algorithms used, initially it was contemplated to classify the ECG signals with random forest, however, since today multiple algorithms are used for comparison purposes, algorithms such as k Nearest were used Neighbors, Linear SVM, RBF SVM, Decision Tree, Neural Net, AdaBoost, Naive Bayes and QDA.

4.1   Metrics

In order to carry out the objective evaluation of the proposed method for the classification of cardiac arrhythmias, 3 aspects were considered, which are mentioned below:

The confusion matrix was considered to evaluate the performance of a classification model, the weighting of correct and incorrect predictions are summarized with the count values and separated by class. This set of predictions are interpreted through metrics derived from the confusion matrix such as: Accuracy, Precision, Recall and F1-Score that are detailed in [26]. The Cohen's Kappa Score (KCS) is used to compare the observed agreement in a data set with respect to the expected agreement as mentioned in [27]. The Mathews Correlation Coefficient (MCC) is a contingency matrix method used to calculate Pearson's product-moment correlation coefficient between actual and predicted values, as discussed in [28].

4.2   Results

The performance of the extraction of characteristics of the wavelets was evaluated through the classification algorithms using the real database of arrhythmias MIT-BIH, which contains 48 extracts of half an hour of ambulatory ECG records. Of those 48 extracts, 23 were collected from a mixed inpatient and outpatient population, the remaining 25 extracts contain rare but clinically significant arrhythmias that cannot be adequately represented in a small random sample.

A subset of data was selected, with a total of 2546 signals from 320 samples each, classified as: Normal rhythm, Premature atrial beat, Premature ventricular contraction, Left bundle branch block beat, and Left bundle branch block beat.

Table 1. Performance results of the proposed classification method

Algorithm	Accuracy	Precision	Recall	F1-Score	CKS	MCC
Nearest Neighbors	0.9133	0.9126	0.9133	0.9121	1.0	1.0
Linear SVM	0.9544	0.9543	0.9544	0.9543	1.0	1.0
RBF SVM	0.1927	0.8465	0.1927	0.0668	0.0	0.0
Decision Tree	0.9026	0.9067	0.9026	0.9029	1.0	1.0
Random Forest	0.9513	0.9511	0.9513	0.9511	1.0	1.0
Neural Net	0.9633	0.9633	0.9633	0.9632	1.0	1.0
AdaBoost	0.3637	0.4074	0.3637	0.3781	0.0	0.0
Naive Bayes	0.89	0.894	0.89	0.8904	1.0	1.0
QDA	0.9578	0.9592	0.9578	0.9581	1.0	1.0

The average quantitative summary for each method and metric considered in the experimentation is presented in Table 1. Of the 99,289 QRS intervals extracted from the ECG recordings, 12730 were considered, because the intervals corresponding to "premature atrial beat" could only be extracted 2546, therefore, that minimum amount was selected to be able to have the classes fully balanced at the time of extracting the statistical characteristics. From the results obtained, it is notable to observe that the neural network, QDA and Linear SVM were the ones that had the best performance when classifying. However, of the 3 mentioned above, it can be seen that the neural network had the best performance of all in the metrics considered.

5   Conclusions

In this research work, a method for the classification of cardiac arrhythmias and normal heart beats was proposed. The results obtained show that the correct treatment of the signals improves the training process of the classification algorithms used during the research, also suggesting that the neural network obtained the best performance for the classification of arrhythmias, since although algorithms such as k -Nearest Neighbors, Decision Trees, Naive Bayes or Random Forest, despite being characterized by being multiclass classification algorithms, do not manage to exceed the performance of the neural network when analyzing

ECG signals. The implementation of high-performance computing equipment is of great help in terms of processing large amounts of electrocardiographic signals, as exemplified in the aforementioned experiment. As future work, since the present work did not use parallel calculations since it only worked with the CPU for the calculation tasks without being able to carry out another experimentation for purposes of comparison with the use of parallelism, it is contemplated in the research an extension where the time-frequency characteristics of the spectrograms can be extracted and subjected to a deep learning model for their classification using a high-performance equipment and making use of the GPU to perform the calculation in parallel.

Acknowledgments. This work was supported by the Tecnológico Nacional de México/CENIDET trough the project entitled "Clasificador para detectar fibrilación auricular en señales electrocardiográficas utilizando una red recurrente profunda entrenada con momentos de tiempo-frecuencia", as well as by CONACYT.

References

1. He, R., Liu, Y., Zhang, H.: Study on automatic classification of arrhythmias. In: Liu, C., Li, J. (eds.) Feature Engineering and Computational Intelligence in ECG Monitoring, pp. 113–141. Springer, Singapore (2020). https://doi.org/10.1007/978-981-15-3824-7_7

2. Ribeiro, A.H., et al.: Automatic 12-lead ECG classification using a convolutional network ensemble. In: Computing in Cardiology, pp. 1–4 (2020). https://doi.org/10.22489/CinC.2020.130

3. Sejersten, M., Wagner, G.S., Pahlm, O., Warren, J.W., Feldman, C.L., Horáček, B.M.: Detection of acute ischemia from the EASI-derived 12-lead electrocardiogram and from the 12-lead electrocardiogram acquired in clinical practice. J. Electrocardiol. **40**(2), 120–126 (2007). https://doi.org/10.1016/j.jelectrocard.2006.08.099

4. Maron, B.J., et al.: Assessment of the 12-lead electrocardiogram as a screening test for detection of cardiovascular disease in healthy general populations of young people (12–25 Years of Age). J. Am. College Cardiol. **64**(14), 1479–1514 (2014). https://doi.org/10.1016/j.jacc.2014.05.006

5. Antink, C.H., Leonhardt, S., Walter, M.: Fusing QRS detection and robust interval estimation with a random forest to classify atrial fibrillation. In: 2017 Computing in Cardiology (CinC), pp. 1–4 (2017). https://doi.org/10.22489/CinC.2017.167-163

6. Tadesse, G.A., et al.: Cardiovascular disease diagnosis using cross-domain transfer learning. In: 2019 41st Annual International Conference of the IEEE Engineering in Medicine and Biology Society (EMBC) (2019). https://doi.org/10.1109/embc.2019.8857737

7. Petmezas, G., et al.: Automated atrial fibrillation detection using a hybrid CNN-LSTM network on imbalanced ECG datasets. Biomed. Signal Process. Control **63**, 102194 (2020). https://doi.org/10.1016/j.bspc.2020.102194

8. Banerjee, S., Mitra, M.: Application of cross wavelet transform for ECG pattern analysis and classification. IEEE Trans. Instrum. Measur. **63**(2), 326–333 (2014). https://doi.org/10.1109/TIM.2013.2279001

9. Xiong, Z., Nash, M.P., Cheng, E., Fedorov, V.V., Stiles, M.K., Zhao, J.: ECG signal classification for the detection of cardiac arrhythmias using a convolutional recurrent neural network. Physiol Meas. **39**(9), 094006. PMID: 30102248; PMCID: PMC6377428 (2018). https://doi.org/10.1088/1361-6579/aad9ed

10. Wang, J., Li, W.: Atrial fibrillation detection and ECG classification based on CNN-BILSTM. arXiv:2011.06187 [cs, eess] (2020)

11. Bazargani, M.H.Z., Pakrashi, A., Mac Namee, B.: The deep radial basis function data descriptor (D-RBFDD) network: a one-class neural network for anomaly detection. arXiv:2101.12632 [cs] (2021)

12. Khan, M.M.R., Siddique, M.A.B., Sakib, S., Aziz, A., Tanzeem, A.K., Hossain, Z.: Electrocardiogram heartbeat classification using convolutional neural networks for the detection of cardiac arrhythmia. In: 2020 Fourth International Conference on I-SMAC (IoT in Social, Mobile, Analytics and Cloud) (I-SMAC), pp. 915–920 (2020). https://doi.org/10.1109/I-SMAC49090.2020.9243474

13. Chen, C.L., Chuang, C.T.: A QRS detection and R point recognition method for wearable single-lead ECG devices. Sensors (Basel). **17**(9), 1969 (2017). PMID: 28846610; PMCID: PMC5621148. https://doi.org/10.3390/s17091969

14. Silva, P., et al.: Towards better heartbeat segmentation with deep learning classification. Sci. Rep. **10**(1), 20701 (2020). PMID: 33244078; PMCID: PMC7692498. https://doi.org/10.1038/s41598-020-77745-0

15. Goldberger, A., et al.: PhysioBank, PhysioToolkit, and PhysioNet: components of a new research resource for complex physiologic signals. Circulation [Online]. **101**(23), e215–e220 (2000)

16. Tung, T.-H., Wang, S.-H., Huang, C.-C., Su, T.-Y., Lo, C.-M.: Use of discrete wavelet transform to assess impedance fluctuations obtained from cellular micromotion. Sensors **20**(11), 3250 (2020). https://doi.org/10.3390/s20113250

17. Amiri, N., and Naderi, I.: DWT-GBT-SVD-based robust speech steganography. arXiv:2004.12569 (2020)

18. Wang, Q., Ju, S.: A mixed classifier based on combination of HMM and KNN. In: 2008 Fourth International Conference on Natural Computation (2008). https://doi.org/10.1109/icnc.2008.680

19. Taneja, S., Gupta, C., Aggarwal, S., Jindal, V.: MFZ-KNN – a modified fuzzy based k nearest neighbor algorithm. In: 2015 International Conference on Cognitive Computing and Information Processing(CCIP) (2015). https://doi.org/10.1109/ccip.2015.7100689

20. Braga-Neto, U.: Fundamentals of Pattern Recognition and Machine Learning, 1a edn. Springer, Cham (2020). https://doi.org/10.1007/978-3-030-27656-0

21. Kroese, D.P., Botev, Z., Taimre, T., Vaisman, R.: Data Science and Machine Learning: Mathematical and Statistical Methods, 1a edn. CRC Press, London (2019)

22. Phillips, J.M.: Clustering. In: Mathematical Foundations for Data Analysis. SSDS, pp. 177–205. Springer, Cham (2021). https://doi.org/10.1007/978-3-030-62341-8_8

23. Fajardo, L.M.R. (s/f).: Aplicación del algoritmo adaboost rt para la predicción del indice colcap y el diseño de un controlador no lineal. https://repository.udistrital.edu.co/bitstream/handle/11349/5232/ReyesFajardoLauraMarcela2017.pdf?sequence=1&isAllowed=y. Accessed 07 May 2021

24. Yang, X.-S.: Introduction to Algorithms for Data Mining and Machine Learning. Academic Press, San Diego (2019). https://doi.org/10.1016/C2018-0-02034-4

25. Faul, A.C.: A Concise Introduction to Machine Learning, 1st edn. Chapman and Hall/CRC, London (2019). https://doi.org/10.1201/9781351204750

26. Chen, H., et al.: GasHis-transformer: a multi-scale visual transformer approach for gastric histopathology image classification (2021). arXiv:2104.14528

27. Samiuc. https://www.samiuc.es/estadisticas-variables-binarias/medidas-de-conco rdancia/kappa-de-cohen/. Accessed 07 May 2021

28. Chicco, D., Jurman, G.: The advantages of the Matthews correlation coefficient (MCC) over F1 score and accuracy in binary classification evaluation. BMC Genom. **21**(1), 6 (2020). https://doi.org/10.1186/s12864-019-6413-7

29. Sun, Z., Chang, C.: Structural damage assessment based on wavelet packet transform. J. Struct. Eng. **128**(10), 1354–1361 (2002). https://doi.org/10.1061/ (ASCE)0733-9445(2002)128:10(1354)

30. Saraswathy, J., Hariharan, M., Vijean, V., Yaacob, S., Khairunizam, W.: Performance comparison of Daubechies wavelet family in infant cry classification. In: 2012 IEEE 8th International Colloquium on Signal Processing and its Applications, pp. 451–455 (2012). https://doi.org/10.1109/CSPA.2012.6194767

Performance Analysis of S-ALOHA Protocol Under Pareto Distributed Packet Arrival

Mario E. Rivero-Angeles[1]([⊠]) and Izlian Y. Orea-Flores[2]

[1] Centro de Investigación en Computación, CIC-IPN, Mexico City, México
mriveroa@ipn.mx
[2] Unidad Profesional Interdisciplinaria en Ingeniería y Tecnologías Avanzadas, UPIITA-IPN,
Mexico City, Mexico
iorea@ipn.mx

Abstract. This article presents a medium access control mechanism based on the very well-known Slotted ALOHA, using Adaptive Traffic Load (ATL) to stabilize the throughput and access delay under long range dependent traffic and Poisson traffic. We consider a system in which users request a data channel for packet data transmission, where arrivals follow a Poisson distribution, if the request is successful, they transmit their data and release the channel at the end of the transmission. If after the first transmission, users have more packets to transmit, they request a data channel again, but the packet inter-arrival times follow a Pareto distribution. At high traffic loads, the basic idea of ATL is to limit the number of packet transmission for both new and retransmitted users, to avoid collisions and keeping the system stability. We show that S-ALOHA, in spite of its simplicity and low throughput, can provide low delay and latency in the second access channel even in high traffic loads by using the ATL scheme limiting the access to the second access channel. Also, a Pareto-based traffic entails lower transmissions compared to the Poisson traffic.

Keywords: S-ALOHA · Adaptive Traffic Load · Access delay · Pareto inter-arrival times

1 Introduction

There are basically two applications for random access protocols. They have been extensively used for packet data transmission of many users sharing a common channel when the activity factor of the users is low. Also, they have been used for users to content for a data channel (collision-less type) in cellular systems, such as EDGE or GPRS. ALOHA random multiple access is preferred in many cases due to its simplicity and because it does not require many operations nor memory to operate [1–4]. Systems based on the ALOHA protocol basically transmit whenever they have a packet ready to convey to the receiver. In the slotted version, the channel is composed by time slots with fixed duration. The idea behind this is for nodes to wait for the beginning of the time slot to transmit, avoiding unnecessary collisions during ongoing transmissions. Even if

© Springer Nature Switzerland AG 2021
M. F. Mata-Rivera and R. Zagal-Flores (Eds.): WITCOM 2021, CCIS 1430, pp. 186–195, 2021.
https://doi.org/10.1007/978-3-030-89586-0_15

S-ALOHA has better performance than the pure ALOHA protocol, it still has an inadequate performance in terms of low throughput 1, measured as the time that the system conveys information to the receiver, especially when the traffic load is high. Indeed, in this case, throughput is near zero and no packets are successfully transmitted [4]. Data services have a bursty characteristic where we can find a high arrival rate to the system at some instants with high probability and no arrivals for a long period of time. Hence, access techniques should be able to allocate many resources in a decentralized way to reduce delay and increase throughput [2].

As the traffic load increases, conventional ALOHA protocols will not be able to support the number of access to the network. Then we have proposed a way to stabilize this protocol to cope with the grow in the number of users for current and future mobile networks. Since data services have quite different characteristics than conventional voice services, it is of great importance to analyze the performance of this protocol under long-range-dependent traffic. In this paper, as opposed to [5], we do not consider limiting the number of retransmissions to stabilize the protocol under high traffic. Instead, we limit the initial access (with Poisson traffic) since, as we will see in Sect. 5, in this way, S-ALOHA never enters the unstable region. We believe our proposal is preferable because users downloading files under Pareto distributed packet arrival times, retransmit their access packets indefinitely until they can access the channel successfully.

The work presented in this work is a continuation of the work reported previously in [15] and [16] where we now extend the ATL strategy to consider Pareto distributions for the packet arrival process. This has not been considered before and the impact of this fractal distribution has still not been studied in the context of the S-ALOHA protocol.

In this paper, we analyze the behavior of the S-ALOHA random access protocol, in terms of throughput and access delay for data users, under long-range-dependent traffic when the initial access is stabilized by using Adaptive Traffic Load as presented in [6]. The rest of the article is organized as follows. In Sect. 2, we present the basic access method for the system. And the basic idea of Adaptive Traffic Load. Traffic model for initial access as well as for data users in the system is explained in Sect. 3. In Sect. 4, we introduce the traffic load estimation algorithm. In Sect. 5, we present some results of the analysis and conclusions are drawn in Sect. 6.

2 Basic Access Method

To study the effect of the long-range-dependent model on the S-ALOHA protocol we consider two access channels. We consider a channel where traffic is Poisson (we call it first access channel), that is, packet inter-arrival times are exponentially distributed random times. Additionally, we consider an access channel where traffic is long-range-dependent (we call it second access channel), that is, packet inter-arrival times for each user are Pareto distributed random times. Hence, we separate access according to the traffic model in the sense that for the first access channel we only have arrivals following a Poisson process, and for the second access channel we only have long-range-dependent distributed random times.

In the first access channel users that have not yet transmitted any packet in the system arrive, that is users who initiate a session. In the second access channel we have arrivals from users that have more data files to download, and they transmit an access packet to contend for a data channel in the network. Once a user has transmitted a successful packet in the first access channel, he gains access to a collision-less data channel in the system and downloads his data. When transmission is finished, he releases the data channel. For subsequent files, he has to gain access in the second access channel. It is clear however, that if the system only has one random access channel, we will have a combination of exponentially distributed random inter-arrival times (from users initiating a session) and Pareto distributed random inter-arrival times (from users continuing their data transmission). Since S-ALOHA protocols have been extensively studied under a Poisson process, we find it especially useful to study this protocol only under a long-range-dependent traffic model and draw some conclusions from it.

Once users have successfully been granted a data channel, it is considered that the system has enough capacity to attend all users that arrive through the access channels. We define g as the traffic load of the first access channel in users per second and for both channels let T be the time slot and the time required to transmit a packet. For both access channels we assume that all packets are always received correctly if they do not suffer collision and that all packets involved in a collision are not successfully received. Packets that fail in correct reception must be retransmitted until correctly received. Hence, for the first access channel, g accounts for both new and retransmitted packets. Packet generation is inhibited when the terminal is in the retransmission mode. For the second access channel, traffic load varies according to the average session time of data users.

It is well known that random access protocols in general, cannot operate adequately when the traffic load increases beyond a certain value, gmax in our case, which correspond to the point where the throughput reaches the maximum value. To address this issue, we proposed the ATL scheme [6], where the new arrivals to the system are limited by assigning a transmission probability, $p(g) = gmax/g$, i.e., new arrivals are allowed to transmit with probability $p(g)$, and their transmission is differed to a future random time with probability $q(g) = 1 - p(g)$, where g is the actual arrival rate to the system. In view of this, the traffic load is not modified when $g < gmax$ while the arrival rate is kept constant at gmax when $g > gmax$. This transmission probability entails a subdivision of the Poisson process, which produces two new Poisson processes [7].

Building on this, the throughput of the S-ALOHA protocol is given by [4].

$$S_{ALOHA} = gTe^{-gT}, \tag{1}$$

while the troughput of the S-ALOHA protocol with the ATL scheme enabled is given by [6]:

$$S_{ATL\ S\text{-}ALOHA} = g_{max}Te^{-g_{max}T}; \quad \text{for } g > gmax \tag{2}$$

where gmax $= 1/T$, therefore:

$$S_{ATL\ S\text{-}ALOHA} = 1/e; \quad \text{for } g > gmax \tag{3}$$

As we can see from description in this section, ATL is only used when the traffic load is increased beyond gmax which is easy to see in the first access channel, however in the second access channel, we need to investigate if the traffic load is higher than gmax and then decide if ATL is required or not.

3 Traffic Models

As communication networks evolve, there is a greater amount of non-voice traffic, mainly generated by social media, streaming services and data communications in general such as the one generates by the Internet of Things (IoT). For traditional traffic models (voice) we have a Poisson arrival process (although self-similar behavior has been identified [17–19]) while multimedia traffic can be characterized by frequent transmissions between active and inactive states (ON/OFF). The ON period represents the file downloading time and the OFF period is the user reading time [8]. The aggregation of independent ON/OFF sources with heavy tailed ON and/or OFF time distributions explains the burst nature of the traffic in packet data networks [9].

For data services, it is reasonable to assume that session arrival is Poisson with an arrival rate of g users per second, and the duration of each session is exponentially distributed [8, 10]. This means that users initiating a session arrive according to a Poisson process, hence, the time between arrivals in the first access channel follow an exponential distribution. And users remain in the system for an exponential distributed random time.

Packet arrival patterns within the session depend on the application. Traffic analysis in different data networks have shown a heavy-tailed, self-similar, fractal, and LRD characteristics, as described in [8]. One of the most important features of the packet traffic is the self-similar characteristic, which implies that the size and time between packets have an infinite variance. This means that for any user, packet inter-arrival time and packet size can be exceedingly long with a non-negligible probability. The Pareto distribution is the simplest heavy tailed distribution and has been used extensively to model the data-packet networks traffic behavior.

In this paper we focused on the www traffic. For www traffic the data traffic models, and their numerical parameters are summarized in Table 1. The ON period distribution is based on the file size and the available downlink bandwidth, were k_{ON} is the minimum file size in bytes during the ON period, we consider only text downloads with sizes less than 1000 bytes. In this paper we consider a data rate of 11.2 kbps, commonly found in cellular systems [11], therefore, the minimum time for the ON period is given by:

$$\text{Minimum Download Time} = \frac{(\text{Minimum File size (kbytes)}) * 8}{11.2 \text{ (kbits/sec)}} = 0.714\,\text{s} \quad (4)$$

The OFF-period distribution is based on the user's reading time, where k_{OFF} is the minimum time required by the user to read a web page and is of 30 s.

Considering this model, users transmit their packets according to Fig. 1. Notice that we want only long-range-dependent traffic in the second access channel, therefore, retransmissions in this channel also follow a Pareto distribution which could lead to higher access delay times as opposed to exponential distributed retransmission times in the first access channel.

The random-access packet has a fixed length and is the same for both the first and second access channels.

Table 1. Values for www traffic model

Period	Distribution	Formula	Parameters
ON	Pareto	$F_{ON}(x) = 1 - \left(\frac{k}{x}\right)^{\alpha}$	$k_{ON} = 1000$ bytes $\alpha_{ON} = 1.1 - 1.5$
OFF	Pareto	$F_{OFF}(t) = 1 - \left(\frac{k}{t}\right)^{\alpha}$	$k_{OFF} = 30$ s $\alpha_{OFF} = 1.5$

4   Traffic Load Estimation

As it will be seen in next section, the use of the ATL protocol has no effect on the second access channel, since traffic load is not high enough to cause the protocol to become unstable due to a high number of collisions, even if bursts of traffic occur.

For the first access channel, the access probability introduced by the ATL protocol requires the exact knowledge of the average traffic load, which is exceedingly difficult. We propose a quite simple algorithm to estimate the traffic load without the use of estimators or previous estimations. In general, there could be two different periods, as proposed by [12]. In one period the traffic load is estimated and in the second period this estimated load is applied to the system. For simplicity we assume that they have the same length. The algorithm estimates the load in an estimation period and this estimate is applied during the whole duration of the next estimation period. The algorithm is as follows:

- Step 1: Estimate the probability of finding an empty slot in an estimation period as:

$$P_{empty\_slot} = \frac{\text{Total Number of Empty Slots}}{\text{Total Number of slots}} \qquad (5)$$

- Step 2: Calculate the estimated traffic load. Theoretically:

$$P_{empty\_slot} = P[\text{No access in T sec}] = e^{-p_{ATL}gT} \qquad (6)$$

where g is the real traffic load. If we know the exact value of g, then $p_{ATL} = g_{max}/g$ and (6) becomes $e^{-g_{max}}$.

Since we do not know the value of the actual traffic load or the value of the authorization probability, we make an overestimation of the traffic load by considering $p_{ATL} = 1$. Hence:

$$g_{est} = -\frac{1}{T}ln(P_{empty\_slot}) \tag{7}$$

- Step 3: If $g > g_{max}$, then $p_{ATL} = 1$
  Else $(g > g_{max})$.

We know that when $g > g_{max}$, the probability of finding an empty slot is given by the probability that no users generate packets or the probability that one user generates a packet and it is not allowed to transmit or the probability that two users generates packets and they are not allowed to transmit them, and so on, hence:

$$P(N(T) = 0) = e^{-G} + \left(1 - \frac{G_{max}}{G}\right)Ge^{-G} + \left(1 - \frac{G_{max}}{G}\right)^2\frac{G^2e^{-G}}{2!} + \cdots$$

$$= \sum_{i=0}^{\infty}\left(1 - \frac{G_{max}}{G}\right)\frac{G^ie^{-G}}{i!} = e^{-G_{max}} \tag{8}$$

Where $G = gT$, substituting (8) and the estimated load of (7) in (8), we get:

$$p_{ATL} = \frac{1}{g_{est}}\left[-\frac{1}{T}ln\left(e^{-g_{max}T}\right)\right] = \frac{g_{max}}{g_{est}} = \frac{g_{max}}{-\frac{1}{T}ln(P_{empty\_slot})} \tag{9}$$

In our previous work presented in [15], we proposed an algorithm to estimate the actual traffic load based on the measurement of the empty slot probability depicted in (9).

5 Numerical Results

In this section we present performance results considering the ATL scheme, using the traffic estimation presented in Sect. 4. For illustrative purposes, we consider the EDGE cellular system parameters [13] to evaluate the performance of our proposal. Specifically, there are 4 access opportunities every 20 ms, once every 4.615 ms. Then, the time slot is settled as $T = 4.615$ ms. The time slot is assumed to be constant and sufficiently large to transmit the data needed to stablish a new packet-based connection. During this session, users transmit packets during the ON periods and remain silent during the OFF periods, where the assigned channel can be assigned to other users active in the network. When more data is required to be transmitted, the node contends to access the system but now in the second access channel.

The throughput of the aforementioned system has been extensively studied before in [15] and [16]. Hence, we do not focus on this performance metric. However, we do not omit to mention that the throughput is maintained constant for traffic loads higher than gmax at both the first and second access channels. Another important observation is that as we increment the average session time, throughput for the second channel is incremented until a certain limit, where it will not be further increased. This is because for extremely high ST (around 10000 s) all users accessing successfully to the system, remain active in the second access channel transmitting, and will not leave the system for the duration of the simulation. Therefore, if we keep incrementing the ST (100000 s) this number of active users in the second access channel remains the same as before. This can be seen in Fig. 1.

Now, we investigate the performance at the second access channel, presented in Fig. 2. In this figure we show the traffic load that successfully entered to the second channel, considering that some transmissions in the first access channels experience collisions or are restricted by the ATL scheme. We can see that the transmission attempts for the Pareto distributed ON and OFF times is lower compared to the Poisson model. Hence, we can conclude that these lower values are not the result of the higher number of collisions but rather, is the result of longer ON/OFF times. For current and future services, this is an important results since it is not necessary to highly limit transmission in the second access channels when LRD-type traffic is presented. Conversely, of the service generates a Poisson traffic in the second access channel, it may have to be further limited to reduce collisions.

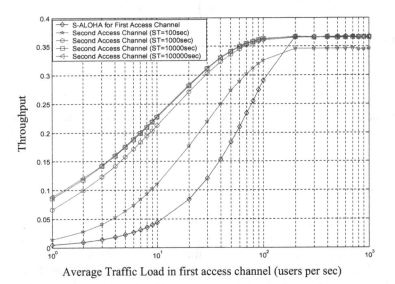

Fig. 1. Traffic load in the first access channel for an infinite population.

For the average access delay in the second access channel, it remains constant at 0.0023 s as depicted in Fig. 3. As we have seen, since the S-ALOHA protocol is in the stable region, access delay is kept constant for all traffic load values and never increases. This effect is caused because the number of collisions is relatively small since in average, we have less than one arrival per slot time and the number of retransmissions is very small. As opposed to the first access channel where for traffic loads higher than gmax access delay is increased exponentially for the conventional protocol and increases linearly for the ATL S-ALOHA protocol. A detailed analysis is presented in [14].

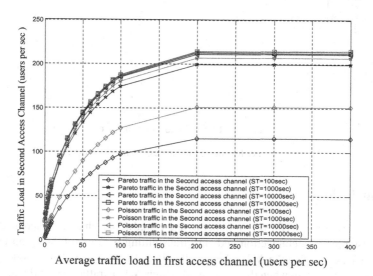

Fig. 2. Traffic load in the second access channel.

The average traffic load changes from 200 to 1000 users per second in steps of 200 users per second. We can see that for light conditions of traffic load, the estimation is very close to the real value, but for high traffic loads (higher than 600 users per second) the estimation is not as accurate. This effect is because the probability of finding an empty slot in a high arrival rate condition is very small and the estimate period is not long enough to accurately measure this probability according to (5). Nonetheless, this error is very small and as we shall see later in this section it does not have a big impact on the performance of the system. We can see that the estimation algorithm can follow the changes in the traffic load in any direction.

To further investigate the effect of the length of the estimation period in the performance of the system we obtain the throughput for different values of this period and observe the degradation in the system as shown in Fig. 3. We can see that the bigger the estimation period is, the more accurate is the estimation of the traffic load. When the estimation period decreases the number of empty slots counted in the estimation period is not reliable to calculate the probability of finding an empty slot, thus causing more error in the estimation of (5), especially for high traffic loads where most of the slots are busy. However, using an estimation period of 500 time slots (2.3075 s), we can see that the error is maintained less than 5% even for very high traffic loads.

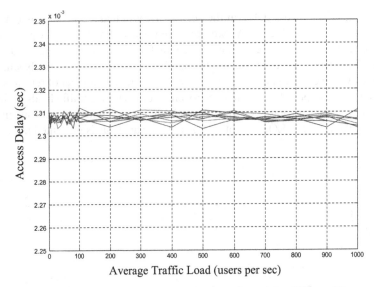

Fig. 3. Access delay for the second access channel for different ST.

6   Conclusions

In this work, we focus on the performance of the second access channel, where nodes have already established a connection and start transmitting packets following an ON/OFF scheme. We can see that the ATL scheme, effectively limits the number of nodes accessing this second channel when the traffic load is high. When traffic load at the first access channel is low, the ATL scheme has no effect on the number of nodes accessing the system. These results are important and can be used as design guidelines in the context of 5G communications systems where latency is a major performance parameter for non-tolerant delay services and low latency applications. Indeed, effectively limiting the number of nodes accessing the second access channel can lead to adequate performance even if a simple random access protocol, such as S-ALOHA is used in conjunction with the ATL scheme.

References

1. Sallent, O., Agustí, R.: Adaptive S-ALOHA CDMA as an alternative way of integrating services in mobile environments. IEEE Trans. Veh. Technol. **49**, 936–947 (2000)
2. Liang, Z.: Advances in ALOHA random multiple access techniques. Int. J. Commun. Syst. **13**, 353–364 (2000)
3. Linnartz, J.P.: Narrow Band Land-Mobile Radio Networks. Artech House, p. 168 (1993)
4. Rom, R., Sidi, M.: Multiple Access Protocols. Performance and Analysis, pp. 47–103. Springer, Heidelberg (1990). https://doi.org/10.1007/978-1-4612-3402-9
5. Harpantidou, Z., Paterakis, M.: Random multiple access of broadcast channels with Pareto distributed packet inerarrival times. IEEE Pers. Commun. **5**, 48–55 (1998)

6. Rivero-Angeles, M., Lara-Rodríguez, D., Cruz-Pérez, F.: A new EDGE medium access control mechanism using adaptive traffic load slotted ALOHA. In: IEEE VTC, Fall 2001, Atlantic City, NJ, pp. 1358–1362, October 2001

7. Gallager, R.G.: Discrete Stochastic Processes. Kluwer Academic Publishers, Boston (1996)

8. Jamalipour, A.: The Wireless Mobile Internet. Wiley, New York (2003)

9. Willinger, W., Taqqu, M.S., Sherman, R., Wilson, D.V.: Self-similarity through high-variability: statistical analysis of Ethernet LAN traffic at the source level. IEEE/ACM Trans. Netw. 5(1), 71–86 (1997)

10. Zukerman, M., Neame, T.D., Addie, R.G.: Internet traffic modeling and future technology implications. In: IEEE INFOCOM 2003, 30 March–3 April 2003, pp. 587–596 (2003)

11. Furuskar, A., Mazur, S., Muller, F., Olofsson, H.: EDGE: enhanced data rates for GSM and TDMA/136 evolution. IEEE Pers. Commun. 6, 56–66 (1999)

12. Naor, Z., Levy, H.: A centralized dynamic access probability protocol for next generation wireless networks. In: IEEE INFOCOM 2001, vol. 2, pp. 767–775 (2001)

13. Qiu, X., Chawla, K., Chang, L.F., Chuang, J., Sollenberger, N., Whitehead, J.: RLC/MAC design alternatives for supporting integrated services over EGPRS. IEEE Pers. Commun. 7, 20–33 (2000)

14. Rivero-Angeles, M., Lara-Rodríguez, D., Cruz-Pérez, F.: Access delay analysis of adaptive traffic load-type protocols for S-ALOHA and CSMA in EDGE. In: IEEE WCNC 2003, New Orleans, March 2003

15. Rivero-Ángeles, M., Lara-Rodríguez, D., Cruz-Pérez, F.: Random access control mechanism using adaptive traffic load in S-ALOHA and CSMA strategies in EDGE. IEEE Trans. Veh. Technol. 54(3), 1160–1186 (2005). ISSN 0018-954

16. Rivero-Ángeles, M., Lara-Rodríguez, D., Cruz-Pérez, F.: Performance evaluation of edge under S-ALOHA and adaptive traffic load S-ALOHA random access protocols. In: IEEE Vehicular Technology Conference, Milan, Italy, Spring - May 2004, vol. 4, pp. 2291–2295 (2004)

17. Vazquez-Avila, J.L., Sandoval-Arechiga, R., Perez-Ramirez, A., Sanchez-Lara, R., Toral-Cruz, H., El Hamzaoui, Y.: A fast simulation model based on Lindley's recursion for the G/G/1/K queue. Math. Probl. Eng. 19, 1–11 (2019). https://doi.org/10.1155/2019/3464389

18. Toral-Cruz, H., Al-Sakib, K.P., Ramírez Pacheco, J.C.: Accurate modeling of VoIP traffic in modern communication networks. In: IET Book Series on Big Data: Modeling and Simulation of Complex Networks, Institution of Engineering & Technology (IET), pp. 175–208 (2019). https://doi.org/10.1049/pbpc018e_ch7

19. Toral-Cruz, H., Al-Sakib, K.P., Ramírez Pacheco, J.C.: Accurate modeling of VoIP traffic QoS parameters in current and future networks with multifractal and Markov models. Math. Comput. Model. J. 57(11–12), 2832–2845 (2013). https://doi.org/10.1016/j.mcm.2011.12.007

Learning Through Interactive Vicarious and Social Experiences, an Alternative to Developing Teaching Training Processes in Ict Skills

L. J. Rengifo-Arcos[1]([✉]) [iD], L. F. Maldonado-Granados[1] [iD],
and Y. A. Méndez-Alegría[2] [iD]

[1] Faculty of Education, University of San Buenaventura Cali, Cali, Colombia
[2] Vice-Rectory of Research. Cybersecurity Research Center, University Mayor,
Providencia, Chile
yenny.mendez@umayor.cl

Abstract. In this writing, we briefly talk about a training proposal for undergraduate students, in which they are involved in two types of learning experiences, which allows them to acquire not only the knowledge in ICT skills necessary for the design of learning content making use of information and communication technologies (ICT) but also manage to apply their resource in a work context such as a class with primary school children.

In the training process, a portion of the graduates is trained with the vicar experience through videos, where a model teacher is shown who develops and applies a learning content of work. The other students are incorporated into a training process with interactive social experience through instructions in a teacher-student relationship to the elaboration and learning content.

The research aims to arrive at results that indicate which of the two experiences allows the greatest acquisition and transfer of ICT skills to the labor field.

Keywords: Teacher training · Teacher competence · ICT · Learning experience · Vicarious experience

1 Introduction

Amid the current landscape and the global crisis, the need to link technology in training processes and work in some professions is increased. This means that teachers must make frequent use of ICTs for teaching; for this, it is necessary to train teachers with new procedures that ensure that their knowledge in the formative stage applies it to their work environment.

In addition to this need, educational proposals have been developed for teachers in training and exercise, some in countries such as Chile [1], Spain [2], Europa [3], Colombia [4], among others, propose skills that allow the development of skills in teachers to effectively involve ICTs in the classroom, which leads to the massification of

---

The original version of this chapter was revised: The authors names have been revised as L.J. Rengifo-Arcos, L.F. Maldonado-Granados, and Y.A. Méndez Alegría. The correction to this chapter is available at https://doi.org/10.1007/978-3-030-89586-0_20

© Springer Nature Switzerland AG 2021, corrected publication 2022
M. F. Mata-Rivera and R. Zagal-Flores (Eds.): WITCOM 2021, CCIS 1430, pp. 196–206, 2021.
https://doi.org/10.1007/978-3-030-89586-0_16

the use of technologies to improve the quality of life, educational processes and promote the modernization of public institutions. However, it is clear that, in work practice, teachers are not making continuous use of technologies for teaching and learning. As part of the development, this study is carried out, a survey of teachers of primary and middle school, in addition to an analysis of the degree programs of the most concurrent universities in the city of Cali, showing formative shortcomings for the learning and transfer of ICT competencies of professionals, which makes them not have the necessary skills to design their learning content and involve them in the development of their classes.

An alternative solution to this problem of teacher training is to develop a contextualized training proposal based on experiences, vicarious and interactive social. In 1977, Bandura proposed the concept of vicar learning within his theory of social learning. It is characterized by its interest in learning by observation or example, and not always through direct strengthening, and it is learned because of vicarious reinforcement when observations are made of the behavior of others and their consequences. In 1995, a team of Italian neurobiologists, led by G. Rizzolatti of the University of Parma, found a mechanism in the brain whose neurobiological basis is neurons of action not before seen, was called mirror neurons because they reflect the action of other individuals in the brain. States that "When these neurons are activated, an internal motor representation of the act that the animal observes is generated, which would make it possible to learn by imitation. That is, it allows the recognition and understanding of the actions of others." [5]. "Most of the images of reality on which we base our actions are truly inspired by the experience we gain through others (vicar experience)" [6]. Other research indicates that television programs, videos, games, and more also influence, allowing to acquire knowledge, skills, standards, patterns of behaviors, beliefs, and strategies. On the other hand, interactive social experience, whether in teacher-student or peer relationships, generates training of concepts and activation of motor actions that lead to the development of metacognitive skills.

In this sense, the research question is: Does learning based on vicar experiences increase the transfer of acquired skills than learning based on interactive social experience? For its development, processes are made to transfer learning ICT skills between environments, specifically from the training environment to the work environment and compare which two experiences is most effective. The methodology carried out focuses on the design of a training proposal that links; the vicarious experience (which in this study is based on the observation of videos) and the interactive social experience (in which symbolic and language elements are introduced into the permanent interaction between the teacher and the student). These experiences should give teachers in training the possibility to learn the ICT skills they require to develop learning content supported by ICT and teach the concept of subject matter. The activities designed for the training of teachers include the problem questions to be solved, questions of the judgment of metamemory, the actions that they must perform for the design of learning content, and finally perform a real practice, where the competencies acquired and transmitted to the labor field are evaluated.

The remainder of this paper is organized as follows. Firs, Sect. 2 presents the development of the research. Then, Sect. 3 describes the results. Finally, Sect. 4 summarizes the concluding remarks and provides some potential avenues for future work.

2 Methodology of Design and Validation

For the development of research, we opt for the design of learning experiences for teacher training, since the learning of complex skills is presented when students observe models that develop them and then practice them, that is, observed the interaction of another subject with elements of their environment obtaining the solution of a problem.

2.1 Graduate Training Based on Learning Experience Design

Neuroscience studies indicate that cognitive processes are influenced by sensorimotor systems, emotions, and body movements. In addition to individuals interacting with their environment, the brain is stimulated to make neural connections that allow it to perceive it, activating the motor system that uses available elements (technological devices), executing actions to control that environment, and making subsequent representations [7]. This sense looks at the training processes; students watch the teachers demonstrate their skills during their practice, providing corrective information to perfect the skill they are learning or already acquired. In a virtual, face-to-face, or mixed classroom environment like the ones we are presenting today in schools, the teacher must create better ways to take advantage of ICT in their field of work, a situation that must activate the sensorimotor capacity of the teacher in training, allowing him to execute actions that lead him to consolidate his skills or expertise.

It is then that this proposal links ICT activities and competences for the elaboration of learning content, selecting the appropriate tools to the contextual and learning needs.

For shaping the activities and competencies, expert validation is used to ensure that the competencies are of the ICT category have educational relevance in research (See the Fig. 1). For this, the revision of the proposal is requested to two expert teachers with knowledge in graduate training and ICT skills.

For the preparation of the proposal, the following questions are considered:

¿Who is it formed for? The activities are designed for two groups of students of bachelor's degree in natural sciences from the University of Valle involved in two types of experiences (vicaria and social-interactive).

¿What is the form? so that future teachers live learning experiences in which they develop the ICT skills necessary for the design and application of learning content supported by ICT, in a real context of virtual, face-to-face, or mixed classroom, taking into account the resources available in homes and educational institutions.

¿What develops? design of learning experiences, content, information systems, and learning to monitor.

¿How does it develop? the group linked to the vicarious experience is formed from the observation of videos, where one teacher models, designs, and executes a natural sciences class making use of ICT, the other group of students are formed through the interactive social experience following instructions and continuous feedback that allows us to maintain a teacher-student relationship using tools such as email, chat, video calls, in the tutorials for the acquisition of knowledge necessary for the development of virtual, face-to-face or mixed educational practice.

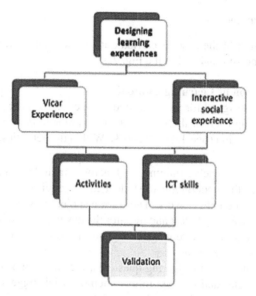

Fig. 1. Formative proposal based on the design of learning experiences.

¿What is it developing with? Both experiences use word processors, email, web browser, applications to develop meetings, chat, designing evaluative games, videos, images.

¿How is it determined that it has been learned? Indicates whether the undergraduate student has learned by the amount and level of assessment of competencies they managed to acquire and transfer in the field of work, the number of problems and exercises they managed to solve, the time required by each student, up to the minimum yield of 75. If the level is lower, an improvement plan is developed to strengthen those competencies.

2.2 Purposes

For the training proposal, it has been established as purposes that:

- From the interactive vicar and social experiences, the trainees can acquire the skills, disciplinary pedagogical, technological, didactic and evaluative, necessary to solve a set of problems that lead them to the design of learning content.
- In developing ICT competencies, the trainees can integrate knowledge with their ability to perceive, emotion and, activate actions when using technological devices.
- The trainees can bring ICT skills to work through the application of the prepared learning content.

2.3 Proposal of Procedure

Below is a description of the process carried out for the methodological design of the training proposal and summarized in the Fig. 2.

Design and Validation of Learning Content

Learning content is designed for vicarious and interactive social experiences. The four activities that make up each of these contents are similar in both experiences and are subject to expert validation (See Tables 2 and 3). Within the activities, they are included:

- ICT competencies for teacher training, each activity includes competencies with the performances that the undergraduate student must acquire during his training and transfer process to the field of work. These were subject to validation.
- A set of learning problems to test and monitor the development of competencies. The number of problems must be representative and linked to the content to identify the learning state of the competencies.
- A set of metamemory trial triggering questions, the two groups of students train to use learning strategies and respond to metamemory trial triggers. It can control the rule out learning autonomy deficiencies as a determining factor in transfer gaps.

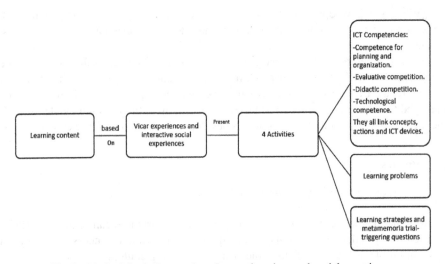

Fig. 2. Methodological procedure. Interactive vicar and social experience.

Design and Validation of ICT Competency Space for Teacher Training

Considering that for the development of this proposal, a person competent in ICT can integrate their knowledge to their ability to perceive the world, activate actions, use devices, self-control, and get excited (knowledge, perception, action, action, devices, emotion). A competence space is designed with a specific ICT concept, actions and devices (See Table 1).

Table 1. ICT competency area for teacher training

Concept	Action						
	Plan	Organize	Expressing strengths and weaknesses	Integrate	To find	Select	Use
Learning content	-Office tools -Multimedia applications	-Office tools -Multimedia applications			-Images -Videos -Text processors -Internet -Multimedia applications	-Images -Videos -Text processors - Internet -Multimedia applications	-Images -Videos -Text processors - Internet -Multimedia applications
Learning process			-Office tools -Multimedia applications				
Classroom practices				-Office tools -Multimedia applications -Internet			

ICT competencies designed with their performances are subject to expert validation (See Table 4). These apply to the work field, activate the perception and motivation or emotion of the subject with a model situation (the one shown in the experience), in the same way, relate the concept to be learned, with the device to be used and generate the motor and analysis actions that allow him to generate the necessary knowledge to create mechanisms of interaction with his work environment.

The ICT competencies developed and validated by experts for this proposal are:

Competence for Planning and Organization. Ability to use office tools and multimedia applications to plan and organize learning content.
    Performance criteria:

CP1: Uses word processor, presentation program among others, in the organization of learning content articulating the curriculum, purposes, and cognitive level of its students.
CP2: Design your learning content in a presentation program, demonstrating pedagogical and disciplinary mastery.
CP3: Links families in the process of training or reinforcing what they have learned through applications that combine text, graphics, sound, images, animation, and video.

Didactic Competence. Ability to integrate office tools, internet browser, and multimedia applications during classroom practices.
    Performance criteria:

CD1: It uses a word processor, presentation program, internet browser, multimedia applications, among others, to carry out its pedagogical practice considering the availability of technological tools and interests of its students.

CD2: Through a video conference application, it promotes some strategies of participation of the students that favor their learning such as posing questions to verify what they have learned, using examples to make clarifications, resolving concerns in class.
CD3: Integrates presentation programs, multimedia applications, among others that generate interest from students and that support the development of the group or individual activities focused on the fulfillment of the purposes, evaluation, and reinforcement of what has been learned and relationship with the context.

Evaluative Competence. Ability to use office tools and multimedia applications to express the strengths and weaknesses of your learning process.
   Performance criteria:

CE1: In a text presentation program, it indicates the advantages and disadvantages over the design of ICT-mediated learning content, observed during its training process.
CE2: Presents through a short video made by cell phone, the strengths and difficulties generated in the application of the learning content with your students and indicates how to correct them.
CE3: Prepares a registration table with the help of a word processor in which it specifies its ease or difficulty in solving the problems, the time it takes, and the effort required to solve them during its training process.

Technological Competence. Ability to search, select and use images, videos, word processors, presentation programs, internet and multimedia applications in the development of learning content.
   Performance criteria:

CT1: Search, choose and download from the Internet the disciplinary content (texts, images and videos) appropriate to the cognitive level of your students, classroom plan and learning purposes.
CT2: Copy, paste or insert text, images, tables, videos among others, to create learning content using word processors and / or presentation programs.
CT3: Create email and event schedule for the development of a virtual class by video conference.
CT4: Makes use of multimedia applications to create evaluative questionnaires for your students.

3   Analysis of Results

A survey[1] is conducted among 18 teachers belonging to three public institutions of primary education. It is found that 89% of teachers recognize the importance of using ICT in their student's teaching and learning processes; but, they do not always use them, sometimes due to an insufficient number of equipment, demanding access to these, or little internet connection in educational institutions. Of these, 33% of teachers do not

---

[1] A survey conducted by researchers.

know the management of programs, platforms, or computer resources to design learning content; they do not have ICT training. These data give us to understand that a significant number of teachers do not keep up to date in pedagogical and didactic knowledge and do not use technological didactic resources or means, even if they have the instruction. Consequently, the academic programs of the faculties of education of the most recognized universities in the city of Cali were reviewed, finding that in two of six universities, they offer ICT training courses to their graduates.

The Universidad del Valle has 14 bachelor's degree programs, but only 50% of these offer ICT training courses; the University Santiago de Cali has seven programs in total but 86%, of these offers training in ICT, the San Buenaventura University has three programs offering 67% of training in ICT, the Antonio José Camacho University Institution has two programs and offers 0%, of ICT training, the Icesi University has five programs and the Catholic University three, both offer 100% ICT training. (See the Fig. 3).

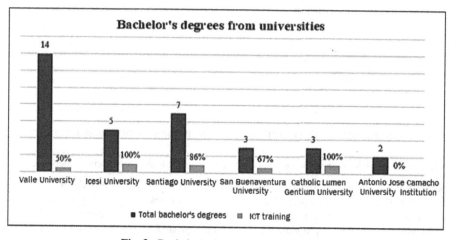

Fig. 3. Bachelor's degrees from universities.

It is essential to address training processes that correctly link the use of ICTs, more in these times than virtual education prevails. It is noted that, as a result of training skills, a considerable number of teachers replicate traditional methods in their field of work, do not design new ICT-supported learning proposals, and if they develop them, they focus on the transfer of knowledge. It is noted that those who have been trained learn to design educational proposals by efficiently integrating ICTs; however, many do not continue with these initiatives in their field of work. The previous training environment that generates experiences can induce future educators' teaching while generating low transfer of what they learn in their training environment to the work exercise.

The observations made by the evaluators against the competencies and training activities are shown in the following tables:

Table 2. Expert validation of activities that make up the vicarious experience.

Activity 1	Activity 2	Activity 3	Activity 4
For validators competencies, resources are appropriate for problem solving and the training strategy from experience is appropriate. One of the validators suggests that there are two teaching models to be observed	For validators competencies, resources are appropriate for problem solving and the training strategy from experience is appropriate. It is suggested to change the problem because the activity is focused on how to obtain the material	For validators competencies, resources are appropriate for problem solving and the training strategy from experience is appropriate. It is suggested that the problem should arise in terms of the characteristics of activities rather than types of activities	For validators competencies, resources are appropriate for problem solving and the training strategy from experience is appropriate

Validation of activity plan for learning content development Vicar Experience

Table 3. Expert validation of activities that make up the interactive social experience

Validation of activity plan for learning content development Interactive Social Experience

Activity 1	Activity 2	Activity 3	Activity 4
Competencies, resources are appropriate for solving the problem and the training strategy from experience is appropriate for one of the validators, but moderately suitable for the other, however so far, the reason is unknown	Competencies, resources are appropriate for solving the problem and the training strategy from experience is suitable for one of the validators, but moderately suitable for others, the observation is to list the characteristics of the materials so that trained teachers choose which one to use	Competencies, resources are appropriate for problem solving and the training strategy from experience is appropriate for validators. However, it is noted that the problem should ask for characteristics without the types of learning	Competencies, resources are appropriate for problem solving and the training strategy from experience is appropriate for validators

Table 4. Validation of ICT skills experts.

Validation of ICT Skills for Teacher Training

Pedagogical competition and discipline	Evaluative Competition	Didactic competition	Technology Competition
Its definition and performance are moderately adequate, since it should be possible to use various office and technological tools, in addition the name of the competition is very broad to deal only with planning actions, in this case in one of the performances the purposes are not developed but are postulated	Its definition and performance are moderately adequate, since it should be given the possibility to use various office and technological tools, and it is also not clear whether it is referred to the learning of the student or the teacher	Its definition and performance are adequate, without embarking the term "technological tools" must be added before listing the possibilities. In addition, you might think that the third performance belongs to a higher level of knowledge such as evaluating or creating	Its definition and performance are adequate. No additional observations are made

4 Conclusions

The research process developed to express whether learning from vicar experiences increases the transfer of skills compared to those acquired by learning based on interactive social experience is still in methodological development. Therefore, no results tell us which of the two experiences best ensures transferring skills from the training field to the work field.

The learning of complex skills is presented when students observe models that develop them and then practice them. In this sense, students watch teachers explain and demonstrate their skills. The practice provides teachers with opportunities to provide corrective information to students to hone the skill acquired that require their students to acquire (Schunk, 2012).

This research intends to open new opportunities to rethink the concept of ICT skills for training and rescue the ability of imitation so that teachers develop learning processes for their excellent development in work practice, whether virtual, face-to-face or mixed.

References

1. Silva Quiroz, J.: ICT Standards for Initial Training Teacher in the Chilean context: Strategies for dissemination and adoption, First edn. Chilean Ministry of Education, Links education and technology center Chile, Valparaiso (2009)

2. Prendes Espinosa, M.P.: ICT skills for teaching at the Spanish public university: indicators and proposals for the definition of good practices: Study and analysis program. Report of project EA2009-0133 of the Secretariat of State of universities and research. Electronic version, pp.1–304. Ministry of Education government of Spain, University of Murcia, Murcia (2010)
3. United Nations Education, Science and Culture Organization: Framework for teachers' competences in ICT UNESCO, pp. 1–64. Unesco, Francia (2019)
4. Ministry of National Education - MEN: ICT skills for teaching professional development, pp. 1–72. United Nations Education, Bogota (2013)
5. Rubia Vila, F.J.: Annals royal national academy medicine. Mirror neurons, 2nd edn., tomo. CXXVIII. Royal National Academy of Medicine, Madrid (2011)
6. Sanchez Sixdos, P.: Albert Bandura and his theory of social learning (TAS) Educational implications, from Cognifit. Health, Brain & Neuroscience (2017). https://blog.cognifit.com/es/al. Accessed 01 Aug 2021
7. Dove, G.: How to go beyond the body: an introduction. Front. Psychol. 6(660), 1–3 (2015)

Analysis of User Generated Content Based on a Recommender System and Augmented Reality

Fernando González[1], Giovanni Guzmán[1(✉)] ⓘ, Miguel Torres-Ruiz[1] ⓘ, Grigori Sidorov[1] ⓘ, and Félix Mata-Rivera[2] ⓘ

[1] Instituto Politécnico Nacional, CIC, UPALM – Zacatenco, 07738 Mexico City, Mexico
{fgonzaleza2021,jguzmanl,mtorres,sidorov}@cic.ipn.mx
[2] Instituto Politécnico Nacional, UPIITA, UPALM – Zacatenco, 07738 Mexico City, Mexico
mmatar@ipn.mx

Abstract. Recommender systems have demonstrated to be very useful in various research areas such as education, e-government, e-commerce, and collaborative and entertainment applications. These systems are based on a set of preferences that aim to help users make decisions by offering different items or services that might interest them. However, by using traditional search approaches, the user often obtains results that do not match the desired interests. Thus, a new search approach is required to use semantic-based retrieval techniques to generate conceptually close results to user preferences. In this paper, a methodology to retrieve information about user preferences based on a recommender system and augmented reality is proposed. As a case study, an Android mobile application was implemented, considering augmented reality to recommend multiplex cinemas that are generated from the genres of movies preferred by users and their geographical location at the time of the search.

Keywords: Augmented reality applications · Recommender system · Semantic similarity computation · Semantic-based retrieval

1 Introduction

Recommender systems assist and provide more information for decision-making by the user. However, there are errors since the recommendations are not precise regarding the requests made by the user and that generally, the search causes that the precise data does not match the parameters convenient for the user. Resnick and Varian proposed a method for making decisions without having experience [1], obtaining information from third parties to offer person-to-person recommendations. These recommendations encompass several fields, including e-commerce, restaurant guides, and tourist attractions.

Thus, the objective of proposing personalized searches is to show users personalized results according to the information users need. The custom search strategy is based on two categories: the first one, is the expansion of the search as developed by Chirita et al. [2], in which reference is made to the possibility of modifying the original search in

© Springer Nature Switzerland AG 2021
M. F. Mata-Rivera and R. Zagal-Flores (Eds.): WITCOM 2021, CCIS 1430, pp. 207–228, 2021.
https://doi.org/10.1007/978-3-030-89586-0_17

two ways, expanding it with other terms, or assigning levels of importance to the terms used in the search; and the second one, reclassifying it, which tailors the search results to personal preferences of the user. Several reclassification strategies try to build a user profile from the point of view of a historical behavior, to be able to use that profile and thus filter the resources that are not of interest to the user. In [3], Pretschner and Gauch proposed structured user profiles with an ontology, which was composed of 4,400 nodes. Moreover, Chirita et al. modeled both user profiles and resources - topical vectors of the Dmoz hierarchy - as well as a match between user interests [2].

In recommendation systems, the user profile is one of the most important data since the system requires user information to be able to recommend or filter the content in a personalized way for each of the users. A system needs a priori information from each of the users to be able to provide results that are adapted to the needs of each one. Generally, the user profile is created based on the information that the system needs or should know about the user. This information can be about general information (for example, name, age, and gender), the behavior of the user, data related to the user's social context, their interests, among others.

The user profile should contain as much information as possible about a user's interests as well as other contextual information about their searches. If the user profile contains the user's real-time location, this can be used to provide results taking into account the distance from the geographic location of both the user and the search results. Displaying the information taking into consideration the geographical location is more relevant for the user than only showing the results since these are not feasible to be used due to their distance from each other. User interests turn out to be the most important information in recommendation systems. User preferences can be used to locate content that best suits their needs [8]. The importance of modeling the user's profile and access to personalized information has increased due to a large amount of information available on the Internet, in digital libraries, and other media. Users require personalized attention in their searches using a large amount of information retrieved according to their interests. The retrieval systems adapt their operation to individual users, processing their preferences during the interaction to build a user profile that can be used in the search process.

The paper is organized as follows: Sect. 2 presents the state-of-the-art concerning this research. Section 3 describes the proposed methodology to tackle the issues. The analysis and experimental results are depicted in Sect. 4. Finally, the conclusion and future work is outlined in Sect. 5.

2 Related Work

Carrer-Neto et al. mentioned that with the arrival of the social web and the growing popularity of Web 2.0 applications, these become relevant and give a boost to the recommendation systems [4]. The recommendations generated by these recommender systems are aimed at providing end-users with suggestions about social elements, features of information, products, or services that could be of interest to the user, for instance, about music or movies recommendations [9, 10]. It is also mentioned that the system's recommendations based on traditional syntactic techniques suffer from a series of deficiencies the which hampers its effectiveness. So, as semantic technologies mature, they provide a consistent and reliable basis to deal with data at the knowledge level, adding techniques semantically empowered for recommender systems, with which they can be improved significantly the overall quality of the recommendations. Christakou & Stafylopatis explained how Artificial Intelligence can help with the problem of finding information successfully [5]. Recommendation systems provide a solution to this problem, giving individualized recommendations, which are based on the content and collaborative filtering; these are generally applied to predict these recommendations. Bobadilla et al. pointed out that research on recommendation systems requires the use of a representative set of public databases to facilitate research on approaches, processes, and algorithms formulated by scientists in the area [6]. With this information, the scenarios to corroborate, compare and enhance the techniques, could be recreated by specialists, to define the characteristics that a user profile should meet, its indicators of interest, and describe some approaches to modeling a user profile such as:

- *Vector representation.* The classic vector space model is used and the profile is represented employing an m-dimensional vector; where each feature represents one dimension.
- *Representation by connection.* This approach uses an associative interconnection of the nodes for representing the user profile.
- *Ontological-based representation.* This representation describes the semantic relationships between information of the user profile. A hierarchy of concepts represents the user profile, where each concept class in the hierarchy defines knowledge in some area of interest of the user profile.
- *Multidimensional representation.* This model is more adequate to describe the semantics of the user profile.

On the other hand, ontologies are ontologies explicit specifications of conceptualizations [11]. The most frequent function of ontologies falls on Linguistics since it serves as a support for Knowledge-Based Machine Translation systems and Termi-nography (Terminology practice). A knowledge base is an advanced form of database that not only aims to store, retrieve and modify large amounts of information, but also it seeks to represent elements of knowledge (generally in the form of facts and inference rules) and the form in which it is to be used [7]. According to [13], the knowledge representation is a method to encode knowledge, beliefs, action, feeling, goals, desires, preferences, and all other mental states in the knowledge base [12]. There are five major models of representations: semantic networks; frames, scripts, and schemata; logic-based representation; procedural representation; and analogical and iconic representation.

3 Methodology

The proposed methodology is based on three main stages: personalization, semantic processing, and visualization. In the *personalization stage*, the modeling of a user profile using a characteristic vector is defined. This profile describes each of the user's preferences that are used as a basis for generating and comparing similarity measures concerning a particular search.

The *semantic processing stage* uses an ontology that includes the entire set of search data, as well as a filtering algorithm that takes into account the characteristic vector constructed in the personalization stage. This stage measures the semantic similarity, considering the distance between nodes of an ontology, since a list is generated by the set of objects closest (conceptually) to the search carried out, ordered in descendent form according to the similarity applied measure.

The *visualization stage* is focused on representing the results obtained in the semantic processing stage. These results can be represented in graphs by using a spatial database listing both the obtained similarity values as well as the geographic locations. In such a way that using SQL queries the list of ordered results can be retrieved based on some specific criteria. These results can be represented visually both on mobile devices and in a web-mapping application. In summary, the proposed methodology is described in Fig. 1.

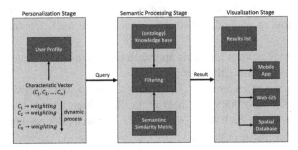

Fig. 1. General framework of the proposed methodology.

3.1 Personalization Stage

This stage aims to represent the user profile that will be made up of the user's preferences on one or more predetermined categories. This user profile is one of the most important features since it is used as a basis by the system to be able to make recommendations or filter content. The information can be general or referring to the interests of the user. Thus, the user profile can also contain the current location of the user, which can be used to offer nearby locations that are of interest to them. Additionally, the dataset that describes the user profile can be stored both on the client-side or on the server-side. On the client-side, the user has the option to customize the search, for example, on a mobile device with which the user can interact and customize their profile when necessary. A characteristic vector (C) is in charge of saving the preferences selected in the user profile. In this case, its length is the number of elements that make up the category as shown in the Eq. 1.

$$C = <c_1; c_2; \ldots; c_n>; \tag{1}$$

where $c_i = [0, 1] \forall c_i \epsilon C$ defines each characteristic that is represented with a binary value, where a value equal to zero indicates that this characteristic is not of interest to the user, while a value equal to one indicates his interest. Additionally, a user profile must be modeled too which and as previously mentioned, a user profile i denoted by U_i that is a label vector composed of pairs of values as follows (see Eq. 2).

$$\vec{U_i} = (t_i, 1 : v_i, 1 : t_i, 2 : v_i, 2 : \ldots, t_i, n : v_i, n), \forall x, t_i, x \in \vec{T_i'} \cup \vec{T_i''}; \qquad (2)$$

where t_i, x is a label that may be of interest to the user i; on the other hand, v_i, x is the degree of preference of user i in the label t_i, x, while n is the number of labels in which the user i may be interested.

3.2 Semantic Processing Stage

In this stage, the process of developing an ontology was divided into three tasks: capturing, encoding, and integrating existing ontologies. Taking into consideration the ontology used, a filtering process is carried out to obtain the results, which are required for the domain that is being used. Thus, knowledge-based filtering was used because it is the one that best adapts to the characteristic vector. This type of filtering can be described as a function that takes partial user preference data as input parameter and produces a list of recommendations for each user as output. First, we have a set E with all the elements that compose it as shown in Eq. 3.

$$E = \{e_1, e_2, \ldots, e_n\}; \qquad (3)$$

where E is the set that contains the elements, and e_i is any subset of the set E. Therefore, the following mapping function described in Eq. 4 is used.

$$f(e_i \in E) \rightarrow c_j \qquad (4)$$

This expression tells us that is possible to define a function f such that each element $e_i \in E$, can be mapped with an element $c_j \in C$ that describes the set of characteristics. This set is defined as indicated in Eq. 5.

$$C = \{c_1, c_2, \ldots, c_n\} \qquad (5)$$

According to the Natural Language Toolkit (NLTK), different similarity measures can be used, one of which can be based on the shortest path connecting each pair of words. In this scenario, the words defined in the taxonomy that are farther apart indicate that they are less similar; since it *is-a* (hyperemia/hypoxemia), its range is between 0 and 1 (unless the path is not found). Additionally, we have at our disposal another technique that does not necessarily use the shortest path but connects the two directions; by definition, this is the deepest common ancestor in taxonomy, which is no closer to the two senses. The probability that a word is an instance of the concept c is given by the following expression, denoted by Eq. 6.

$$P(c) = \frac{\sum w \in words(c)count(w)}{N}; \qquad (6)$$

where $words(c)$ are the words included under the concept c and N is the number of words in the corpus used. So, the probabilities $p(c)$ of each concept are shown in the root word that is equal to 1 (since it contains all the words); while the concept located in the lower part of the hierarchy is represented with the lowest probability. Thus, the information content of a concept is determined employing Eq. 7.

$$IC(c) = -\log P(c) \tag{7}$$

Another way to obtain the similarity is by considering the information content (*IC*), which takes into account the differences between two concepts *A* and *B*.

$$\begin{aligned} Communality : IC(common(A, B)) \\ Difference : IC(description(A, B)) - IC(common(A, B)) \end{aligned} \tag{8}$$

For which, the NLTK Similarity Theorem is used to say that the similarity between two concepts *A* and *B* is measured by the ratio between the amount of information necessary for the commonality of *A* and *B* and the information necessary to fully describe *A* and *B*.

$$sim_{lin}(A, B) = \frac{common(A, B)}{description(A, B)} \tag{9}$$

Once the similarity technique has been selected, a similarity table is generated showing the diagonal in which that value will be compared with itself, so the result will be equal to 1 $\left(S(c_j, c_j) = 1\right)$, while in the other cells the corresponding similarity value will be assigned. One example of a lexical database for English similarity retrieval techniques is the *wup_similarity* method (Wu & Palmer), which calculates the depth of two concepts in the UMLS, along with the depth of the LCS (less common) as described in Eq. 10 [14].

$$score = 2 * depth(lcs)/(depth(s_1) + depth(s_2)) \tag{10}$$

This means that $0 < score \leq 1$. The score cannot be equal to zero because the depth of the LCS is never zero (the depth of the root of taxonomy is one). The score is 1 if the two input concepts are the same. Another example of similarity quantification techniques is *path_similarity*, which is based on the shortest path that connects the words [16], its range is between 0 and 1 (unless it is not in the path), and comparing with itself the result is 1, the expression to quantify the similarity using this technique is given by Eq. 11.

$$sim\_path(c_1, c_2) = -log(len\_path(c_1, c_2)) \tag{11}$$

A third example is similarity measure *lch_similarity* that was proposed by Leacock and Chodorow [15], and defined by Eq. 12.

$$-log(length/(2*D)); \tag{12}$$

where *length* is the length of the shortest path between the two concepts (using node counting), and *D* is the depth of the taxonomy. The similarity will have a value between 0 and 1 as long as the values of both *i* and *j* are less than or equal to *m* (See Eq. 13).

$$0 \leq S(c_i, c_j) \leq 1 \forall i, j \leq m \tag{13}$$

Next, a vector corresponding to the user profile defined by the following expression denoted in Eq. 13 is generated.

$$P(U_i) = \{c_1, c_2, \ldots, c_n\} \qquad (14)$$

Thus, many components greater than or equal to 1 are obtained, but it is less than or equal to the amount of data in set C, which is defined in Eq. 15.

$$1 \le k \le m \, \forall \, c_i \in C \qquad (15)$$

To retrieve the points of interest (POI), a spatial database that contains a set of points indexed by a unique numeric identifier (id) was developed. Additionally, each element includes the name, the domain to which that value belongs, as well as a geographic location represented by a two-dimensional point that contains longitude and latitude; that point can be represented within a domain as described by Eq. 16.

$$O_g = \{o_1, o_2, \ldots, o_s\} \qquad (16)$$

These points can be obtained from different sources of geospatial information, for example, Google Maps, OpenStreetMap, Bing Maps, Here Maps, Yandex Maps, among others, or these can be designed to feed a database of spatial data with the sites of interest that are required. It is important to highlight the importance of having updated information. In such a way that there is both a consistency between the information that is generated by a result of the queries and the existence of a site of interest. An example of how information can be represented for retrieval in this methodology is described in Table 1.

Table 1. Information representation for the query retrieval.

Id	Type	Name	Geographic Location
1796526675	cinema	Cinépolis	0101000020E6100000CB1B458397D058C0F6E3BB5E355E3340
2682499791	school	Colegio Cristóbal Colón	0101000020E6100000BFB476458ED058C0A6ED5B9F0A823340
851950234	university	ITESM, Campus Santa Fe	0101000020E610000032B19D898CD058C0F10AC0700E5C3340
1835887102	school	Primaria Montessori	0101000020E610000069475D5B77D058C0B85BAAC24F7A3340
2682477325	bank	Banco BanBajio	0101000020E61000001027B0F80BD058C09F6E2262A77F3340
1975929160	hospital	Star Médica	0101000020E6100000B5FB392D0BD058C0E137DFF6B87F3340
1975911013	gas_station	PEMEX	0101000020E610000070826C77F9CF58C0A3D20F56237F3340
1041569607	restaurant	Vips Axomiatla	0101000020E6100000D8300527EACF58C0D073CA3F75573340
3750094501	coffe_center	Dunkin Donuts	0101000020E61000001272A9EAD5CF58C022C29C28CC4E3340
331139119	parking	Free Parking	0101000020E610000082AAB801D1CF58C080CD6E0B8F6A3340
1975915768	cinema	Cinemark	0101000020E61000008902D660D0CF58C06C3A9FE3E17E3340
2682518329	fast_food	McDonald's	0101000020E6100000545D9968C1CF58C0CD284940927E3340
2768795271	fuel	Pemex	0101000020E61000005087D63BBCCF58C0C9F001C239613340
1836060878	university	FES Acatlán	0101000020E6100000CC0B47B6B3CF58C05E8CF596577B3340
2383430377	townhall	Delegación Magdalena Contreras	0101000020E6100000EFAF3A5774CF58C024F9772D0B4E3340
2324761563	hospital	Hospital Infantil M. Contreras	0101000020E6100000D76264144CCF58C0252B0D74C5513340
330800673	fountain	Fuente	0101000020E6100000A6491E8722CF58C0555C998DEA6A3340
1098346877	school	Escuela Primaria: Manuel E. Álvarez	0101000020E6100000CD41412C17CF58C04B3356FBDE743340
1836064691	theatre	Teatro Ciudad Bicentenario	0101000020E610000012DF9DD703CF58C00F03E7F5667A3340

3.3 Visualization Stage

The experimental results obtained with the proposed methodology represent one of the following features: Web-GIS, Mobile-GIS (including the augmented reality in the visualization), and also the visualization of the result employing a spatial query.

The Web-GIS represents the geospatial data with the latitude and longitude information in a web-mapping application. So, to visually represent this type of data, a mapping of the spatial attributes is carried out generating a map. Additionally, the type of input, the structures, and the data that will be used must be known. If the data is external, a cleaning process is required.

The Mobile-GIS uses the sensors embedded into the mobile device for the visualization, and the use of the Android operating system and Apple's iOS are considered to develop a mobile application to offer further features such as the use of augmented reality. The following sensors are used in the present research work, according to the definition proposed by [18].

- *Motion sensors.* They measure the acceleration and the rotational forces along three axes. This category includes accelerometers, gravity sensors, gyroscopes, and rotating vector sensors.
- *Environmental sensors.* These sensors measure various environmental parameters such as ambient air temperature and pressure, lighting, and humidity. The category includes barometers, photometers, and thermometers.
- *Position sensors.* They measure the physical position of a device. This category includes orientation sensors and magnetometers. With the use of motion and position sensors, it is possible to obtain some issues such as the current location, the speed at which the owner of the mobile device is moving, as well as the direction in which the device is being pointed.

On the other hand, this work considered the application of the *augmented reality*, to enrich the real-world environment with a certain amount of synthetic information. These must meet three basic requirements: mixing of real and virtual images, real-time execution, as well as the alignment of virtual objects with real-world structures. Special attention must be taken when replacing the structures since inadvertent increases could cause loss of information useful for the operation. Another problem that may arise is the visual interaction between the real and virtual representations because the use of the parameters is the same, but the object in the real world is different, and therefore the results may not be optimal. Similarly, caution should be exercised in the perception as the depth signals illustrated are those that can be found in a single image including occlusion, relative size, relative height, detail, atmospheric perspective, shadows, or lineal perspective. Additionally, the synchronization of the parameters of the virtual and the real scenario should allow the camera to align real and virtual pictorial depth signals; however, the management of the occlusion defines that the results may be shown incorrectly (superimposed). To solve this problem, phantom objects are used in the occlusion handling algorithm and it is necessary to have good control of the characteristics of the edges to improve the result with an edge detector and preserve those that are necessary. Another aspect to take into consideration is the outstanding characteristics related to the preservation of the edges of the occlusion elements; which helps to maintain context and improve spatial perception. Thus, the class diagram used in the mobile application is depicted in Fig. 2.

Moreover, the visualization of the result in a spatial query is supported by a geospatial database These differ from SQL queries, which are not spatial since they allow us to

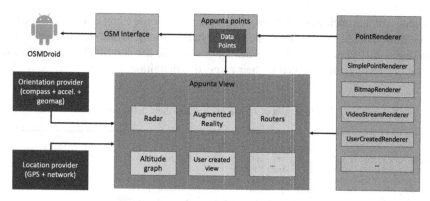

Fig. 2. Mobile application class hierarchy.

use geometric data such as points, lines, and polygons because of their relationships are geometric and topological. The query can include a buffer that can offer us more appropriate results. Thus, it allows us to retrieve the set of geographic objects that are within a certain radius concerning the current position of the user. So, consider the spatial query presented in Table 2 that is based on a current position (latitude, longitude) equal to (−99.143887 19.510518) as an example.

Table 2. Example of spatial query.

```
SELECT name, st_astext (way)
FROM planet_osm_point
WHERE st_dwithin(way, st_geographyfromtext('SRID=4326;
    POINT(-99.143887 19.510518)'), 3000)
AND name LIKE '%Cine%'
```

4   Results

This section describes the results obtained with the proposed methodology. As a case study, a mobile application was developed for the Android operating system in which the user defines his profile using his preference regarding the genres of cinema films. Based on this information and current geographic location, a screen is displayed using Augmented Reality. This is for the user can locate movie theaters that show films that conceptually are of interest to him.

4.1   Results of the Personalization Stage

According to the definition of the user profile, the case study is focused on mastering films shown in movie theaters. So, to customize the user profile, it is required to have a complete set that includes the types of genres in which the films can be classified and the definition of each genre. Thus, the list was built from the WordNet ontolo-gy, and its meaning was obtained from the English language. The list described in Table 3 shows the set of movie genres, as well as their respective definition.

Table 3. Set of movie genres and their definition.

```
Action: The series of events that form a plot.
Adventure: A wild and exciting undertaking (not necessarily lawful).
Animation: The making of animated cartoons.
Biography: An account of the series of events making up a person's life.
Comedy: Light and humorous drama with a happy ending.
Crime: (criminal law) An act punishable by law; usually considered an evil act.
Documentary: A film or TV program presenting the facts about a person or event.
Drama: An episode that is turbulent or highly emotional.
Family: An association of people who share common beliefs or activities.
Fantasy: Action with a large amount of imagination in it.
History: A record or narrative description of past events
Horror: Intense and profound fear.
Music: An artistic form of auditory communication incorporating instrumental or
vocal tones in a structured and continuous manner.
Musical: A play or film whose action and dialogue is interspersed with singing
and dancing.
Mystery: Something that baffles understanding and cannot be explained.
Romance: a relationship between two lovers.
Sci-fi: A literary work based on the imagination and not necessarily on fact.
Sport: An active diversion requiring physical exertion and competition.
Thriller: A suspenseful adventure story or play or movie.
War: The waging of armed conflict against an enemy.
Western: A film about life in the western United States during the period of
exploration and development.
```

In Fig. 3, a partial list displayed in the Android application is presented. This has the option of selecting each of the genres that are of interest to the user with the restriction that at least one of the genres must be selected for the correct operation of the application.

In the implementation, an XML resource of type *PreferenceScreen* was created in which a *PreferenceCategory* is generated to store the user's name. Subsequently, an additional *PreferenceCategory* was created, which helps us to generate the view and make the selection of genres to later save the user's preferences through an XML file based on the *CheckBoxPreference* component (see Table 4).

Table 4. CheckBoxPreference layout file.

```
<CheckBoxPreference                    <CheckBoxPreference
android:key="action"                   android:key="adventure"
android:title="Action"                 android:title="Adventure"
android:defaultValue="false"/>         android:defaultValue="false"/>
```

Moreover, the *getSharedPreferences* method was used to generate the characteristic vector, where each genre classified populates the vector to represent the user's preferences.

Fig. 3. Selection of movie genres.

4.2 Semantic Processing Stage

In this research work, the WordNet ontology [17] was proposed as the lexical database for English *synsets* as well as the application of three semantic similarity measures. In this way, the similarity measures that were used to generate the recommendation employed a list that contains all the combinations and the quantification of the similarity between each pair of genders. Table 5 shows the similarities obtained by applying the similarity measures: *lch* (Leacock and Chodorow), *wup* (Wu and Palmer), and *path_length* (path length). Due to space limitations, we present only the results for 6 genres of film classification.

In addition, the graphics that represent the similarity values concerning the applied measures are shown in Fig. 4.

According to the graphs depicted in Fig. 4, the *lch* and *wup* measures obtained better results because their calculates are more accurate. In contrast, the *path_length* measure does not generate a representative difference between the points that compose the series, tending to have very close values while with the *wup* metric, despite the similarity values being between 0 and 1, there is a more pronounced variation between the results. In conclusion, the *lch* ranges of similarity were located between 0 and 0.63758616; the results are displayed in greater detail and the similarity measures can be more precise.

Concerning the filtered out, once the user profile and relational tables are available to obtain the filtering (server), an SQL query must be carried out to obtain the set of movies whose genres are most similar in terms of user preferences. So, the list of genres

Table 5. Similarity values obtained by applying the *lch*, *wup* and *path_length* similarity measures.

ID	Genre 1	Genre 2	lch	wup	path_length
1	action	Action	3.63758616	1	1
2	action	Adventure	0.864997437	0.210526316	0.0625
3	action	Animation	0.747214402	0.19047619	0.055555556
4	action	Biography	1.072636802	0.333333333	0.076923077
5	action	Comedy	1.15267951	0.352941176	0.083333333
6	action	Crime	0.864997437	0.210526316	0.0625
7	action	documentary	0.929535959	0.222222222	0.066666667
8	action	drama	0.99852883	0.235294118	0.071428571
9	action	family	0.99852883	0.235294118	0.071428571
10	action	fantasy	2.028148247	0.777777778	0.2
11	action	history	1.15267951	0.352941176	0.083333333
12	action	horror	1.15267951	0.153846154	0.083333333
13	action	music	1.335001067	0.4	0.1
14	action	musical	0.929535959	0.222222222	0.066666667
15	action	mystery	2.251291799	0.842105263	0.25
16	action	romance	1.84582669	0.736842105	0.166666667
17	action	fiction	2.251291799	0.823529412	0.25
18	action	sport	0.929535959	0.222222222	0.066666667
19	action	thriller	2.028148247	0.8	0.2
20	action	war	0.99852883	0.235294118	0.071428571
21	action	western	0.864997437	0.210526316	0.0625
22	comedy	action	1.15267951	0.352941176	0.083333333
23	comedy	adventure	1.072636802	0.25	0.076923077
24	comedy	animation	0.929535959	0.222222222	0.066666667
25	comedy	biography	1.335001067	0.4	0.1
26	comedy	comedy	3.63758616	1	1
27	comedy	crime	1.072636802	0.25	0.076923077
28	comedy	documentary	1.15267951	0.266666667	0.083333333
29	comedy	drama	1.239690887	0.285714286	0.090909091
30	comedy	family	1.239690887	0.285714286	0.090909091
31	comedy	fantasy	1.335001067	0.4	0.1
32	comedy	history	1.440361582	0.428571429	0.111111111

(*continued*)

Table 5. (*continued*)

ID	Genre 1	Genre 2	lch	wup	path_length
33	comedy	horror	1.440361582	0.2	0.111111111
34	comedy	music	1.691676011	0.5	0.142857143
35	comedy	musical	1.15267951	0.266666667	0.083333333
36	comedy	mystery	1.239690887	0.375	0.090909091
37	comedy	romance	1.239690887	0.375	0.090909091
38	comedy	fiction	1.440361582	0.428571429	0.111111111
39	comedy	sport	1.15267951	0.266666667	0.083333333
40	comedy	thriller	1.15267951	0.352941176	0.083333333
41	comedy	war	1.239690887	0.285714286	0.090909091
42	comedy	western	1.072636802	0.25	0.076923077
43	drama	action	0.99852883	0.235294118	0.071428571
44	drama	adventure	1.440361582	0.5	0.111111111
45	drama	animation	1.239690887	0.444444444	0.090909091
46	drama	biography	1.15267951	0.266666667	0.083333333
47	drama	comedy	1.239690887	0.285714286	0.090909091
48	drama	crime	1.440361582	0.5	0.111111111
49	drama	documentary	1.558144618	0.533333333	0.125
50	drama	drama	3.63758616	1	1
51	drama	family	1.239690887	0.285714286	0.090909091
52	drama	fantasy	1.15267951	0.266666667	0.083333333
53	drama	history	1.239690887	0.285714286	0.090909091
54	drama	horror	1.440361582	0.2	0.111111111
55	drama	music	1.440361582	0.333333333	0.111111111
56	drama	musical	1.558144618	0.533333333	0.125
57	drama	mystery	1.072636802	0.25	0.076923077
58	drama	romance	1.072636802	0.25	0.076923077
59	drama	fiction	1.239690887	0.285714286	0.090909091
60	drama	sport	1.558144618	0.533333333	0.125
61	drama	thriller	0.99852883	0.235294118	0.071428571
62	drama	war	1.691676011	0.571428571	0.142857143
63	drama	western	1.440361582	0.5	0.111111111
64	history	action	1.15267951	0.352941176	0.083333333

(*continued*)

Table 5. (*continued*)

ID	Genre 1	Genre 2	lch	wup	path_length
65	history	adventure	1.072636802	0.25	0.076923077
66	history	animation	0.929535959	0.222222222	0.066666667
67	history	biography	2.944438979	0.933333333	0.5
68	history	comedy	1.440361582	0.428571429	0.111111111
69	history	crime	1.072636802	0.25	0.076923077
70	history	documentary	1.15267951	0.266666667	0.083333333
71	history	drama	1.239690887	0.285714286	0.090909091
72	history	family	1.239690887	0.285714286	0.090909091
73	history	fantasy	1.335001067	0.4	0.1
74	history	history	3.63758616	1	1
75	history	horror	1.440361582	0.2	0.111111111
76	history	music	1.691676011	0.5	0.142857143
77	history	musical	1.15267951	0.266666667	0.083333333
78	history	mystery	1.239690887	0.375	0.090909091
79	history	romance	1.239690887	0.375	0.090909091
80	history	fiction	1.440361582	0.428571429	0.111111111
81	history	sport	1.15267951	0.266666667	0.083333333
82	history	thriller	1.15267951	0.352941176	0.083333333
83	history	war	1.239690887	0.285714286	0.090909091
84	history	western	1.072636802	0.25	0.076923077
85	fiction	action	2.251291799	0.823529412	0.25
86	fiction	adventure	1.072636802	0.25	0.076923077
87	fiction	animation	0.929535959	0.222222222	0.066666667
88	fiction	biography	1.335001067	0.4	0.1
89	fiction	comedy	1.440361582	0.428571429	0.111111111
90	fiction	crime	1.072636802	0.25	0.076923077
91	fiction	documentary	1.15267951	0.266666667	0.083333333
92	fiction	drama	1.239690887	0.285714286	0.090909091
93	fiction	family	1.239690887	0.285714286	0.090909091
94	fiction	fantasy	2.944438979	0.933333333	0.5
95	fiction	history	1.440361582	0.428571429	0.111111111
96	fiction	horror	1.440361582	0.2	0.111111111

(*continued*)

Table 5. (*continued*)

ID	Genre 1	Genre 2	lch	wup	path_length
97	fiction	music	1.691676011	0.5	0.142857143
98	fiction	musical	1.15267951	0.266666667	0.083333333
99	fiction	mystery	2.538973871	0.875	0.333333333
100	fiction	romance	2.538973871	0.875	0.333333333
101	fiction	fiction	3.63758616	1	1
102	fiction	sport	1.15267951	0.266666667	0.083333333
103	fiction	thriller	2.251291799	0.823529412	0.25
104	fiction	war	1.239690887	0.285714286	0.090909091
105	fiction	western	1.072636802	0.25	0.076923077
106	thriller	action	2.028148247	0.8	0.2
107	thriller	adventure	0.864997437	0.210526316	0.0625
108	thriller	animation	0.747214402	0.19047619	0.055555556
109	thriller	biography	1.072636802	0.333333333	0.076923077
110	thriller	comedy	1.15267951	0.352941176	0.083333333
111	thriller	crime	0.864997437	0.210526316	0.0625
112	thriller	documentary	0.929535959	0.222222222	0.066666667
113	thriller	drama	0.99852883	0.235294118	0.071428571
114	thriller	family	0.99852883	0.235294118	0.071428571
115	thriller	fantasy	2.028148247	0.777777778	0.2
116	thriller	history	1.15267951	0.352941176	0.083333333
117	thriller	horror	1.15267951	0.153846154	0.083333333
118	thriller	music	1.335001067	0.4	0.1
119	thriller	musical	0.929535959	0.222222222	0.066666667
120	thriller	mystery	2.251291799	0.842105263	0.25
121	thriller	romance	1.84582669	0.736842105	0.166666667
122	thriller	fiction	2.251291799	0.823529412	0.25
123	thriller	sport	0.929535959	0.222222222	0.066666667
124	thriller	thriller	3.63758616	1	1
125	thriller	war	0.99852883	0.235294118	0.071428571
126	thriller	western	0.864997437	0.210526316	0.0625

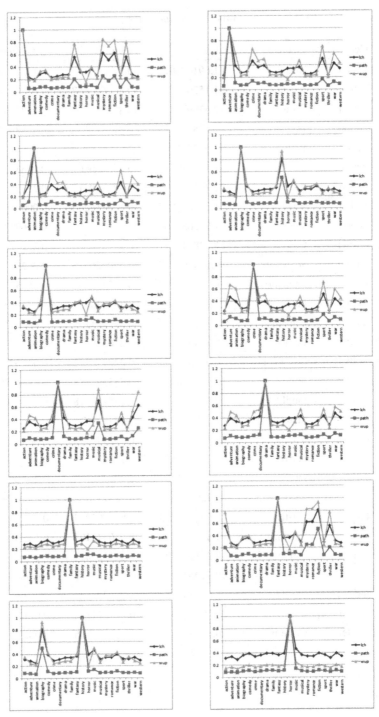

Fig. 4. Graphics that represent the similarity values of movie genres regarding the applied measures.

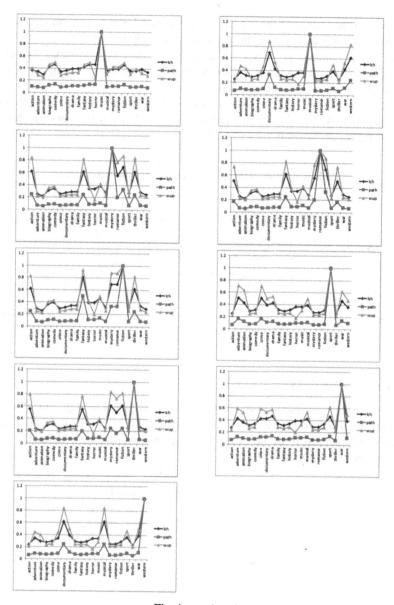

Fig. 4. continued

that represent the interest of the user must be obtained. Later, a query to send to a PHP web service is generated by using the Laravel framework. A response to a POST request is returned that contains an array with the set of recommended movies. Likewise, it is possible to send the web service request from Android in the following way and with the string that was previously generated.

The response of the web service is an arrangement that depending on the tastes that were selected in the profile by the user (see Table 6). Since it is an arrangement, it is given the necessary handling for its visualization.

Table 6. Results of the response concerning the web service.

```
{"title":"Deadpool","classification":"B15","genre":"action","similarity":"3.64"},
{"title":"Legend","classification":"B","genre":"action","similarity":"3.64"},
{"title":"The 5ᵗʰ Wave","classification":"B","genre":"action","similarity":"3.64"},
{"title":"600 Miles", " classification": "B", " genre": "thriller", " similarity":"2.03"},
{"title":"Knock Knock","classification":"C","genre":"thriller","similarity":"2.03"},
{"title":"Carol","classification":"B15","genre":"thriller","similarity":"2.03"},
{"title":"I saw the devil","classification":"B15","genre":"thriller","similarity":"2.03"},
{"title":"By the see","classification":"B15","genre":"romance","similarity":"1.85"},
{"title":"Suite française","classification":"B","genre":"romance","similarity":"1.85"},
{"title":"Pride and Prejudice and Zombies","classification":"B","genre":"romance","similar-
ity":1.85"}
```

4.3 Visualization Stage

At this stage, two databases were used: the first is obtained through OpenStreetMap (www.openstreetmap.org) and the rest is depicted in Fig. 5. The data of the points of interest were obtained from the OpenStreetMap and with the help of the Osm2pgsql tool, we exported the points to PostGIS.

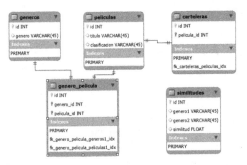

Fig. 5. Database model.

It can be appreciated that in the table of "genres", there are the 21 most used genres in the classification of films. In the table of "movies", the information related to the titles that are projected at that moment on the billboard or a more complete list is stored. On the other hand, in the "billboards" table there is the relationship of the tables that are currently on the billboard, the "genre_film" table maintains the relationship with the "genres" and "movies" table since it is a relationship many-to-many. Thus, to retrieve a server-side spatial query, a web service, and through SQL (see Table 7).

Table 7. Query used in the visualization stage.

```php
<?php
Class PuntosController extends Controller {
  public function PostIndex(Request $request) {
    $points = $request->all();
    $lat = $points['latitud'];
    $lon = $points['longitud'];
    $cinemas = DB::select("SELECT name, st?astext(way)
      FROM planet_osm_point
      WHERE st_dwithin(way, st_geographyfromtext('SRID=4326;
      POINT($lon, $lat)'), 3000) and name LIKE '%Cine%'")
    return response->json($cinemas, 200);
  }
}
?>
```

With the previous information, an arrangement of points is retrieved that represent all the cinemas in the specified distance within the buffer of 3 km. In addition, the Appunta API was used for this representation. Thus, we can start the drawing of the retrieved points, in Fig. 6 and Fig. 7 the recovery of the points corresponding to movie theaters is shown. Moreover, helping us with the orientation of the camera, only the movie theaters which are in that range of vision appear (see Fig. 8).

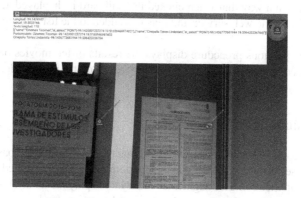

Fig. 6. Obtained results using the location 1.

On the other hand, the top part shows the current location, which is updated as the user moves and calculating again the points to retrieve. It can be appreciated that the retrieved arrangement shows the point where the latitude and longitude of the movie

Fig. 7. Obtained results using the location 2.

Fig. 8. Obtained results using the location 2 with camera rotation.

theater are located as well as the name of the movie theater found. Each icon works as a button in such a way that when clicked the billboard is displayed according to the data retrieved from the web service and thus it is added to the list to be displayed on the screen.

Finally, the previous procedure displays the results of ten movies on the billboard with a greater coincidence using the similarity regarding the user's selections in terms of preferred genre tastes, the user profile.

5   Conclusions and Future Work

In this paper, a novel approach to retrieve semantically information based on current location and user preferences applying semantic metrics was presented. The Android mobile device application uses augmented reality to display the most-closed conceptual movies to user genres preferences is also proposed.

The main advantage of the proposed approach is that the semantic processing stage uses different similarity formulas to determine the most adequate metric. On the other hand, this stage could be adapted to implement other similarity metrics to analyze and retrieve the desired information. Future work is oriented towards developing and implementing the mobile device application using other frameworks, like Flutter, in order to provide a mobile device application that can be used both in Android and iOS devices, and applying this methodology with other datasets, related to location services such as banks, commercial centers, among others.

Acknowledgements. This work was partially sponsored by Instituto Politécnico Nacional under grants 20210162, 20211579 and 20210541, and Consejo Nacional de Ciencia y Tecnología (CONACyT) under grants PN-2016/2110 and 7051.

References

1. Resnick, P., Varian, H.R.: Recommender systems. Commun. ACM **40**(3), 56–58 (1997)
2. Chirita, P.A., Nejdl, W., Paiu, R., Kohlschütter, C.: Using ODP metadata to personalize search. In: Proceedings of the 28th Annual International ACM SIGIR Conference on Research and Development in Information Retrieval, pp. 178–185. Association for Computing Machinery, New York (2005)
3. Pretschner, A., Gauch, S.: Ontology based personalized search. In: Proceedings 11th International Conference on Tools with Artificial Intelligence, pp. 391–398. IEEE, November 1999
4. Carrer-Neto, W., Hernández-Alcaraz, M.L., Valencia-García, R., García-Sánchez, F.: Social knowledge-based recommender system. Application to the movies domain. Expert Syst. Appl. **39**(12), 10990–11000 (2012)
5. Christakou, C., Vrettos, S., Stafylopatis, A.: A hybrid movie recommender system based on neural networks. Int. J. Artif. Intell. Tools **16**(05), 771–792 (2007)
6. Bobadilla, J., Ortega, F., Hernando, A., Gutiérrez, A.: Recommender systems survey. Knowl.-Based Syst. **46**, 109–132 (2013)
7. Arano, S.: La ontología: una zona de interacción entre la Lingüística y la Documentación (2), (2004). www.hipertext.net
8. Gao, M., Liu, K., Wu, Z.: Personalisation in web computing and informatics: theories, techniques, applications, and future research. Inf. Syst. Front. **12**, 607–629 (2010). https://doi.org/10.1007/s10796-009-9199-3
9. Dauban, N., Sénac, C., Pinquier, J., Gaillard, P.: Towards a content-based prediction of personalized musical preferences using transfer learning. In: 2021 International Conference on Content-Based Multimedia Indexing (CBMI), pp. 1–6 (2021). https://doi.org/10.1109/CBMI50038.2021.9461911
10. Parida, P.P., Gourisaria, M.K., Pandey, M., Rautaray, S.S.: Collaborative-based movie recommender system—a proposed model. In: Satapathy, S.C., Bhateja, V., Favorskaya, M.N., Adilakshmi, T. (eds.) Smart Computing Techniques and Applications. SIST, vol. 225, pp. 561–571. Springer, Singapore (2021). https://doi.org/10.1007/978-981-16-0878-0_55
11. Guarino, N., Oberle, D., Staab, S.: What is an ontology? In: Staab, S., Studer, R. (eds.) Handbook on Ontologies. IHIS, pp. 1–17. Springer, Heidelberg (2009). https://doi.org/10.1007/978-3-540-92673-3_0
12. Patel, A., Jain, S.: Formalisms of representing knowledge. Procedia Comput. Sci. **125**, 542–549 (2018)
13. Partridge, D.: Representation of knowledge. In: Artificial Intelligence, pp. 55–87. Academic Press (1996)
14. Wu, Z., Palmer, M.: Verbs semantics and lexical selection. In: Proceedings of the 32nd Annual Meeting on Association for Computational Linguistics (ACL 1994), pp. 133–138. Association for Computational Linguistics, USA (1994). https://doi.org/10.3115/981732.981751

15. Leacock, C., Miller, G.A., Chodorow, M.: Using corpus statistics and WordNet relations for sense identification. Comput. Linguist. **24**(1), 147–165 (1998)
16. Gomaa, W.H., Fahmy, A.A.: A survey of text similarity approaches. Int. J. Comput. Appl. **68**(13), 13–18 (2013)
17. Fellbaum, C.: A Semantic Network of English Verbs. WordNet: An Electronic Lexical Database, no. 3, pp. 153–178 (1998).
18. Griol, D., García-Herrero, J., Molina, J.M.: A novel approach for data fusion and dialog management in user-adapted multimodal dialog systems. In: Proceedings of the 17th International Conference on Information Fusion, p. 1/17. IEEE, Salamanca (2014)

An Improved Riesz s-Energy-Based Archive to Handle Dominance Resistant Solutions

Jesús Guillermo Falcón-Cardona[✉]

Tecnológico de Monterrey, Escuela de Ingeniería y Ciencias,
Monterrey, Nuevo León 64849, México
jfalcon@tec.mx

Abstract. Recently, the potential energy functions, which come from physics, have been successfully applied to increase the performance of multi-objective evolutionary algorithms (MOEAs). The increase in performance is notable in terms of the generation of evenly distributed Pareto front approximations regardless of the associated manifold geometry. A remarkable potential energy function is the Riesz s-energy which has been employed to assess Pareto front approximations and to promote the design of selection mechanisms of MOEAs, such as archiving strategies. However, an important issue of the Riesz s-energy and some other potential energy functions is that they reward the existence of dominance resistant solutions (DRSs) in a Pareto front approximation even though DRSs are harmful solutions. In this paper, we propose a mechanism to improve the performance of a Riesz s-energy-based archive which is embedded into the MOEA based on decomposition (MOEA/D). Our proposed mechanism incorporates the density-based clustering of applications with noise (DBSCAN) and a penalization function into the Riesz s-energy-based archive to let it handle DRSs. Our experimental results show that this improved archive allows MOEA/D to generate, with a higher probability, DRS-free Pareto front approximations when tackling especially multi-frontal multi-objective optimization problems.

Keywords: Riesz s-energy · Archiving strategy · Dominance resistant solutions · Multi-objective optimization

1 Introduction

Multi-objective evolutionary algorithms (MOEAs) are population-based and derivative-free metaheuristics based on the principles of natural evolution [2]. These metaheuristic techniques have been typically applied to tackle multi-objective optimization problems (MOPs), i.e., problems in which an objective function cannot be optimized without worsening another one. When tackling a MOP, the main goal of a MOEA is to generate a high-quality Pareto front approximation. According to Zitzler *et al.* [21], a good Pareto front approximation should

© Springer Nature Switzerland AG 2021
M. F. Mata-Rivera and R. Zagal-Flores (Eds.): WITCOM 2021, CCIS 1430, pp. 229–243, 2021.
https://doi.org/10.1007/978-3-030-89586-0_18

fulfill the following characteristics: (1) it should be as close as possible to the true Pareto front which implies a high degree of convergence; (2) the solutions composing the Pareto front approximation should be spread all along the Pareto front, covering it completely; and (3) the solutions should be configured producing an even distribution. In recent years, MOEAs have demonstrated to be useful methods to generate good Pareto front approximations which have attracted the attention of several specialized communities to tackle MOPs related to several scientific, engineering, and industrial fields.

Despite the notable advantages of MOEAs when tackling MOPs, in recent years, some drawbacks have been pointed out about their performance. In 2017, Ishibuchi et al. [17] showed that the performance of some MOEAs is overspecialized when tackling MOPs whose Pareto front geometries are highly correlated with the shape of a simplex (we call them *regular Pareto front shapes*). The reason for this behavior is that most MOEAs employ a set of convex weight vectors[1] (which produces a $m-1$-dimensional simplex) to guide the evolutionary process and, then, find the intersections between the Pareto front and these convex weight vectors. Moreover, some commonly employed test suites such as the Deb-Thiele-Laumanns-Zitzler (DTLZ) [4] and the Walking-Fish-Group (WFG) [15] have MOPs with regular Pareto front shapes. Hence, when a MOEA that uses convex weight vectors is tested on a MOP with a regular Pareto front shape, it is likely that it performs well in terms of convergence, coverage, and distribution. However, when these MOEAs are tested on MOPs with irregular Pareto front shapes (i.e., geometries not correlated with the shape of a simplex), they do not exhibit good performance, as shown by Ishibuchi et al. [17].

To overcome the overspecialization of MOEAs, several methods have been proposed [9,11,14,19]. Among the different proposals, the use of potential energy functions has recently arisen as a promising research direction to increase the performance of MOEAs when tackling MOPs with irregular Pareto front shapes [9]. In physics, the potential energy functions represent the energy hold by an object because of its position relative to other objects, thus, they measure the inter-object interaction. In the context of multi-objective optimization, the potential energy functions have been utilized in three directions. Since a potential energy function measures the interaction between objects, these functions have been recently employed to assess the diversity of Pareto front approximations by taking into account the interaction (using a kernel function) between the objective vectors that compose the Pareto front approximation. In this regard, the Riesz s-energy function is a remarkable example [6,8]. This potential energy function employs the Riesz kernel to measure the interaction between objective vectors and, due to its mathematical properties, it prefers configurations of points with a high degree of diversity regardless of the geometry of the related manifold [12]. On the other hand, the second utilization of these energy functions is as part of density estimators and archives of MOEAs [7,9,11]. The underlying idea is to exploit their preferences for well-diversified manifold discretizations. Finally, the

---

[1] A vector $\vec{w} \in \mathbb{R}^m$ is denoted as a convex weight vector if and only if $\sum_{i=1}^{m} w_i = 1$ and $w_i \geq 0$ for all $i = 1, 2, \ldots, m$.

third research direction is the design of methods to construct reference sets that are employed by MOEAs as part of selection mechanisms or to calculate quality indicators [1,10].

Despite the notable properties of potential energy functions when embedded into MOEAs, there is still a lot of room for improvement. In this paper, we focus on improving the performance of a Riesz s-energy-based archive to handle dominance resistant solutions. A dominance resistant solution (DRS), in multi-objective optimization problems, has very good values for some objective functions and very bad values for other ones which makes them very difficult to being deleted [16]. According to Falcón-Cardona et al. [9], potential energy-based selection mechanisms (such as density estimators and archives) exhibit issues to handle DRSs. The reason for this behavior is that the potential energy functions (e.g., the Riesz s-energy) do not take into account the convergence of the solutions and they reward objective vectors which are not clusterized as in the case of DRSs. To overcome this issue, in this paper, we propose a Riesz s-energy-based archive that can detect and delete DRSs. To this aim, we propose to couple the density-based clustering of applications with noise (DBSCAN) [5] into the Riesz s-energy-based archive to detect the presence of DRS (which in principle are outlier solutions) and, then, we employ a penalization function to delete them. Our experimental results show that the improved Riesz s-energy-based archive allows handling DRSs in a better way than the raw Riesz s-energy-based archive proposed in [9].

The remainder of this paper is organized as follows. Section 2 presents the background concepts employed throughout the paper to make it self-contained. Section 3 is devoted to describe our proposed approach. Section 4 outlines the experimental results and, finally, our main conclusions and future work are presented in Sect. 5.

2 Background

In this section, we describe the basic terms employed throughout the paper. First, we provide the formal definition of a MOP. Secondly, the Riesz s-energy is introduced, emphasizing their mathematical properties.

2.1 Multi-objective Optimization

In this paper, we consider, without loss of generality, unconstrained MOPs for minimization which are defined as follows:

$$\min_{\vec{x} \in \Omega} f(\vec{x}) := (f_1(\vec{x}), f_2(\vec{x}), \dots, f_m(\vec{x}))$$

where $\vec{x}$ is a vector of decision variables, $\Omega \subseteq \mathbb{R}^n$ is the decision space, $f(\vec{x})$ is the vector of $m \geq 2$ objective functions such that $f_i : \Omega \to \mathbb{R}$ for $i = 1, 2, \dots, m$. The solution of a MOP, denoted as the *Pareto set*, is a set of vectors of decision variables that represent the best-possible trade-offs among the objective functions. In this regard, given $\vec{x}, \vec{y} \in \Omega$, we say that $\vec{x}$ Pareto dominates $\vec{y}$ (denoted as $\vec{x} \prec \vec{y}$) if and only if $f_i(\vec{x}) \leq f_i(\vec{y})$ for all $i = 1, 2, \ldots, m$ and there exists at least an index $j \in \{1, 2, \ldots, m\}$ such that $f_j(\vec{x}) < f_j(\vec{y})$. Based on the Pareto dominanance relation, it is possible to identify *Pareto optimal solutions*. A solution $\vec{x}^* \in \Omega$ is Pareto optimal if there does not exist another $\vec{x} \in \Omega$ such that $\vec{x} \prec \vec{x}^*$. The set of all Pareto optimal solutions constitutes the Pareto set and its image in the objective space is known as the *Pareto front*.

2.2 Riesz *s*-Energy

In general, a potential energy function (U) assigns a real value to a set of objects (particles), by measuring their interaction. If U is exclusively focus on measuring the interaction between pairs of particles, it is denoted as a pair-potential function and it is defined as follows:

$$U(\mathcal{A}) = \sum_{i=1}^{N} \sum_{j=1 \wedge j \neq i}^{N} \mathcal{K}(\vec{a}_i, \vec{a}_j) \qquad (1)$$

where $\mathcal{A} = \{\vec{a}_1, \ldots, \vec{a}_N\}, \vec{a}_i \in \mathbb{R}^m$ is a non-empty set of N particles and $\mathcal{K} : \mathbb{R}^m \times \mathbb{R}^m \to \mathbb{R}$ is a kernel function that measures the interaction between two given m-dimensional particles.

In recent years, the discrete Riesz s-energy function [12] has been employed in evolutionary multi-objective optimization in different research directions [1,7–11]. The Riesz s-energy (E_s) is a pair-potential function, thus, it follows the scheme of Eq. 1 but it uses a particular kernel function $\mathcal{K}_s$ (called the Riesz kernel), given by the next formula:

$$\mathcal{K}_s(\vec{a}_i, \vec{a}_j) = \begin{cases} \|\vec{a}_i - \vec{a}_j\|^{-s}, & s > 0 \\ -\log \|\vec{a}_i - \vec{a}_j\|, & s = 0 \end{cases}, \qquad (2)$$

where $\|\cdot\|$ denotes the Euclidean distance, and $s \geq 0$ is a parameter that controls the emphasis on rewarding a uniform distribution of the particles in $\mathcal{A}$. As $s \to \infty$, a more uniform distribution is rewarded [10]. It is worth noting that s is independent of the geometry of the underlying manifold of $\mathcal{A}$, according to Hardin and Saff [12,13]. It is worth noting that the lower the Riesz s-energy, the better.

3   Handling Dominance Resistant Solutions

The Riesz s-energy has been embedded into the selection mechanisms of MOEAs by using the concept of contribution [7,10,11]. Given a Pareto front approximation $\mathcal{A} = \{\vec{a}_1, \ldots, \vec{a}_N\}$, where each $\vec{a}_i \in \mathbb{R}^m$ is an objective vector, the individual contribution C of a point $\vec{a} \in \mathcal{A}$ is given as follows:

$$C_s(\vec{a}, \mathcal{A}) = E_s(\mathcal{A}) - E_s(\mathcal{A} \setminus \{\vec{a}\}). \qquad (3)$$

Using the contribution to the Riesz s-energy, a backward elimination process can be defined. Supposing that the cardinality of $\mathcal{A}$ is $N + 1$ but $\mathcal{A}$ must be of size N, the worst-contributing solution ($\vec{a}_{\text{worst}}$) to the Riesz s-energy could be deleted, where $\vec{a}_{\text{worst}} = \arg\max_{\vec{a} \in \mathcal{A}} C_s(\vec{a}, \mathcal{A})$. This heuristic elimination process approximates the solution to the Riesz s-energy-based subset selection, i.e., select a subset of solutions from $\mathcal{A}$, aiming to minimize the Riesz s-energy of the resulting subset [10].

Despite the notable advantages of the Riesz s-energy-based selection mechanisms to improve the diversity of Pareto front approximations, some issues have been observed when handling dominance resistant solutions. Figure 1 shows a Pareto front approximation $\mathcal{A} = \{(0, 2),\ (0.02, 0.98),\ (0.25, 0.75),\ (0.5, 0.5),\ (0.75, 0.25),\ (0.98, 0.02),\ (2, 0)\}$, where the color of each point emphasizes its contribution to the Riesz s-energy and the continuous line represents the true Pareto front. Even though the objective vectors $(0, 2)$ and $(2, 0)$ are DRSs, they have the lowest Riesz s-energy contribution values (3.728545). In consequence, if a solution should be deleted to decrease the cardinality of $\mathcal{A}$, neither $(0, 2)$ nor $(2, 0)$ will be dropped. Instead, the objective vector $(0.5, 0.5)$, that has the greatest Riesz s-energy contribution value (7.685571), will the deleted from $\mathcal{A}$ even when it is a Pareto optimal solution. This example shows the inability of a Riesz s-energy-based selection mechanism to delete DRSs although they are harmful solutions.

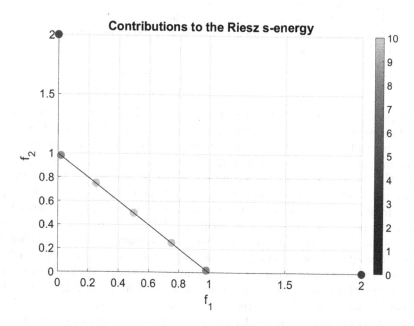

Fig. 1. The colormap emphasizes the individual Riesz s-energy contributions of a set of objective vectors that represent a Pareto front approximation, where the continuous line is the true Pareto front. The points $(0, 2)$ and $(2, 0)$ are DRSs but they have the lowest contribution values to the Riesz s-energy.

To overcome the inability of a Riesz s-energy-based selection mechanism to handle DRSs, we propose to use a clustering technique to detect the presence of these undesirable objective vectors and apply a penalization function to delete them. We employed the framework proposed by Falcón-Cardona et al. [9] where the MOEA based on Decomposition (MOEA/D) [20] is unidirectionally connected to a Riesz s-energy-based archive. The archive stores the best solutions, according to the Riesz s-energy, that MOEA/D has produced throughout the evolutionary process.

Algorithm 1. MOEA/D using Riesz s-energy-based archive

Require: N: population size; T: neighborhood size; $A_{\max}$: maximum archive size
Ensure: Main population and archive as Pareto front approximations
1: Initialize N weight vectors $\lambda^1, \ldots, \lambda^N$
2: Determine the T nearest neighbors of each λ^j
3: Randomly initialize the main Population $P = \{\vec{x}_1, \ldots, \vec{x}_N\}$
4: Calculate $f(P) = \{f(\vec{x}_1), \ldots, f(\vec{x}_N)\}$
5: Initialize archive $\mathcal{A} = f(P)$
6: **while** Stopping criterion is not satisfied **do**
7:     **for** $j = 1$ to N **do**
8:         Select mating parents from the neighborhood of λ_j
9:         Generate a new solution $\vec{y}$ by using variation operators.
10:         $\mathcal{A} = \text{Insert}(\mathcal{A}, f(\vec{y}))$
11:         Evaluate $f(\vec{y})$, using a scalarizing function g_{λ_j}
12:         Update the main population P and the neighborhood structure
13:     $\mathcal{A} = \text{Prune}(\mathcal{A}, A_{\max})$
14: **return** $\{P, \mathcal{A}\}$

Algorithm 1 shows the general framework of MOEA/D where it is necessary to provide as inputs the population size N, the size T of the neighborhood structure, and since the Riesz s-energy archive is bounded, it is necessary the maximum archive size $A_{\max}$. First, MOEA/D constructs a set of N weight vectors $\{\lambda^1, \ldots, \lambda^N\}$ to guide the evolution of the N individuals which are randomly initialized in line 2 to shape the population P. The objective vectors of the individuals in P constitute the initial state of the Riesz s-energy-based archive (denoted as $\mathcal{A}$). The main loop of MOEA/D comprehends lines 6 to 13, where a new iteration is ensured whenever the stopping criterion is fulfilled. For each weight vector λ_j, two parent solutions are selected from the neighborhood structure of λ_j to generate a new solution $\vec{y}$, using variation operators. In line 10, the objective vector $f(\vec{y})$ is inserted in $\mathcal{A}$, utilizing Algorithm 2 that returns the updated archive. Afterward, a scalarizing function (SF) $g : \mathbb{R}^m \to \mathbb{R}$ related to λ_j evaluates $f(\vec{y})$ to determine if it is a better solution to the single-objective optimization problem (SOP) defined through this SF. If $\vec{y}$ represents a better solution, the neighborhood structure of λ_j and the main population P are updated. When all the weight vectors have been processed for an iteration of the main loop, a pruning process based on the Riesz s-energy backward elimination is executed to reduce the cardinality of $\mathcal{A}$ and ensure that $|\mathcal{A}| = A_{\max}$.

Algorithm 2. Insert

Require: $\mathcal{A}$: archive; $\vec{a}^*$: solution to be inserted
Ensure: Updated archive $\mathcal{A}$
1: **for all** $\vec{a} \in \mathcal{A}$ **do**
2:    **if** $\vec{a}^* \prec \vec{a}$ **then**
3:        $\mathcal{A} = \mathcal{A} \setminus \{\vec{a}\}$
4:    **else if** $\vec{a} \preceq \vec{a}^*$ **then**
5:        **return** $\mathcal{A}$
6: $\mathcal{A} = \mathcal{A} \cup \{\vec{a}^*\}$
7: **return** $\mathcal{A}$

The Riesz s-energy-based archive is updated by two separate processes. On the one hand, whenever MOEA/D generates a new solution, its objective vector is tested for insertion into $\mathcal{A}$, using Algorithm 2. The insertion mechanism uses the Pareto dominance relation to identifying if the newly created objective vector $\vec{a}^*$ is mutually nondominated with respect to all the elements $\vec{a} \in \mathcal{A}$. The algorithm ensures that all the objective vectors $\vec{a} \in \mathcal{A}$ Pareto dominated by $\vec{a}^*$ are deleted from $\mathcal{A}$. In case that no $\vec{a} \in \mathcal{A}$ Pareto dominates $\vec{a}^*$ and $\vec{a}^*$ is a different objective vector, then it is inserted into $\mathcal{A}$. However, if at least an objective vector $\vec{a} \in \mathcal{A}$ Pareto dominates or is equal to $\vec{a}^*$, the latter is not inserted into the archive.

Algorithm 3. Prune

Require: $\mathcal{A}$: archive; $A_{\max}$: maximum archive size
Ensure: Updated archive $\mathcal{A}$
1: Calculate $z_i^{\min} = \min_{\vec{a} \in \mathcal{A}} a_i, \forall i = 1, 2, \ldots, m$
2: Calculate $z_i^{\max} = \max_{\vec{a} \in \mathcal{A}} a_i, \forall i = 1, 2, \ldots, m$
3: $\mathcal{A}' = \text{Normalize}(\mathcal{A}, \vec{z}^{\min}, \vec{z}^{\max})$
4: **while** $|\mathcal{A}'| > A_{\max}$ **do**
5:    **if** DBSCAN finds outliers (DRSs) in $\mathcal{A}'$ **then**
6:        $\vec{a}_{\text{worst}} = \arg\max_{\vec{a} \in \mathcal{A}'} \psi(\mathcal{A}') - \psi(\mathcal{A}' \setminus \{\vec{a}\})$
7:    **else**
8:        $\vec{a}_{\text{worst}} = \arg\max_{\vec{a} \in \mathcal{A}'} C_s(\vec{a}, \mathcal{A}')$
9:    $\mathcal{A}' = \mathcal{A}' \setminus \{\vec{a}_{\text{worst}}\}$
10:    Delete from $\mathcal{A}$ the non normalized objective vector related to $\vec{a}_{\text{worst}}$
11: **return** $\mathcal{A}$

The second process that updates the Riesz s-energy-based archive is a pruning scheme (see Algorithm 3). The pruning ensures that the maximum archive size is not exceeded. First, it is mandatory to obtain a normalized version of $\mathcal{A}$. Hence, the vectors $\vec{z}^{\min}$ and $\vec{z}^{\min}$ that contain the minimum and maximum objective values, respectively, are calculated. By using these vectors, it is possible to normalize the components of all the objective vectors of $\mathcal{A}$ as follows: $a_i' = (a_i - z_i^{\min})/(z_i^{\max} - z_i^{\min}), i = 1, 2, \ldots, m$. The normalization process is necessary because DBSCAN and the Riesz s-energy employ Euclidean distance calculations and we aim to avoid the effect of different measuring scales of the objective functions. In case that the cardinality of the normalized Riesz s-energy-based archive $\mathcal{A}'$ is greater than $A_{\max}$, its cardinality must be reduced iteratively. At each iteration, DBSCAN looks for outlier solutions, i.e., DRSs. The main reason to use DBSCAN is that the number of clusters does not need to be specified by the user, thus, DBSCAN automatically determines this number. DBSCAN only requires the user to specify the maximum distance ϵ between two samples for one to be considered as in the neighborhood of the other, and the number α of samples in a neighborhood for a point to be considered as a core point. If DBSCAN detects DRSs, it is not possible to utilize the elimination scheme based on the contributions to the Riesz s-energy. Hence, we propose to use a penalization function which is defined as follows:

$$\psi(\mathcal{A}) = \sum_{i=1}^{N} \sum_{j=1 \wedge j \neq i}^{N} \|\vec{a}_i\|^{\gamma} \|\vec{a}_j\|^{\gamma}, \tag{4}$$

where $\gamma > 1$ is a parameter that controls the degree of penalization. ψ is in essence the same as the potential energy defined in Eq. (1) but it uses the kernel function $\mathcal{K}(\vec{a}_i, \vec{a}_j) = \|\vec{a}_i\|^{\gamma} \|\vec{a}_j\|^{\gamma}$ that penalizes the existence of DRSs. Since a DRS is far away from the principal cluster that composes the Pareto front approximation, it is expected that its norm is greater than the norm of the rest of objective vectors. Hence, when the norm of the DRS is raised to the power of γ, its contribution to ψ will considerably increase. To verify the above argument, let's analyze Fig. 2 that considers the same approximation set $\mathcal{A} = \{(0, 2),$ $(0.02, 0.98), (0.25, 0.75), (0.5, 0.5), (0.75, 0.25), (0.98, 0.02), (2, 0)\}$ as in Fig. 1 but using the contributions to the ψ function. In contrast to the contributions to the Riesz s-energy, the DRSs $(0, 2)$ and $(2, 0)$ have the greatest contributions (1107.332275) to the ψ function while the objective vector $(0.5, 0.5)$ is related to the lowest contribution (11.742808). Hence, in a backward elimination process that considers the contributions to ψ, either $(0, 2)$ $(0, 2)$ will be deleted from $\mathcal{A}$. Retaking Algorithm 3, if DBSCAN does not find any DRS in $\mathcal{A}'$, the usual Riesz s-energy-based elimination process is executed in line 8. Then, $\vec{a}_{\text{worst}}$ is deleted from $\mathcal{A}'$ and the corresponding non normalized objective vector related to $\vec{a}_{\text{worst}}$ is dropped from $\mathcal{A}$. Finally, when the cardinality of $|\mathcal{A}'|$ reached the maximum archive size, the updated $\mathcal{A}$ is returned.

4   Experimental Results

In this section, we compare the performance of the improved Riesz s-energy-based archive with the raw Riesz s-energy- based archive proposed in [9,10] when they are undirectionally connected to MOEA/D which gives rise to MOEA/D-IRSE and MOEA/D-RSE, respectively. We performed comparisons using the test

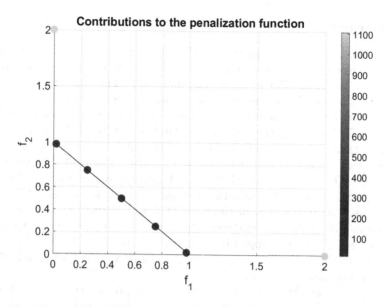

Fig. 2. The colormap emphasizes the individual contributions to the penalization function ψ of a set of objective vectors that represent a Pareto front approximation, where the continuous line is the true Pareto front. The points $(0, 2)$ and $(2, 0)$ are DRSs and they have the greatest contribution values to ψ.

problems: DTLZ1, DTLZ2, DTLZ3, DTLZ5, and DTLZ7 with 2 to 5 objective functions. The number of decision variables was set to $n = m + K - 1$, where m is the number of objective functions and $K = 5$ for DTLZ1, $K = 10$ for DTLZ2, DTLZ3, and DTLZ5, and $K = 20$ for DTLZ7. For a fair comparison, the population size and the maximum archive size were set to $N = A_{\max} = C_{m-1}^{H+m-1}$ for MOEA/D-IRSE and MOEA/D-RSE, where $H = 119, 14, 8, 6$ for $m = 2, 3, 4, 5$, respectively. Hence, $N = 120, 120, 165, 210$ solutions for $m = 2, 3, 4, 5$, respectively. The previous combinatorial number corresponds to the use of the Das and Dennis scheme to generate a set of convex weight vectors [3]. For all cases, the stopping criterion was set to 50,000 function evaluations. We set the neighborhood size T of MOEA/D equal to 20 and we employed the achievement scalarizing function as SF in all cases. Additionally, both Riesz *s*-energy-based archives utilized $s = m$ as recommended in [10]. DBSCAN used $\epsilon = 0.25$ and $\alpha = 3$ for each MOP being tackled. For each test instance, we performed 20 independent executions. We assessed the generated Pareto front approximations using the quality indicators: inverted generational distance indicator (IGD), the pure diversity indicator (PD), and the maximum spread (MS) [18]. To have statistical significant confidence, we selected the Wilcoxon rank-sum test with a significance value of 0.05.

4.1 Discussion of Results

Tables 1 and 2 show the statistical results of the IGD and PD quality indicators. It is worth noting that IGD aims to measure the convergence towards the Pareto front and PD is a diversity indicator. The numerical results are related to the quality of the final Pareto front approximations contained in the improved and raw Riesz s-energy-based archives and the main population of MOEA/D. Regarding the IGD values, MOEA/D-RSE is the best algorithm since it obtained the first rank in 14 out of 20 test instances. However, in not all the cases, MOEA/D-RSE exhibits statistically significant differences with respect to MOEA/D-IRSE or MOEA/D. A possible reason that explains why MOEA/D-IRSE does not obtain the best places is due to the use of DBSCAN and its sensibility to DRSs. Sometimes, DBSCAN may detect a DRS but it is not which implies the utilization of the penalization function that has disruptive consequences in Pareto front approximations that do not have DRSs. Despite this situation, MOEA/D-IRSE is competitive with MOEA/D and MOEA/D-RSE in terms of convergence.

Regarding the diversity of Pareto front approximations (see Table 2), MOEA/D-IRSE is the second-best algorithm, producing well-diversified Pareto front approximations for problems DTLZ1, DTLZ2, and DTLZ3. In contrast, MOEA/D-RSE performs better on problems DTLZ5 and DTLZ7. It is worth noting the good performance of MOEA/D-IRSE on problems DTLZ1 and DTLZ3 which are multi-frontal MOPs which implies that it is very likely that some MOEAs have difficulties when solving them due to the presence of DRSs solutions. This is an insight that MOEA/D-IRSE can handle DRSs in comparison with MOEA/D-RSE that uses a raw mechanism based on the Riesz s-energy.

The most important results are shown in Table 3. The maximum spread is a quality indicator that measures the extension of a Pareto front approximation, thus, the greater, the better. In our case, the Table 3 does not show the original MS values. Instead, we proposed to measure the deviation or MS error with respect to a reference set. For each test instance, we measured the MS of a reference set that has Pareto optimal solutions and, then, the MS value obtained by each algorithm for given execution, is subtracted and the absolute value is obtained. Table 3 shows the absolute values of the MS errors which implies that a lower value is desirable. Using this MS error, it is possible to observe if a Pareto front approximation has DRSs. By inspecting the MS error values, it is clear that MOEA/D-IRSE produces minimal errors. It is worth emphasizing the good results obtained for all the DTLZ1 and DTLZ3 test instances where MOEA/D-IRSE outperforms MOEA/D-RSE. As mentioned above, DTLZ1 and DTLZ3 are multi-frontal MOPs which increases the probability of finding DRSs. Despite this search difficulty, the use of DBSCAN and the penalization function effectively help the Riesz s-energy-based archive to handle DRSs in comparison with the raw Riesz s-energy-based archive.

An Improved Riesz s-Energy-Based Archive to Handle DRSs · 239

Table 1. Mean and, in parentheses, the standard deviation of the IGD indicator. The two best values are shown in grayscale, where the darker tone corresponds to the best value. Each algorithm has a superindex that indicates its rank in the comparison, regarding the specific test instance. A symbol # is placed when the best algorithm is significantly better than another based on a one-tailed Wilcoxon rank-sum test, using a significance value of 0.05.

MOP	Dim.	MOEA/D-IRSE	MOEA/D-RSE	MOEA/D
DTLZ1	2	1.765381e-03³ (2.951912e-05)	1.763096e-03² (4.060932e-05)	1.757573e-03¹ (2.945205e-05)
	3	2.214821e-02³# (8.111276e-03)	2.018786e-02²# (1.085348e-03)	1.839714e-02¹ (1.794726e-04)
	4	1.094340e-01³# (4.928752e-02)	4.490666e-02²# (6.768629e-03)	3.569464e-02¹ (3.331017e-04)
	5	1.999242e-01³# (5.366179e-03)	6.123662e-02²# (5.233885e-03)	5.509006e-02¹ (5.221755e-03)
DTLZ2	2	4.017268e-03³ (7.042589e-05)	3.847392e-03¹ (5.543338e-05)	4.007811e-03²# (7.818638e-05)
	3	5.138691e-02³# (8.376789e-04)	5.058494e-02¹ (6.376267e-04)	5.109632e-02²# (3.682269e-04)
	4	1.113878e-01³ (1.126123e-02)	1.078459e-01¹ (1.588022e-03)	1.100120e-01²# (6.911561e-04)
	5	3.258679e-01³# (4.030240e-02)	1.628234e-01¹ (2.448217e-03)	1.725457e-02²# (3.204019e-03)
DTLZ3	2	1.445326e-02³ (3.869865e-02)	5.672151e-03¹ (2.245857e-03)	5.778942e-03² (2.159958e-03)
	3	5.448137e-02¹ (4.216985e-03)	6.655254e-02³# (9.092362e-03)	5.459176e-02² (1.675502e-03)
	4	2.132814e-01³# (5.135204e-02)	1.458089e-01²# (1.710334e-02)	1.263613e-01¹ (4.534342e-03)
	5	4.060815e-01³# (5.690587e-02)	2.755108e-01¹ (8.245491e-02)	3.505978e-02²# (6.399568e-02)
DTLZ5	2	4.043606e-03²# (5.511395e-05)	3.899034e-03¹ (7.431707e-05)	4.052253e-03³# (4.391626e-05)
	3	4.416428e-03² (1.376315e-04)	4.369882e-03¹ (1.565813e-04)	1.463719e-02³# (1.494721e-03)
	4	1.141291e+00³# (5.699563e-01)	2.855679e-01¹ (1.502847e-01)	4.848101e-01²# (9.984195e-02)
	5	1.868546e+00³# (6.277563e-02)	4.660935e-01¹ (1.591882e-01)	1.224684e+00²# (1.113428e-01)
DTLZ7	2	4.187879e-02² (1.657725e-01)	4.184643e-01¹ (1.657802e-01)	5.827623e-02³# (1.619276e-01)
	3	2.927412e-01² (3.042324e-01)	2.926167e-01¹ (3.035277e-01)	3.732797e-01³# (2.526018e-01)
	4	9.501427e-01³ (7.348565e-01)	5.438005e-01¹ (4.061689e-01)	6.742633e-01² (3.278840e-01)
	5	2.082227e+00³# (3.876818e-01)	7.763881e-01¹ (3.337216e-01)	8.782614e-01²# (2.768392e-01)

Table 2. Mean and, in parentheses, the standard deviation of the PD indicator. The two best values are shown in grayscale, where the darker tone corresponds to the best value. Each algorithm has a superindex that indicates its rank in the comparison, regarding the specific test instance. A symbol # is placed when the best algorithm is significantly better than another based on a one-tailed Wilcoxon rank-sum test, using a significance value of 0.05.

MOP	Dim.	MOEA/D-IRSE	MOEA/D-RSE	MOEA/D
DTLZ1	2	$9.475881e+02^1$ $(1.150879e+02)$	$9.427541e+02^2$ $(1.516818e+02)$	$8.621348e+02^3$ $(2.243885e+02)$
	3	$8.790323e+04^2\#$ $(8.641114e+03)$	$9.752972e+04^1$ $(6.923369e+03)$	$7.775064e+04^3\#$ $(6.053274e+03)$
	4	$1.027459e+06^3\#$ $(4.983131e+05)$	$1.872398e+06^1$ $(1.603719e+05)$	$1.312965e+06^2\#$ $(8.083613e+04)$
	5	$3.473268e+06^3\#$ $(4.249283e+05)$	$1.888104e+07^1$ $(2.218963e+06)$	$1.204043e+07^2\#$ $(5.169360e+05)$
DTLZ2	2	$1.603279e+03^2$ $(1.739102e+02)$	$1.638375e+03^1$ $(1.770145e+02)$	$1.361727e+03^3\#$ $(2.819667e+01)$
	3	$2.319167e+05^1$ $(7.810479e+03)$	$2.157439e+05^3\#$ $(9.364599e+03)$	$2.209627e+05^2\#$ $(5.759652e+03)$
	4	$5.194310e+06^1$ $(4.913880e+05)$	$5.152298e+06^2\#$ $(1.420711e+05)$	$4.757376e+06^3\#$ $(1.365248e+05)$
	5	$2.234238e+07^3\#$ $(3.946828e+06)$	$5.357264e+07^1$ $(1.428071e+06)$	$4.131016e+07^2\#$ $(1.417407e+06)$
DTLZ3	2	$1.699056e+03^1$ $(2.731840e+02)$	$1.684652e+03^2$ $(2.599049e+02)$	$1.443312e+03^3\#$ $(2.592329e+02)$
	3	$2.244211e+05^1$ $(1.132192e+04)$	$2.214208e+05^2$ $(1.252536e+04)$	$2.151144e+05^3\#$ $(8.915982e+03)$
	4	$2.732829e+06^3\#$ $(6.388076e+05)$	$5.414597e+06^1$ $(6.446635e+05)$	$4.481422e+06^2\#$ $(1.928407e+05)$
	5	$2.025342e+07^3\#$ $(3.940449e+06)$	$5.661190e+07^1$ $(7.531485e+06)$	$3.093718e+07^2\#$ $(5.035226e+06)$
DTLZ5	2	$1.603279e+03^2$ $(1.739102e+02)$	$1.638375e+03^1$ $(1.770145e+02)$	$1.361727e+03^3\#$ $(2.819667e+01)$
	3	$7.507559e+04^2$ $(1.107521e+04)$	$7.664379e+04^1$ $(1.229666e+04)$	$7.390840e+04^3$ $(5.220011e+03)$
	4	$1.661487e+06^3\#$ $(9.353890e+05)$	$4.464226e+06^1$ $(5.300488e+05)$	$1.846526e+06^2\#$ $(1.983593e+05)$
	5	$7.055536e+06^3\#$ $(3.282323e+06)$	$7.323082e+07^1$ $(1.196163e+07)$	$1.499190e+07^2\#$ $(1.702245e+06)$
DTLZ7	2	$1.902792e+03^1$ $(4.273779e+02)$	$1.798986e+03^2$ $(3.619931e+02)$	$1.282927e+03^3\#$ $(2.277793e+02)$
	3	$1.650314e+05^2$ $(5.300562e+04)$	$1.745703e+05^1$ $(5.378708e+04)$	$1.111419e+05^3\#$ $(3.228849e+04)$
	4	$2.324478e+06^2\#$ $(2.084259e+06)$	$3.790350e+06^1$ $(1.124334e+06)$	$1.696666e+06^3\#$ $(6.281333e+05)$
	5	$3.310794e+06^3\#$ $(2.386713e+06)$	$4.371677e+07^1$ $(9.917871e+06)$	$1.155342e+07^2\#$ $(2.651953e+06)$

Table 3. Mean and, in parentheses, the standard deviation of the Maximum Spread error. The minimum MS error is shown in a dark gray tone. A symbol # is placed when the best algorithm is significantly better than the other based on a one-tailed Wilcoxon rank-sum test, using a significance value of 0.05.

MOP	Dim.	MOEA/D-IRSE	MOEA/D-RSE
DTLZ1	2	$4.074505e\text{-}03^1$ (7.583751e-03)	$1.602263e\text{-}01^2$ (5.883193e-01)
	3	$4.198815e\text{-}02^1$ (5.642272e-02)	$9.778035e\text{+}00^2\#$ (1.824319e+01)
	4	$4.312057e\text{-}01^1$ (2.697792e-01)	$1.910796e\text{+}01^2\#$ (2.468276e+01)
	5	$8.821180e\text{-}01^1$ (2.687321e-02)	$2.340224e\text{+}01^2\#$ (2.721487e+01)
DTLZ2	2	$6.638047e\text{-}03^1$ (8.365472e-03)	$6.638047e\text{-}03^2$ (8.365472e-03)
	3	$4.719683e\text{-}02^1$ (5.533349e-02)	$6.409624e\text{-}02^2$ (8.291718e-02)
	4	$1.542336e\text{-}02^1$ (1.438000e-02)	$2.365202e\text{-}01^2\#$ (2.173191e-01)
	5	$1.662610e\text{-}01^1$ (7.334514e-02)	$1.929353e\text{-}01^2$ (1.897331e-01)
DTLZ3	2	$2.941448e\text{-}02^1$ (1.026508e-01)	$5.088926e\text{-}01^2$ (9.854949e-01)
	3	$4.251307e\text{-}02^1$ (6.438561e-02)	$2.387676e\text{+}01^2\#$ (4.204014e+01)
	4	$4.112837e\text{-}02^1$ (4.086863e-02)	$1.007667e\text{+}02^2\#$ (1.051022e+02)
	5	$3.501596e\text{+}00^1$ (1.013009e-01)	$7.213689e\text{+}01^2\#$ (5.990598e+01)
DTLZ5	2	$5.954024e\text{-}03^1$ (8.365472e-03)	$5.954024e\text{-}03^2$ (8.365472e-03)
	3	$1.812251e\text{-}02^1$ (2.541738e-02)	$2.346386e\text{-}02^2$ (3.254165e-02)
	4	$1.645332e\text{+}00^2\#$ (8.313557e-01)	$4.991810e\text{-}01^1$ (3.068282e-01)
	5	$5.907144e\text{+}00^2\#$ (1.335852e-01)	$2.533410e\text{+}00^1$ (5.763297e-01)
DTLZ7	2	$7.583095e\text{-}02^1$ (2.594852e-01)	$7.583095e\text{-}02^2$ (2.594852e-01)
	3	$1.052157e\text{+}00^2$ (7.593803e-01)	$8.785969e\text{-}01^1$ (7.909809e-01)
	4	$2.901494e\text{+}00^2$ (2.069453e+00)	$2.485241e\text{+}00^1$ (1.633103e+00)
	5	$6.583654e\text{+}00^2\#$ (2.179359e-01)	$1.960445e\text{+}00^1$ (2.214462e+00)

5 Conclusions and Future Work

The Riesz s-energy is a pair-potential function that has been recently incorporated into the selection mechanisms of MOEAs. The most important benefit of using this pair-potential function is the generation of Pareto front approximations with good diversity regardless of the Pareto front geometry of the associated MOP. Despite the advantages of Riesz s-energy-based selection mechanisms, they have critical problems handling dominance resistant solutions. A selection mechanism of this nature is unable to delete DRSs even though they are harmful solutions. Hence, in this paper, we proposed an improved Riesz s-energy-based archiving strategy that can detect and delete DRSs. To this aim, we embedded the density-based clustering of applications with noise to detect the presence of DRSs. In case of a DRS is detected, a penalization function is applied to delete such solutions. Our experimental results showed that our proposed improved Riesz s-energy-based archive outperforms a raw Riesz s-energy-based archive when handling multi-frontal MOPs that have a considerable number of DRSs. As part of our future work, we aim to analyze the effect of the parameters required to DBSCAN aiming to reduce the number of false-positive detections of DRSs. Moreover, we aim to balance the performance of the improved Riesz s-energy-based archive when tackling MOPs with disconnected Pareto front shapes.

References

1. Blank, J., Deb, K., Dhebar, Y., Bandaru, S., Seada, H.: Generating well-spaced points on a unit simplex for evolutionary many-objective optimization. IEEE Trans. Evol. Comput. **25**, 48–60 (2020)
2. Coello Coello, C.A., Lamont, G.B., Van Veldhuizen, D.A.: Evolutionary Algorithms for Solving Multi-Objective Problems, 2nd edn. Springer, New York (2007). https://doi.org/10.1007/978-0-387-36797-2ISBN 978-0-387-33254-3
3. Das, I., Dennis, J.E.: Normal-boundary intersection: a new method for generating the pareto surface in nonlinear multicriteria optimization problems. SIAM J. Optim. **8**(3), 631–657 (1998)
4. Deb, K., Thiele, L., Laumanns, M., Zitzler, E.: Scalable test problems for evolutionary multiobjective optimization. In: Abraham, A., Jain, L., Goldberg, R. (eds.) Evolutionary Multiobjective Optimization. Advanced Information and Knowledge Processing, pp. 105–145. Springer, London (2005). https://doi.org/10.1007/1-84628-137-7_6
5. Ester, M., Kriegel, H.P., Sander, J., Xu, X.: A density-based algorithm for discovering clusters in large spatial databases with noise. In: Proceedings of the Second International Conference on Knowledge Discovery and Data Mining, KDD 1996, pp. 226–231. AAAI Press (1996)
6. Falcón-Cardona, J.G., Coello, C.A.C.: Convergence and diversity analysis of indicator-based multi-objective evolutionary algorithms. In: Proceedings of the Genetic and Evolutionary Computation Conference, GECCO 2019, pp. 524–531. ACM Press, New York (2019). https://doi.org/10.1145/3321707.3321718
7. Falcón-Cardona, J.G., Coello Coello, C.A., Emmerich, M., et al.: CRI-EMOA: a pareto-front shape invariant evolutionary multi-objective algorithm. In: Deb, K.

(ed.) EMO 2019. LNCS, vol. 11411, pp. 307–318. Springer, Cham (2019). https://doi.org/10.1007/978-3-030-12598-1_25

8. Falcón-Cardona, J.G., Coello Coello, C.A.: A multi-objective evolutionary hyper-heuristic based on multiple indicator-based density estimators. In: 2018 Genetic and Evolutionary Computation Conference (GECCO'2018), pp. 633–640. ACM Press, Kyoto (2018)

9. Falcón-Cardona, J.G., Covantes Osuna, E., Coello Coello, C.A., et al.: An overview of pair-potential functions for multi-objective optimization. In: Ishibuchi, H. (ed.) EMO 2021. LNCS, vol. 12654, pp. 401–412. Springer, Cham (2021). https://doi.org/10.1007/978-3-030-72062-9_32

10. Falcón-Cardona, J.G., Ishibuchi, H., Coello Coello, C.A.: Riesz s-energy-based reference sets for multi-objective optimization. In: Proceedings of the 2020 IEEE Congress on Evolutionary Computation, pp. 1–8 (2020)

11. Falcón-Cardona, J.G., Ishibuchi, H., Coello Coello, C.A., Emmerich, M.: On the effect of the cooperation of indicator-based multi-objective evolutionary algorithms. IEEE Trans. Evol. Computat. 1–15 (2021). https://doi.org/10.1109/TEVC.2021.3061545

12. Hardin, D.P., Saff, E.B.: Discretizing manifolds via minimum energy points. Not. AMS **51**(10), 1186–1194 (2004)

13. Hardn, D.P., Saff, E.: Minimal Riesz energy point configurations for rectifiable d-dimensional manifolds. Adv. Math. **193**(1), 174–204 (2005)

14. Hernández Gómez, R., Coello Coello, C.A.: A hyper-heuristic of scalarizing functions. In: 2017 Genetic and Evolutionary Computation Conference (GECCO 2017), pp. 577–584. ACM Press, Berlin (2017). ISBN 978-1-4503-4920-8

15. Huband, S., Hingston, P., Barone, L., While, L.: A review of multiobjective test problems and a scalable test problem toolkit. IEEE Trans. Evol. Comput. **10**(5), 477–506 (2006)

16. Ishibuchi, H., Matsumoto, T., Masuyama, N., Nojima, Y.: Effects of dominance resistant solutions on the performance of evolutionary multi-objective and many-objective algorithms. In: Proceedings of the 2020 Genetic and Evolutionary Computation Conference, GECCO 2020, pp. 507–515. Association for Computing Machinery, New York (2020). https://doi.org/10.1145/3377930.3390166

17. Ishibuchi, H., Setoguchi, Y., Masuda, H., Nojima, Y.: Performance of decomposition-based many-objective algorithms strongly depends on pareto front shapes. IEEE Trans. Evol. Comput. **21**(2), 169–190 (2017)

18. Li, M., Yao, X.: Quality evaluation of solution sets in multiobjective optimisation: a survey. ACM Comput. Surv. **52**(2), 26:1-26:38 (2019)

19. Tian, Y., Cheng, R., Zhang, X., Cheng, F., Jin, Y.: An indicator-based multiobjective evolutionary algorithm with reference point adaptation for better versatility. IEEE Trans. Evol. Comput. **22**(4), 609–622 (2018)

20. Zhang, Q., Li, H.: MOEA/D: a multiobjective evolutionary algorithm based on decomposition. IEEE Trans. Evol. Comput. **11**(6), 712–731 (2007)

21. Zitzler, E., Thiele, L., Laumanns, M., Fonseca, C.M., da Fonseca, V.G.: Performance assessment of multiobjective optimizers: an analysis and review. IEEE Trans. Evol. Comput. **7**(2), 117–132 (2003)

Analysis of the Level of Geographic Criminal Risk Oriented to Women

Jonathan Hernández[1], Dennise Jiménez[1], Roberto Zagal[1] (ID), Félix Mata[2](✉) (ID), and Jose Antonio Leon Borges[3] (ID)

[1] ESCOM-IPN, Mexico City, Mexico
rzagalf@ipn.mx
[2] UPIITA-IPN, Mexico City, Mexico
mmatar@ipn.mx
[3] Universidad de Quintana Roo, Campus Cancún, Chetumal, Quintana Roo, Mexico
jleon@uqroo.edu.mx

Abstract. In this research, a methodology is presented to estimate and visualize the level of insecurity in geographical areas, using spatio-temporal analysis and data mining techniques focused in crimes against women. Data sources used are from official crime reports and news media, classified as: femicide, armed robbery and rape. Data were extracted using web scrapping in digital media publications and were collected from open databases provided by the Mexican government. It is distinguished the crimes reports against women, based on the fact they are classified in news media as feminicides while in open data appears as gender violence. The case study is focused on the municipality of Ecatepec de Morelos, State of Mexico due to its high crime density according to official reports. The results show a geographical and temporal description of the crime behavior in space and time. It allows estimating the level of risk for women in a geographical area at the suburb level and a day granularity. The approach was tested using a web tool that facilitates decision-making based on the representativeness of crime behavior, the dataset includes around 20,000 records in the years from 2018 to 2019. Future work includes the integration of the machine learning process to possible forecast and discover correlations, validations and filtering of possible fake news is other possible direction, and include other municipalities of Mexico.

Keywords: Crime analysis · Spatial and temporal analysis · Integration information

1 Introduction

In Mexico, violence can occur both in public and private spaces and is one of the causes of death in the population between 15 and 44 years of age according to reports from National Institute of Geography Statistics and Informatics in Mexico (INEGI) [11]. Despite this, violence against women and girls is one of the most serious, widespread, deep-rooted and tolerated human rights violations in the world (https://www.unfpa.org/gender-based-violence). According to publications of the United Nations (UN), globally,

M. F. Mata-Rivera and R. Zagal-Flores (Eds.): WITCOM 2021, CCIS 1430, pp. 244–255, 2021.
https://doi.org/10.1007/978-3-030-89586-0_19

1 in 3 women has suffered physical and/or sexual violence throughout their lives, and in some countries this proportion increases to 7 out of every 10, in most countries, less than 40 percent of women who experience violence seek some form of help. Among the women who do so, the majority turn to family and friends, but very few trust official institutions and mechanisms, such as the police or the Health services; Less than 10 percent of those women who sought help after having suffered an act of violence did so by going to the police [1].

In Mexico, at least 6 out of 10 women have faced an incident of violence; 43 percent of women have been victims of sexual violence and, in its most extreme form, 9 women are murdered a day (http://www.diputados.gob.mx/sedia/sia/se/SAE-ISS-22-15. pdf). Among the ten entities that present the highest rate of Female Deaths with Presumption of Homicide in Mexico (DFPH) are Baja California Sur, Colima, Chihuahua, Baja California, Guerrero and Zacatecas. The ten municipalities that concentrated the largest number of DFPHs are: Tijuana, Juárez, Acapulco de Juárez, Ecatepec de Morelos, Chihuahua, Los Cabos, Victoria, León, Culiacán and Manzanillo, which together account for one out of every five DFPH that occur in the country (http://www.iaca.net/ Publications/Whitepapers/es/iacawp_es_2011_01_patron_de_delito.pdf).

The crime phenomenon is complex because it requires the intervention of various disciplines and consequently there is a range of techniques, algorithms and methods that can be applied to each element present in crime reports. In this sense, there are descriptive approaches, others classifying, others in the predictive and grouping order that, on the one hand, present local solutions or novel methods that allow the crime phenomenon to be viewed from another context. Now we will make a brief summary of these works in recent years, and the differences with the approach presented in this work.

In [8] authors assesses and the association between geographic variations and sociodemographic determinants of crime incidence in Nigeria. They used a mixed Poisson model was formulated to incorporate spatial dependency (clustering) effects and state-specific heterogeneity effects of offenses. The results show that the unemployment rate was positively associated with rape, kidnapping, and armed robbery, but negatively associated with robbery. No web data was used and the approach is focused in analysis techniques based in Bayesian and Markov mechanisms.

In the line to use demographic data or immigration data, there is a work in [9] where based on the hypothesis of the common belief that immigration increases crime. Using data from Chile, spanning 10 years, they analyzed the relationship between immigration and crime through a dynamic Durbin Spatial Model (SDM),. they conclude that there is no statistical evidence linking an increase in the number of immigrants with an increase in the rate of any type of crime.

In [10] they state that accurate crime predictions in real time help reduce the crime rate, for this reason they propose various visualization techniques and machine learning algorithms to predict the distribution of crime in an area, and present a work support in crime prevention based on these predictions with spatial analysis.

Other similar work oriented to crimes but related to women, is presented in [5]. They show how is the behavior of crimes during covid-19, and after and analyzing possible mechanisms for reducing crimes. They showed coincidence between the victim and the offender and the prohibition of the sale of alcohol are related to a greater decrease in crime.

In [4] a research addressed to analyze the possible asymmetric impact of crime on the labor force participation rates of men and women in India. But the approach does not considers social or web reports in the study.

While, in [3] an overview of current methods used for the analysis of spatial phenomena in relation to different available data, and discusses a solution for the analysis of crime data to level country.

For the other side, authors of [6] they examine the association between crime and health outcomes if it has been hampered by the lack of reliable data on crime in small areas. Then, they evaluate the accuracy of synthetically estimated crime rates for use in health research and the case of study is centered in preterm birth.

Our research works a different granularity level and with subset of crimes classified and related to women.

Overall, this paper presents a framework methodology to estimates and visualizes the level of insecurity at street level, based on the current or desired location within Ecatepec de Morelos municipality of state of Mexico and considering reports from criminal activities (femicide, rape, violence against women and robbery of bystanders with violence) with the aim of informing and helping the user's decision-making.

The rest of paper is organized as follows: Sect. 2 presents the data sources and how they were obtained, Sect. 3 Methodology, and Sect. 4 experiments and preliminary results; Finally, conclusions and further work are discussed.

2 Data Sources Description

The data sources used is provided by the government through the transparency portal and open data (http://datos.edomex.gob.mx/), it has data on different types of crimes and ranges from 2016 to 2018. Data structure is denormalized, they contains the following domains: crime, year, date, hour, municipality, suburb, street and in some cases the latitude and longitude.

Given that the data source provided by the government does not have data records catalogued as oriented to women, it was decided to complement it with information extracted from the media news. The following domains are selected to be extracted: title of the note, the date of the note and body of the note.

In addition, geographic information of political division of municipality of Ecatepec was used with data from 334 suburbs. See Fig. 1.

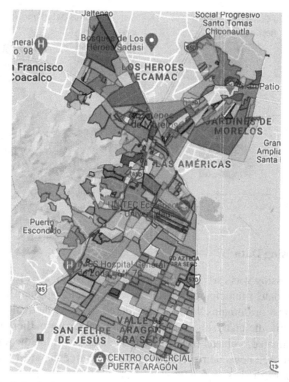

Fig. 1. Suburbs in municipality of Ecatepec de Morelos, State of Mexico

3   Methodology

Methodology is based on the CRISP-DM methodology [12] and implemented in a framework of three stages, the first one consist of collecting and extracting information from
open databases and some digital newspapers. The second stage is composed of data Mining process, application of nature language processing (NLP) implemented in python,
and Spatial analysis of overlapping and buffer actions, an implementation of algorithm
to estimate of crime risk based on location. The third one stage is a the display of a dashboard with general statistics based on radius of the location, filtered by type of crime
and type of data source used. The Fig. 2 depicts the methodology.

The CRISP-DM methodology was used to divides the data mining process into three
steps: a) understanding of women crime in official reports, and news data, b) preparing
the data, c) modeling and implementation. Each phase is broken down into second-
level traditional and well-known documented tasks (e.g. cleaning, stops word removal,
duplicity records) using NLP libraries (https://scikit-learn.org/). The preparing of data
consists of integration of open database and news to obtain an integrated database (
catalogued as crime oriented to women).

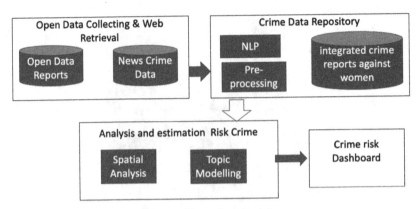

Fig. 2. Framework methodology.

3.1 Preprocessing Data

A data pre-processing was carried out in the open data where is extracted the following domains: crime, date, municipality, street, between streets, neighborhood, latitude and longitude. The rest or domains was not considered because the quality of data are not enough to perform the analysis (several nulls and numerous outliers identified). Stop words were eliminated, a cluster of all the words contained within the text was made and the top words of each news item were found. To determine the most used words across the entire digital media base.

The star model was used (which is very similar to a normalized database) but oriented to perform a query for statistical purposes, it contains a fact table and different catalog tables. the generation of their respective catalogs and their table of facts was carried out from the values obtained in the tables. Subsequently, based on the information contained in the star model, the building of data cubes starts to be used as a source in the queries in domains spatial temporal for several crimes.

Data exploration and transformation, include some steps was carried out to obtain the geographic coordinates from a postal address and later convert the denormalized table to a star model. First, the extracted notes were processed through a new model implemented in Spacy (https://spacy.io/), to classify news items identifying those that contain postal addresses (neighborhood, avenue and street); This attributes are used to apply reverse geocoding using Geopy (https://pypi.org/project/geopy/).

This process is illustrated in algorithm 2.

Algorithm 2 Data insertion by Reverse Geocoding.

1. Begin
2. Data extracted from web news
3. Data processing
4. Geographic information extraction
5. Processing with reverse geocoding
6. Generate Data with coordinates
7. If location is within Ecapetec

8. Store record in a database table news_ecatepec_coordinates
9. else
10. Discard record and return to 5
11. End

Subsequently, the denormalized table was converted to the star model manually, that is, the creation of their respective catalogs and their table of facts. Next, the data cubes are built and based on exploration of them, the level of risk is computed.

3.2 Level Crime Risk Estimation

The calculation of the level of risk is performance in two phases 1) based on the proximity analysis method well-known as buffer [13] and 2) a prototype to estimated risk crime level proposed in this work.

Buffer analysis is the determination of a zone around a geographic feature that contains locations that are within a specific distance of that feature, the buffer zone in this case is the crime incidence frequency. It this work it was implemented considering the following parameters: i) geographical location of people or person, ii) the selection of their filters (crimes and sources).

The calculation of the search radius (buffer) uses the Haversine equation [2] depicted in Eq. 1:

$$radius = 2 * \left(\sqrt{\left(\frac{\phi_2 - \phi_1}{2} \right) + cos\, cos\, \phi_1 \phi_2 \left(\frac{\lambda_2 - \lambda_1}{2} \right)} \right) \tag{1}$$

where:

ϕ_1 : Latitude of center point
ϕ_2 : Latitude of the point obtained from the database.
λ_1 : Center point length
$\lambda 2$: Length of the point obtained from the database.
Land radius = 6371 km

The estimation of the level of risk is computed using the Eq. 2:

$$Risk\ level\ estimation = \frac{\#\ of\ crimes\ within\ buffer\ zone}{\#\ total\ crimes\ in\ the\ municipality} \tag{2}$$

Where:
The # of crimes within a given range is the set of data found within a radius of less than 500 m, considering three domains: location, data source and type of crime.

The # of total crimes in the municipality will be the total of the data set in relation to the selected data source.

4 Experiments and Results

The first experiment, consists of estimate the level risk for a user located in Ecatepec, dashboard allows to select type of data source (open or official), crime type (femicide, armed robbery and rape) and the geographical location of people. Figure 3 shows a snippet of the result for people located in surroundings of Ecatepec municipality, open data selected and armed robbery).

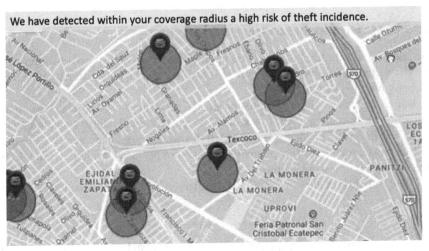

Fig. 3. Map of buffer zones with high risk (Armed robbery).

Fig. 4. Suburbs with major percentage of violence against women in Ecatepec Municipality (names in Spanish).

The second experiment consist in obtain the statistics regarding to main suburbs with reports of crimes oriented to women and not oriented to women to compare between them and distinguish if exists some similarities in frequency (names of suburbs are in Spanish) it is shown in Fig. 4.

As is shown in Fig. 4 suburbs are reported with major violence against women, in contrast when all the crimes are considered 8 suburbs appears with the major incidence of reports and some of them change of place in the ranking, it is depicted in Fig. 5.

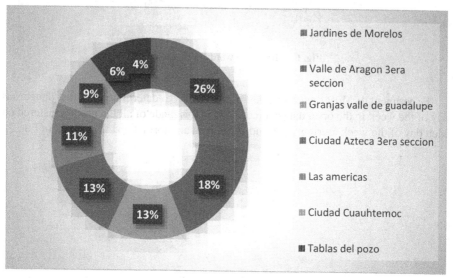

Fig. 5. Suburbs with major percentage of violence (both genders) in Ecatepec Municipality (names in Spanish).

Experiment 3: Identifying the most used words in digital media. One of analysis to show in the dashboard is topic modeling, which consists of showing the most relevant words found in reports crime. The data cube displayed the following results (Table 1).

Table 1. Snippet most used words in digital.

Word	Counting
Year	1168
Women	1151
Suburb	1149
Couple	1141
Justice	1188
Feminicide	1100

Graphically, the following cloud is generated to show the results in the Fig. 6.

Fig. 6. Most used words in digital media

Experiment 4: Most dangerous day of the week. To determine the most dangerous day of the week in the open data source, a count was made of all the news registered on each day of the week, during 2018 and 2019, data are normalized. It appears in Fig. 7.

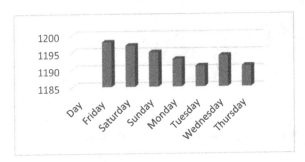

Fig. 7. Data cube Most dangerous day of the week

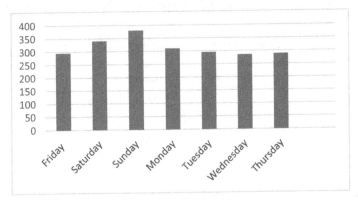

Fig. 8. Most dangerous day of the week (Open data)

Experiment 5: Comparing the most dangerous days of the week in open data and news media in crimes addressed to women. It is shown in Fig. 8.

Now in Fig. 9 we can see some variations because in Open Data the day more reported is Sunday while in news media you can see the most dangerous day is Saturday (although we can consider in global form that weekends are the most dangerous days for women in all reports collected.

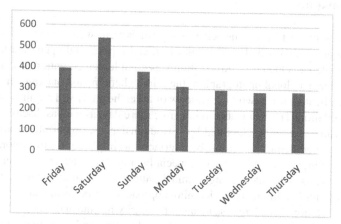

Fig. 9. Most dangerous day of the week (News data)

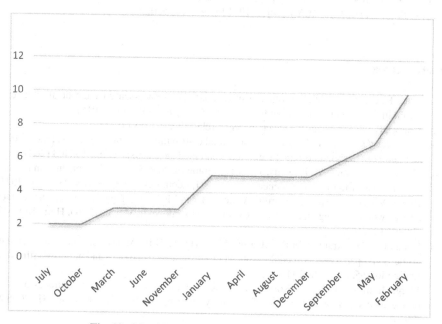

Fig. 10. Monthly behavior of crime reports (femicides)

Finally, in Fig. 10 you can see the behavior of crimes reported as feminicides in news by month (2018–2019).

We can see, July is the month with minor reports catalogued as feminicides in news digital media, while February is the most dangerous month, with the high index of reports of crimes against women. Data are normalized to generate the graph.

5 Conclusions

The approach allows to know the behavior of crimes against women (classified as femicides in the news of verified media) but in official reports and open data they appear as gender violence. Open data information was complemented with news information, allowing to have a global photograph of the crime phenomenon, having a first approximation of its behavior in a two-year window of time, the study still requires carrying out external validations and being able to integrate more data as well as discussing the way in which crimes are being classified by various instances, organizations and not only those of the government. In addition, an interface was implemented to explore and visualize points of high level of insecurity, especially aimed at women in a geographic area. Future work consists of identifying criminal patterns in the municipality of Ecatepec. In addition to integrating machine learning approaches to perform analyzes to identify possible correlations on a larger scale and granularity in time and space.

As well as implementing mechanisms for debugging and identifying possible fake news in order to grant greater certainty to this research in progress.

Acknowledgments. Authors of this paper, we thank to God, COFAA-IPN, Project SIP-20210541 y SIP-20211639, and CONACYT project 7051 by their support.

References

1. Mata, F., et al.: A mobile information system based on crowd-sensed and official crime data for finding safe routes: a case study of Mexico City. Mob. Inf. Syst. (2016)
2. Sinnott, R.W.: Virtues of the haversine. Sky Telesc. **68**(2), 158 (1984)
3. Lisowska-Kierepka, A.: How to analyse spatial distribution of crime? Crime risk indicator in an attempt to design an original method of spatial crime analysis. Cities 103403 (2021)
4. Mishra, A., Mishra, V., Parasnis, J.: The asymmetric role of crime in women's and men's labour force participation: evidence from India. J. Econ. Behav. Organ. **188**, 933–961 (2021)
5. Hoehn-Velasco, L., Silverio-Murillo, A., de la Miyar, J.R.B.: The great crime recovery: crimes against women during, and after, the COVID-19 lockdown in Mexico. Econ. Hum. Biol. **41**, 100991 (2021)
6. Gobaud, A.N., Kramer, M.R., Stearns, E.R., Haley, D.F.: Measuring small-area violent crime: a comparison of observed versus model-estimated crime rates and preterm birth. Ann. Epidemiol. **55**, 27–33 (2021)
7. Margagliotti, G., Bollé, T., Rossy, Q.: Worldwide analysis of crimes by the traces of their online media coverage: the case of jewellery store robberies. Digit. Investig. **31**, 200889 (2019)

8. Adeyemi, R.A., Mayaki, J., Zewotir, T.T., Ramroop, S.: Demography and crime: a spatial analysis of geographical patterns and risk factors of Crimes in Nigeria. Spatial Statistics **41**, 100485 (2021)
9. Leiva, M., Vasquez-Lavín, F., Oliva, R.D.P.: Do immigrants increase crime? Spatial analysis in a middle-income country. World Dev. **126**, 104728 (2020)
10. ToppiReddy, H.K.R., Saini, B., Mahajan, G.: Crime prediction & monitoring framework based on spatial analysis. Proc. Comput. Sci. **132**, 696–705 (2018)
11. statistics for the purpose of the international day for the elimination of the violence against women, INEGI. https://www.inegi.org.mx/contenidos/saladeprensa/aproposito/2018/violencia2018_nal.pdf. Accessed May 2021
12. Wirth, R., Hipp, J.: CRISP-DM: Towards a standard process model for data mining. In: Practical Applications of Knowledge Discovery and Data Mining, vol. 1. Springer, London (2000)
13. Chakraborty, J., Armstrong, M.P.: Exploring the use of buffer analysis for the identification of impacted areas in environmental equity assessment. Cartogr. Geogr. Inf. Syst. **24**(3), 145–157 (1997)

Correction to: Learning Through Interactive Vicarious and Social Experiences, an Alternative to Developing Teaching Training Processes in Ict Skills

L. J. Rengifo-Arcos⊙, L. F. Maldonado-Granados⊙,
and Y. A. Méndez-Alegría⊙

Correction to:
Chapter "Learning Through Interactive Vicarious and Social Experiences, an Alternative to Developing Teaching Training Processes in Ict Skills" in: M. F. Mata-Rivera and R. Zagal-Flores (Eds.): *Telematics and Computing*, CCIS 1430, https://doi.org/10.1007/978-3-030-89586-0_16

In the originally published version of chapter 16 the names of the authors were indicated in a wrong format. The authors names have been revised as L. J. Rengifo-Arcos, L. F. Maldonado-Granados, and Y. A. Méndez Alegría.

The updated original version of this chapter can be found at
https://doi.org/10.1007/978-3-030-89586-0_16

Author Index

Printed in the United States
by Baker & Taylor Publisher Services